Warlord Politics

PRAEGER LIBRARY OF CHINESE AFFAIRS

PRAEGER LIBRARY OF CHINESE AFFAIRS

General Editor: Donald W. Klein, Columbia University

China is one of the world's oldest civilizations and one of the least known or understood. Its rich history has much to contribute to our understanding of man; its experiences in modernization are relevant to other developing nations; its crucial role in Asian and world politics makes imperative a fuller comprehension of the Chinese past and present.

The volumes in this multidisciplinary series will explore central issues of China's political, social, and economic structure, its philosophy and thought, and its history, civilization, and culture. The contributors to the series represent a wide variety of approaches and attitudes, and all are specialists in their respective fields. Included in the series are the following works:

Ralph C. Croizier, ed., *China's Cultural Legacy and Communism* (1970)

Alexander Eckstein, ed., *China Trade Prospects and U.S. Policy* (1971)

Donald G. Gillin, *History of the Chinese Civil War, 1945–50* (1972)*

James P. Harrison, *A History of the Chinese Communist Party* (1972)*

Li Jui, *Comrade Mao Tse-tung's Early Revolutionary Activities,* trans. by Anthony W. Sariti, with an introduction by Stuart R. Schram (1972)*

Michel Oksenberg and Frederick C. Teiwes, eds., *The Chinese Communist Bureaucracy at Work* (1972)*

Lucian W. Pye, *Warlord Politics: Conflict and Coalition in the Modernization of Republican China* (1971)

Theodore Shabad, *China's Changing Map: Regional Development, 1949–70,* rev. ed. (1971)

William W. Whitson, with Chen-hsia Huang, *The Chinese Communist High Command: A History of Military Politics, 1927–70* (1972)*

* Title and publication date are not yet final.

Warlord Politics

CONFLICT AND COALITION IN THE
MODERNIZATION OF REPUBLICAN CHINA

Lucian W. Pye

PRAEGER PUBLISHERS
New York · Washington · London

To

Mary Toombs Waddill Pye
and to all that went into
being a
graduate student's wonderful wife;

and

to the life of the
graduate student at a
time when aspiring scholars
need to be humored
and the joys of being
a student affirmed

PRAEGER PUBLISHERS
111 Fourth Avenue, New York, N.Y. 10003, U.S.A.
5, Cromwell Place, London SW7 2JL, England

Published in the United States of America in 1971
by Praeger Publishers, Inc.

© 1971 by Praeger Publishers, Inc.

Library of Congress Catalog Card Number: 70–153394

Printed in the United States of America

CONTENTS

TABLES

PREFACE

Twenty years ago, when this study was essentially completed, the Chinese Communists had just come to power and it appeared as though ideology and party were about to take complete command of one hundred years of Chinese revolutionary change. When I first decided on the topic of warlord politics for my thesis at Yale, the fate of China was being decided by military means, and therefore a study of an earlier phase of military-political history seemed reasonably relevant to the contemporary concerns of that day. In the ensuing years, the possibility of the military's playing a dominant role or the evolution of a more pragmatic and competitive form of politics seemed increasingly unlikely. Also my own intellectual interests shifted. So there was little pressure to transform the manuscript into a book until Donald Klein proposed this spring that the book be published in the Praeger Library of Chinese Affairs.

Because I had been very impressed by James E. Sheridan's study of Feng Yü-hsiang and Donald Gillin's work on Yen Hsi-shan, I was hesitant to respond to Klein's invitation, but, in the end, my feeling about the importance and fascination of the Republican period won out, and I decided that it might be useful to add to the literature on that period, particularly since my study had dealt with the warlords as a distinctive political system and thus complemented their more recent studies of individual warlords. It is true that I used Feng Yü-hsiang as an important case, but, on reviewing Sheridan's outstanding study, I felt that we still complemented each other, for he had relied mainly on Feng's autobiography and I had used more his published diary. Donald Gillin's work dealt with the man who governed the province I grew up in, who inspired some of my first political sentiments, and who must have in some subtle way directed me to my sympathy for the problems the warlords faced, but who, I now find, quite oddly, hardly appeared in my study of the wardlord system.

Whether one is inclined to see the current importance of the People's

vii

Liberation Army as proof of the continuing significance of the military in Chinese politics or one is merely curious about an earlier stage in China's modernization, there is clearly a case to be made for more scholarly attention being given to the phenomenon of Chinese warlordism. As for biases that may have colored this study, I believe that it should be clear that I feel that it was unfortunate that the workings of the warlord system failed to create a more popular and acceptable form of competitive politics for China. While accepting the historical verdict that the operations of the warlord system contributed to the Chinese search for one-party rule, I still feel that there is more to be said for the warlords than contemporary opinion allowed. A fundamental paradox of Chinese modernization is that the phase of military domination brought competitive politics to China while the periods of party domination have brought monolithic authority and the denial of open competition—the exact reverse of the typical pattern in the currently developing countries.

Although recent scholarship has added to our understanding of the Republican period in China and the evolution of the Chinese Communist system provides us with new perspectives for viewing the record of Chinese political development and modernization, I have decided to leave this study essentially as it was originally written. Nothing in subsequent developments in either scholarship or the current history of China seems to require changes in either assumptions or conclusions, and the original emphasis upon the role of power relations in shaping Chinese politics still seems to offer a valuable and underutilized approach. I must, however, confess that if I were to have done this study afresh I would have felt it necessary to deal more with human and cultural factors.

Nevertheless, the theoretical approach of analyzing behavior according to "the logic of power," which so clearly identifies the limits of the possible and the paramountcy of mere political survival, does have general value, particularly for studying periods of political confusion and disorder. It can bring a vivid sense of realism to the study of political development in the new states of Asia and Africa. Leaders in such contexts must, before they can concern themselves with questions of ultimate values in national development, cope, as the warlords did in their day, with the painful limits of their power and with the need to compete with others for power. The process of nation-building is always shaped by the dynamics of such domestic power relationships.

Viewed from such an approach, fundamental calculations about power provide a "rational" underpinning for political behavior in the developmental process. On the other hand, there are always some cultural differences in the "styles" of such pragmatic calculations. Therefore, the logic of warlord politics may illuminate basic Chinese attitudes toward competition over decentralized power, a situation that may in a limited fashion recur in domestic Chinese politics and that will certainly exist in the area of foreign affairs, where the Chinese will have to compete, and possibly even align themselves, with others.

Thus possibly this investigation of an earlier period of Chinese political development may still have relevance for understanding contemporary China and the general problem of political development in transitional societies.

It is hard to decide where to begin, or end, in acknowledging help in this study. David N. Rowe was tolerant of my interests, but demanding in his standards, and thus an admirable thesis director. At the time I was writing this study, my interest in power analysis was greatly influenced by Arnold Wolfers, William T. R. Fox, Bernard Brodie, Klaus Knorr, Gabriel Almond, Frederick S. Dunn, Percy Corbett, and William W. Kaufmann. George Kennedy and Tien-yi Li helped me overcome my then semi-illiteracy in Chinese. During the time that I was working in the National Archives and the Library of Congress, John and Jo Hicks provided warm hospitality.

Above all, however, I owe an immeasurable debt of gratitude to Mary Pye, who worried with me through every stage of this study and substantially contributed to the collecting of data, the editing for style, and the typing of the drafts and of the final thesis. She truly deserves to be recognized as a co-author, an honor that convention denies wives of graduate students but that should be demanded by those anxious for justice for women.

Finally, I am indebted to Breda Hollingsworth and Molly Morell, for helping to prepare and retyping segments of the final manuscript.

In the light of all this help and inspiration, it is important to recognize that I alone am responsible for all the inadequacies in this study.

Cambridge, Massachusetts
April, 1971

Warlord Politics

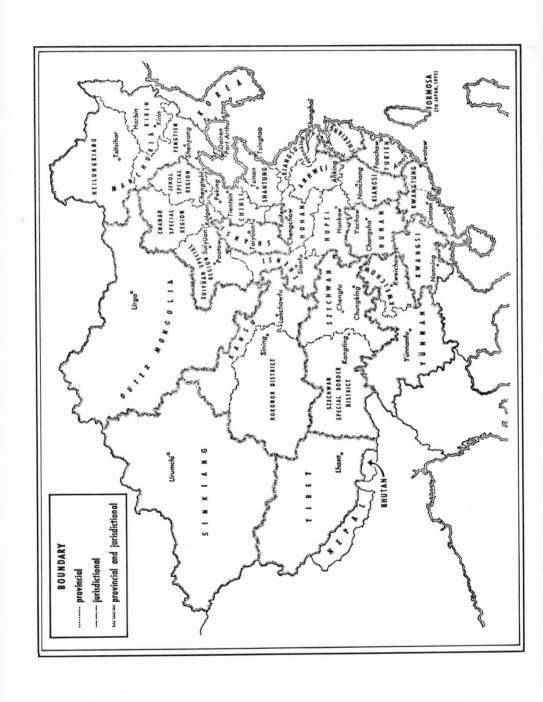

CHINA IN THE WARLORD ERA: mid-1924, at the peak of Chihli power, with the Nationalist movement centered at Canton

Jurisdiction	Ruling Figure or Group
Area under Peking regime	Chihli faction leaders: Ts'ao K'un, Wu P'ei-fu
Manchuria	Commander in Chief of Three Eastern Provinces Chang Tso-lin
Shansi	*Tuchün* Yen Hsi-shan
Chekiang	*Tuchün* Lu Yung-hsiang (Chang Tso-lin man)
Fukien	*Tuchün* Chou Yin-jen
Eastern Kwangtung	Ch'en Chiung-ming
Kwangtung	Sun Yat-sen's Nationalists
Kwangsi	*Tuchün* Lu Jung-t'ing; Shen Hung-ying; Li Tsung-jen
Hunan	Commander in Chief Chao Heng-t'i
Yunnan-Kweichow	Commander in Chief T'ang Chi-yao
Szechwan	Military Affairs Rehabilitation Commissioner Yang Sen (Wu P'ei-fu man); Border Defense Commissioners Liu Ts'un-hou, Liu Hsiang; Liu Ch'eng-hsun
Kansu	*Tuchün* Lu Hung-t'ao
Sinkiang	*Tuchün* Yang Tseng-hsin
Tibet	*De facto* independent, Thirteenth Dalai Lama
Outer Mongolia	*De facto* independent, *Hutukhtu*

From O. Edmund Clubb, *Twentieth Century China*. © 1964 Columbia University Press. Reprinted by permission of Columbia University Press.

1. THE PLACE OF WARLORDS
IN CHINESE POLITICS

In no country in the world have soldiers dominated politics as extensively or for so long as in China. Modern Chinese politics has revolved around armies and military figures. Yet the convention of Chinese historiography has been to minimize, if not ignore, the role of the military in Chinese history. In truth, at each stage of Chinese history, soldiers and armies have generally been more important than contemporary observers or subsequent historians have allowed. Even though every dynasty was established by military force and the rule of all emperors depended ultimately upon their armies, the Confucian interpretation of government insisted that soldiers were insignificant and ranked near the bottom of the social scale. What was true in traditional China is still largely true today in Communist China. At a time when the People's Liberation Army has become the key to government in China, the formal doctrines of Communism, while acknowledging the merits of martial qualities, continue to suggest that events are shaped more by peasants and workers than by soldiers.

In the early years of the Republic, however, it was impossible to deny that the military was decisive in public affairs. Enlightened Chinese were mortified, partly by the conduct of the warlords and possibly even more by the shame of having to admit that the arbiters of Chinese society were the military—the very element the Chinese always liked to treat as insignificant. It is not only that military calculations and actions have been decisive in the establishment of every regime in China since 1911; in the daily operations of government for sixty years, armies have never been far from the center of the stage. For example, even during one of the most dramatic and apparently politically inspired periods of modern Chinese politics, the Cultural Revolution, when students and Red Guards seemed to be in aggressive command and when the structure of the party was being torn apart, it was the People's Liberation Army that was in fact becoming the vital institution of rule; Mao's rhetoric was of

3

revolution, but his decisions, as with all modern Chinese political leaders, tended to give operational power to the army.

One can sympathize with the Chinese spokesmen of the Republican, Nationalist, and Communist eras who have tried to minimize or to justify as only temporary the critical role of the military; yet, for the student of Chinese politics, the intriguing questions are: Why does the importance of this particular institution persist in Chinese society, and what has been the underlying pattern of the role of the military? The answers to such fundamental questions call for the analysis of, first, the structural characteristics of an evolving Chinese society as it broke from its traditional civilization in response to the modern world and, second, the attitudinal or cultural characteristics of those involved in calculating and manipulating power in such a society.

Although the same basic problems of structure and attitude are to be found in both the Nationalist and Communist periods, they are in many respects best studied during the warlord period. An analysis of the nature of warlord institutions and the logic of their power relationships may be of great importance in providing us with a better understanding of the upheaval of the Chinese polity since the collapse of the imperial system, and it can point to the underlying power dynamics of the subsequent Nationalist and Communist periods, during which the military continued to be the ultimate institution of Chinese politics.

Only recently has the warlord phase of Republican China received the careful study and attention that have been given to other periods of modern Chinese history. Few people have believed that there could be any value in trying to untangle the complex and contorted relations of the warlords. The interest of serious scholars of modern China when confronted with this period has generally shifted to the international scene, where such events as the declaration of the Twenty-one Demands, the Versailles Conference, and the Washington Conference were taking place. The sordid story of domestic events in China has been treated as the "great aberration" of a grand society that had lost its direction and fallen onto evil times. The reason for China's weakness appeared all too obvious and hardly deserving of serious analysis: China lacked a strong governmental organization, and the actions of the military, with their greedy and petty wars, were bleeding China of its material and spiritual power. What formal government did exist was nothing more than a "phantom republic."

The conventional history of China in the 1920's has tended to focus, first, upon the skill of Chinese diplomacy in holding off the Japanese and winning international sympathy for a weak and mistreated country; second, upon the emergence of the Kuomintang in Canton and the heroic efforts to ensure that Sun Yat-sen's theories of politics, and especially his Three Principles, would become the guiding inspiration of a more democratic China; and, third, upon the conspiratorial efforts of the early Communists who were busy during the decade learning about the complexities of party discipline and the dynamics of a Chinese revolution. The decade was an exciting one because it began with the awakening of Chinese nationalism and the frantic activities of the May Fourth Movement, which committed Chinese intellectuals irrevocably to nationalism. Yet, in spite of all the drama of nationalism and Communism, the basic political fact of the decade was that China was ruled by warlords—the very people that the interpreters of China wanted to ignore.

However, during the 1920's, it was still necessary for students of Far Eastern affairs to offer some general explanations as to the cause and the probable outcome of the disease that had stricken the Chinese body social. The usual explanation was that China was passing through a period of interregnum characteristic of its history whenever one dynasty collapsed and before another took over. The period was interpreted as the dark hour before the dawn of another great day in Chinese history, when some leader or some group would rise up and, crushing all opposition, reunify China and return it to its rightful place among the world's great societies. Thus, the events of 1927, when the Northern Expedition of the Nationalist armies was establishing a degree of unity unknown in China since the death of Yüan Shih-k'ai, were interpreted as a sign that all the nightmares of the previous period could be forgotten and discounted.

The warlord period as an interregnum was generally interpreted as qualified by the Western impact upon Chinese society—a new ingredient not present during the other periods of turmoil between dynasties. There was now the demand that China practice some form of republican government and constitutional rule. The warlord era could thus be interpreted as a period when, although the symbols and slogans of republicanism were recognized as essential, the population as a whole was not qualified to contribute to the success of such a government. China had only partially and imperfectly assimilated the Western ideals of constitutional government and was therefore unable either to institute a workable republican government or to return to the old system of traditional rule.

These theories, although possibly valid as far as they went, do not adequately explain the phenomenon of warlordism in terms that make meaningful either the complex relationship of the participants or the relation of this period to the previous system of social organization or to the later Nationalist and Communist eras. It is necessary to consider the period in terms of the process of cultural change in which one can distinguish elements of continuity from the previous period as well as elements of discontinuity. The movement was away from a society that had been highly systematized and toward a condition of greater cultural heterogeneity. Various aspects of Chinese society had been subject to differing degrees of transformation. Thus, the failure of the republican system to function rested upon far more critical factors than just the lack of appreciation for, and understanding of, constitutional and democratic values. The institutions and ordering of the total society were not oriented to the support of such a system of government.

Thus, if we are to view warlordism as an aspect of the Chinese process of modernization and political development, we must at the outset note some of the basic features of traditional China. What is called for is not a detailed analysis of a great civilization but rather a general characterization of the traditional order that identifies its more salient features. In particular, we need to note the manner in which power was once organized, the basis of the political and social order, and the immediate consequences of the collapse of that order.

The traditional Chinese social order was striking in the relative simplicity of its form. At the top of both the governmental and social structures were the Emperor and his immediate advisers. At the bottom of the order were the great masses of the people. The society, being agrarian in nature, was highly sedentary, with an economic order that was both extremely simple and relatively stable. This gave to the great bulk of the members of the society a uniform outlook on life and a minimum of conflict over basic values. The pattern of values was fully recognized by the people and served as a positive framework by which they regulated their behavior. The problems that arose were met with traditional answers, and there was little need for governmental organizations to regulate the actions of the masses. What conflicts of interests did develop were usually solved if possible through informal means. Thus, government in the formal sense was not a primary concern of the people.[1]

The social and political core of traditional China was the body of literati who functioned through the bureaucratic organization of formal government. This was the key element that gave to traditional China its distinctive political and social life. Members of this group were the carriers of the higher social values of the society, and they established and propagated the idealized patterns of social behavior.

The literati recognized Confucianism as a formal and valid scheme of general values that were compatible with and reinforced by the general conditions of the agrarian society. The importance placed upon knowledge of a script and the necessity of acting through a bureaucracy did lead to a strikingly rational orientation of much of the behavior of the literati. However, this rational approach proceeded from the acceptance of traditional values and did not develop into "critical rationalism," whereby the traditional values would have been subjected to attack. As Max Weber has observed, the rationalism of the bureaucrat is conditioned by such factors as the senses of duty and office and the recognition of hierarchy.[2] Also, the Chinese literati developed much of their rationalism out of the need to solve pragmatic problems of government, such as collection of taxes and management of irrigation projects.[3] The solution of these problems did not require the work of theoreticians or the use of abstract conceptual devices. Thus, both the rationalism of the Chinese literati and the traditional values they defended were means for maintaining the elite position of this group in the society. This was quite different from the situation in the West, where the rise of rational attitudes was associated with the appearance of a new elite that was seeking to destroy the traditional values of the former elites. Thus, in so far as rationalism in the West was associated with the rise of capitalism and Protestantism, it possessed revolutionary qualities, whereas rationalism in China became a technique of those who were maintaining the *status quo*. There was thus a broad consensus within this segment of Chinese society as well as within the total society.

The bureaucracy, in addition to being the bulwark of the government, represented the single arena within which individuals competed to achieve the highest social and political prestige and honors offered by the society. Social prestige, economic security, and political power were all to be realized by entering this field of endeavor. Whatever the particular personal aims of the individual, the greatest opportunity for realizing them was to be found in complying with the same general pattern of behavior as would be followed to achieve other, and what in different cultures would seem to be unrelated, aims. The consequence of this situation was the existence of what may be described as a highly monolithic social and state structure.

This monolithic state structure produced a distinctive type of political life. There was a striking paucity of organized associations, parties, or pressure groups competing for political power in order to achieve particular objectives. The trade and craft guilds, secret religious societies, provincial clubs, and clan organizations did serve as informal organs of political control. However, their objectives were of a limited nature and did not include the demand for control of the formal organs of government or for the direction of government policy. These groups directed their energies toward receiving favors from, rather than securing the direction of, the official hierarchy and became critical factors during periods when the structure of government had collapsed.[4] Rather than interest-group politics, there was a high incidence of personal competition, or "palace politics." Thus, in the formation of cliques, the important factors were personalities, friendships, and family relationships and not general principles and values. The existence of a bureaucracy with departments serving particular functions did not, as might be expected, lead to a high degree of competition among offices, bureaus, boards, and departments. This condition can be understood if we realize that these offices were staffed, not by technical experts with a career interest vested in the power and position of a particular office, but by officials moving freely from one office to another. Competition was for rank within the total civil service structure rather than for status in the particular office in which one was working at the moment.[5]

The impact of the West, with its new technology and new social and political values, weakened this monolithic structure. With the Revolution of 1911, the destruction of the formal monolithic structure of government was complete. However, the process had not yet gone far enough to lead to the fractionalization of the society. Interest groups were beginning to appear, but they were not strong enough to form active pressure groups or associations geared to the seeking of political power. Few formally organized groups closely related to the interests of the total society, or even of particular segments of the society, were directed to, and capable of, seeking political power to carry out specific policies.

The only organizations that were in any sense able to seek political power were those in the military field. The military leaders had at their command armies that were personally loyal to them, and these semi-private armies became the only effective organizations with which to compete for political power. In addition to the organizations at their disposal, the military commanders had control of the means of violence to achieve political and economic objectives. Political power therefore gravitated to these men because the rest of the society was devoid of groups that could effectively contend for governmental control.

When viewed in this light, the period of warlord politics takes on an added significance. It becomes the essential link between the old, stable, monolithic society, with its uniform values and limited arena of political activity, and the development of a more diversified society. There was no single alignment of power that could easily direct China through such a period of transition. The politics of the warlords represented the extreme break toward a fractionalized society. However, this break was not absolute, and, in terms of the total society, there was still a high degree of stability in such fields as economic and social organization. As yet, no cleavages had run completely through Chinese society. In terms of the plane of life of the masses of the people, the old order was still strong and the bonds of traditional behavior still valid. However, on the governmental plane, the old system had dissolved completely, and no new order had been able to fill the void.

The warlords and their politics represented all the anachronisms that characterized the transitional phases of Chinese history. Their power rested on the fact that they possessed the only organizations capable of seeking political power. However, these organizations were not bound together by ideological values that could be stated in terms of political objectives. They did not represent clearly defined interest groups or particular segments of the society. Thus, the personal form of politics characteristic of the previous period continued. The values that the warlords sought were primarily personal values, and the ties and allegiances of political life were also based on personal relationships. At the same time, however, the warlords and their organizations were the prime basis for the organization and distribution of power for Chinese society. As such, they represented a revolutionary development signaling the transformation from a monolithic and hierarchical ordering of power to a more fragmented distribution of power. The question of power in Chinese society now became a more openly competitive matter.

Thus, China experienced a disjointed process of political change, in which, at the level of political values, the traditional pattern of personalized concerns continued to have force, while, in the sphere of power distribution, the tendency was toward greater open competitiveness and, in this sense, toward a more modern form of politics. In this view, the warlords represented continuity with respect to values and discontinuity with respect to the organization of power.

Significantly, few progressive Chinese intellectuals appreciated this distinction, and, frustrated over the continued dominance of the old political values, they were not prepared to recognize that, for the development of a more modern organization of power, the warlords were potentially a force for creating a more open and competitive style of politics. Consequently, by confusing the competitiveness and decentralized politics of the warlords with the persistence of nonideological and essentially traditional politics, these intellectuals felt that the salvation of China called for a restoration of a monolithic power structure directed toward more modern values. Repugnance toward the styles and objectives of the warlords became repugnance toward a competitive power pattern.

This analysis suggests that the military, in the form of the warlords, performed a significantly different function in Chinese political development than has the military in many of the currently developing countries. In these latter cases, it has been common for there to be, after independence, a period of competitive politics under the aegis of civilian politicians and party leaders, which is seen by some as excessive; when this competition threatens the civil order, the military would intervene as the ultimate guardian of the state structure. In China, it was the military itself, in the form of the warlords, which engaged in the competitive process that seemed to threaten the social order; then came the armies of, first, the Nationalists and, later, the Communists, both of which performed the role of guardians of the state structure, much as the military has done in such countries as Pakistan, Korea, Indonesia, Ghana, and all the other lands in which the military has come to rule. In this sense, the military in China has been both the agent of competitiveness and, later, the ultimate champion of a single established authority.

Thus, in terms of the changing structure of Chinese politics, the warlords, on the one hand, and the military under the Nationalists and Communists, on the other, performed different functions. Yet, in terms of their approaches to politics and their styles of calculating power, there may not have been such a sharp break between the warlords and their military successors. In part, this may be true because the Nationalist armies were not a monolithic force defending the state structure but actually coalitions of still relatively autonomous commanders, and the Communist army, although a more centralized force, is still divided into the five surprisingly autonomous field armies that emerged out of the Civil War. Thus, although the trend in China since the warlord period has certainly been in the direction of a more centralized military under the command of civilian authorities, the relationships of commanders and their patterns of alliances and mutual competition still have qualities similar to the admittedly more extreme relations among the warlords. To the extent that this is true, a detailed analysis of how the warlords felt compelled to play their competitive politics may be suggestive of underlying tendencies in present-day Communist China, at a time when the People's Liberation Army and its regional commanders have become a basic institution of rule.

In this same vein, it can be argued that the study of warlord politics can also be of great relevance in revealing basic Chinese styles of pragmatic political calculation in a highly competitive power situation. Specifically, a central theme of this study is that the warlords understood they were caught up in a complex balance of power and that they responded with certain distinctive modes of calculation. For example, they displayed great sensitivity to any threat to their organizations and their bases of power. This meant, in turn, that their perspective in evaluating their interests and judging their power prospects tended to focus almost entirely upon short-run considerations, to the point that, even when faced with the manifest "external" threat of the Nationalist armies advancing toward Central and North China, the warlord "system" of a balance of power could not evolve into a united opposition.

The pragmatic style of the warlords also took the form of overly complex and highly involuted lines of reasoning and calculation. Realism for the warlords meant that one could not accept things as they appeared on the surface, but rather that it was necessary to assume that others were engaged in extremely subtle and devious designs. Thus, the pragmatic view meant that, when power was at stake, no one could trust anyone else.

At the same time, the pragmatic approach of the warlords was also consistent with a temperate, accommodating, and highly moralistic style. Realism required accepting the existence of others and the limits of one's power and generally appreciating the value of proclaiming to others where virtue and vice lay. The moral posturing of the warlords was related to their sense of vulnerability in competition with others, and it did not contain the notion that power demanded responsibility of a moral nature. Therefore, the moralism of the warlords did not become emotional or fanatical, and they never allowed their rhetoric to become confused with policy commitments.

These characteristics of Chinese pragmatism in calculating power are some of the themes that will emerge from this study of warlord politics and that may be of value in understanding more contemporary patterns of Chinese politics. Granted, it may seem a bit farfetched to suggest that men presumably steeped in the "thoughts of Mao Tse-tung" would have much in common with the warlords of the 1920's. Yet, in a sense, the warlords were Chinese pathbreakers in trying to discover how security should be sought in a competitive world in which friends could easily become foes and adjustments in one's own behavior had to be made in the light of the relations that others had with each other. Certainly, in the years ahead, the Chinese will again have to accept the idea that power in a modern world cannot be unambiguously structured in the form of a monolithic hierarchy, and therefore they will have to learn how to behave in response to a more complex and competitive distribution of power, both domestically and internationally. To the extent that this happens, the Chinese leaders are likely to reflect some of the same cultural propensities that the warlords did. Pragmatism, after all, does not follow universal laws but is highly sensitive to personal and cultural differences. The tightfistedness of the warlords concerning power, their extreme sensitivity to the dangers of overstating their enmity, their readiness to seek isolation when things went wrong, and the general intensity and shortsightedness of their power calculations are qualities that also seem to emerge in the behavior of Chinese Communists when they must deal with a pluralistic power situation, as they must particularly in foreign affairs.

We are, however, getting ahead of our story, which will deal primarily with the scene in China, north of the Yangtze, from 1920 to 1928. We shall begin with a historical review of the warlord period in which we will seek to outline the main developments and the general sequences of conflicts and alliances. Then we shall turn to an analysis of the warlord organizations: What was the character of the warlord's power? How did he control his following? What were the typical relationships that developed in these organizations, and what were the critical factors in maintaining these groups under the stress of competitive politics?

The word "warlord" has a pejorative quality, and to call the leading figures of Chinese politics of the 1920's "warlords" or to identify the decade as the "warlord period" is to express a degree of criticism of Chinese developments. In many respects, our analysis would be more objective if we were to avoid the term and speak of *tuchün* politics or the *tuchün*. To use the Chinese term, however, would be rather pretentious; and "warlord" is, after all, the common English label. Therefore, we shall use the term "warlord" and hope that readers will not be put off by its pejorative connotations.

After the Revolution of 1911, the military governors of the eighteen provinces were given the title of *tute*, which suggested supreme military and civil authority. After the death of Yüan Shih-k'ai, in 1916, an attempt was made to separate the offices of civil and military governors. The civil governors were called *sheng-chang*, and the military governors were given the title of *tuchün*. Those who became known as warlords in English were almost without exception *tuchüns*, which initially was an honorable title but by 1924 had become rather tarnished. In that year, an effort was made to change the image of the military governors and end the stigma associated with the title of *tuchün* by changing the title to *tuli*, but *tuchün* was retained in common usage.

From this analysis of the organizational and independent power bases of the warlords, we shall go to the problem of the relationships among the warlords and examine in some detail the processes by which alliances were formed and then broken and new ones formed. This will set the stage for studying the complex balance of power that was decisive in shaping the politics of the era. The manner in which this power balance operated suggests much about the Chinese style of coping with a competitive power situation.

The warlords were very much the prisoners of their balance of power, as we shall see when we examine how these power considerations influenced their public relations and propaganda, their dealings with the civilian government and especially their appointment of cabinet ministers, and finally their relations with the two groups in Chinese society who might have given them significant competition, the intellectuals and the financial and business community.

One hopes the cumulative consequence of this analysis will demonstrate that the warlord system of politics was an entirely plausible historical development. The warlords were not up to the task of bringing modern republican government to China; but then neither was anyone else. They responded to their circumstances in entirely understandable ways, and hence they were as rational as any political class.

2. THE SEQUENCE OF POWER STRUGGLES

Only in a few other periods of human history have the affairs of a great nation been so hopelessly tangled and lacking in apparent purpose as in the time of the warlords of Republican China. Only confusion seemed to reign, and, at the time, Chinese and Westerners alike generally despaired of piecing together the details of warlord actions in the hope of finding some ultimate coherence. To the Chinese, the confusion was frightening and distressing, for it violated their basic craving for order and harmony. To Westerners, the scene was bizarre and could only make sense if treated as empty sound and fury. S. J. Perelman, writing in the *New Yorker*, in the early 1930's, expressed the sentiments of many observers when he confessed his nightmare confusion about who was doing and saying what to whom among such unlikely figures as the "Old Marshal" Chang, "Young" Chang, Yen the "Model Governor," the "Dog Meat General," and "Feng, who is called the Christian Marshal (as opposed to Feng, the Jewish Marshal, I guess)."

Confusing as the events were at the time, the details did add up to a pattern. The changing distribution of power in China followed a course that revealed the ambitions and the limitations of those who could realistically seek to rule. A warlord was the prisoner of: first, the conditions at the time of the imperial system's dissolution; second, the limits of his own abilities to mobilize resources and power; and, third, the competitive power of the other warlords.

The pattern began with the effort of the last dynasty to create a modern military machine. In the first phase of the Republican period, events dramatized the fatal gap between the impotence of civilian institutions and formal officeholders, on the one hand, and the realities of the sordid power of the individual military commanders, on the other. Gradually, the pattern took the form of individual warlords competing to emerge as the new authority of the nation. Soon, however, it became apparent that no single contender could hope to become the ruler of the country, and thus the pattern shifted increasingly to the forming of alliances and the creation of a relatively stable balance of power that was marred on the surface by a few forlorn attempts by individual commanders to capture all by *coup d'état*.

This pattern, as well as many other features of the warlord system, can be seen in the brief historical résumé with which we shall begin our analysis.

DIVISION WITHIN THE PEIYANG ARMY

The pattern of early warlord politics had its inception at the time when the Manchu Empire attempted to standardize its military organization and create a "model army." When, in 1895, Yüan Shih-k'ai was recalled from Korea and commissioned to organize the model army, his chief assistants were Feng Kuo-chang, Wang Shih-chen, and Tuan Ch'i-jui.[1] The organization that Yüan Shih-k'ai developed was known as the Peiyang Army, and it became the most effective military force in China since the armies of Tsêng Kuo-fan, Tso Tsung-t'ang, and Li Hung-chang, which were raised to suppress the Taiping Rebellion and which were the direct prototypes of Yüan's model army. Not only did Yüan copy many of the organizational arrangements of these armies, with certain Western modifications, but he followed their example in making the Peiyang Army a personal force in which he, as commander, was responsible for the selection of officers and the obtaining of finances. Thus, the Peiyang Army, as had been the case with the personal armies during the Taiping period, was highly autonomous and not under the direct control of the Throne.[2]

When Yüan Shih-k'ai was forced to retire to Honan after the death of his patroness, the Empress Dowager Tz'u-hsi, the Peiyang Army was nominally under the control of a Manchu, T'ieh-liang, who was a direct appointee of the Throne. However, the actual command and control of the army was in the hands of Feng Kuo-chang and Tuan Ch'i-jui.[3] Although there was as yet no clear-cut division within the ranks of the Peiyang forces, an informal alignment began to form with Tuan and Feng each establishing a group of loyal subordinate officers.[4]

When Yüan Shih-k'ai was recalled by the Manchus in 1911 to suppress the Revolution, he again took command of the Peiyang Army and found Tuan Ch'i-jui in control of the forces in the area of the capital, while Feng commanded the Imperial forces in the Hankow area.[5] Yüan was assisted by Tuan in his efforts to obtain the abdication of the Manchus. Although Yüan was successful in his attempt to obtain from the Throne free control of the Imperial forces, it soon became apparent that he no longer had complete domination over that group. During Yüan's period of absence, both Tuan and Feng had achieved a degree of independence of action that Yüan could not easily overcome. The officers of the army had become accustomed to receiving their orders from either Tuan or Feng. Also, with the abdication of the Manchus and the success of the revolutionists, the political and military picture in China became confused, and, with the decrease in the possibilities of making effective predictions as to future eventualities, the military officials tended more and more to gravitate toward those leaders with whom they had the closest association. This factor served to strengthen further the positions of Tuan and Feng.

Yüan Shih-k'ai, after gaining control of the Republican government, moved to weaken the positions of Tuan and Feng by trying to further the split between them. He named Tuan Ch'i-jui as minister of war, a post of great nominal authority but one which would weaken its holder's contacts with those elements of the Peiyang forces that were loyal to him. Tuan, however, set about attempting to re-establish the old Peiyang Army as the new National Army and thereby strengthen his own hand. Feng Kuo-chang was appointed Military Governor of Chihli—an office that was of less prestige value but left him in direct command of those elements of the Peiyang that were loyal to him personally. Yüan Shih-k'ai, in the meantime, turned his attention to the establishment of a new model army, depending upon lesser generals, such as Lu Yung-t'ing, Chang Hsün, Lung Chi-kuang, and Hsü Pao-chan, to strengthen his own position.[6]

In 1913, with the Second Revolution, Yüan Shih-k'ai and Tuan Ch'i-jui ordered Feng Kuo-chang to move down to the Yangtze Valley to suppress the revolt. After his success in defeating the revolutionists, Feng was appointed *tute* of Kiangsu. The transfer of Feng from Chihli to Kiangsu removed him from immediate contact with the power struggle at the capital, and both Yüan and Tuan were now in a position to dominate the scene in the North. Feng, however, found himself in a strategic position in Kiangsu and was soon able to build up his power in the Yangtze Valley unhampered by interference from Peking. Before the arrival of Feng, the immediate political control in the Yangtze area had been divided among a group of minor military commanders, none of whom had the strength to achieve a position of dominance. It was this lack of any primary control in the area that opened the way to the Second Revolution in 1913. However, when Feng Kuo-chang moved into the area, he immediately became the central figure around whom the lesser military and political figures clustered. Feng also had the advantage of being well received in the area because his pre-Revolution position as Military Commander at Hankow had made him well known in the Yangtze Valley.

Yüan Shih-k'ai, in the meantime, was strengthening his position in North China, seeking control over the weak Parliament and planning to capture the Mandate of Heaven, restore the Imperial rule, and install himself on the Dragon Throne.[7] However, with Yüan's death, on June 6, 1916, the pattern of authority that he had been seeking to create fell apart. The main stabilizing force in Chinese politics collapsed, and all the underlying divisions and frictions revealed themselves, the most important of which was the split among the factions in the Peiyang Army.

THE PRESIDENCY OF LI YÜAN-HUNG, JUNE, 1916–JULY, 1917

The scene was now set for a test of power among the military leaders. Although the groupings that this conflict would produce were unmistakably clear, the actual struggle was held in abeyance because the military commanders found themselves temporarily united over the issues that arose over the succession of the Vice-President, Li Yüan-hung, to the office of the Presidency. Li had been selected as the Vice-President of the new Republic as a result of the compromise reached in 1912 between the representatives of the northern group under Yüan Shih-k'ai and the elements led by Dr. Sun Yat-sen.[8] However, the possibility that the Vice-President should become President had never been seriously contemplated by the military leaders. When Li Yüan-hung did succeed to the Presidency in 1916, the military commanders considered it an accident that interfered with the normal considerations of seniority within the ranks of the military hierarchy. As a result, the new President soon found that he had little control over the *tuchüns*, who continued to consider him a subordinate military commander.

Doubtless, if the accidents of history had placed a civilian in the office of the Vice-Presidency of the infant Republic there still would have been considerable stress between constitutional authority and the realities of military power. However, early in the experiment with Republican rule, the sense of propriety of the most powerful generals was to be blatantly challenged by what was considered the absurd elevation of a subordinate military officer to the supposed highest office in the land. This did more to undermine the entire effort of Republican institution-building than has been generally recognized. From that time on, generals who understood and appreciated the realities of their military hierarchy could only look upon constitutional offices as lacking substance and undeserving of their respect.

Whatever successes Li might have had as President depended upon his ability to elicit sufficient support for the formal institutions of the Republican government to check the power of the military leaders. Thus Li, who had never previously been an outspoken advocate of Republican rule, became, as President, one of the most active champions of constitutional methods. His support would have come from Parliament, but this body was of little help, as it was crippled by the divisions among the Kuomintang representatives and those loyal to either Feng or Tuan.

The sharp break between the formal or constitutional leaders and the holders of the actual power, such as the military leaders Tuan Ch'i-jui and Feng Kuo-chang, made it impossible for the government to function as a policy-making group. The functioning of the government along formal channels was temporarily stabilized by the President's move to appoint Tuan and Feng as Premier and Vice-President, respectively. Li hoped, by this step, to be able to force the military leaders to conform to the constitutional pattern, thereby strengthening the government and improving his own position. However, it was soon apparent that he had only opened the way for Tuan, who controlled the cabinet, to dominate the government.

Failing to control the military by constitutional methods, the President turned to a policy of attempting to meet the threat of the military commanders on their own terms. That is, he began to strengthen his own military position. For this purpose, he sought to gain the support of the lesser military commanders who were not under the influence of the Peiyang Army. He enlisted the support of the same group of commanders that Yüan Shih-k'ai had employed in his efforts to balance off the two factions of the Peiyang Army. In particular, Li found what appeared to be a willing supporter in Chang Hsün, who, although not a Manchu, had been one of the most active defenders of the Imperial family in 1911 and still had strong loyalties to the old dynasty.

The tension between the President and Tuan came to a head over the issue of China's role in World War I.[9] Premier Tuan saw, in the issue of breaking diplomatic relations with the Central Powers, the opportunity not only of gaining the support of the Allies but also a means of winning over the Parliament, thus weakening the position of President Li. However, on this issue, Li was able, on March 14, 1917, to gain a majority in Parliament opposing China's entry into the war. Tuan Ch'i-jui, after this defeat at the hands of the President and Parliament, turned to a definite policy of building up the power of the military commanders under his control. By moving his headquarters to Tientsin and strengthening his dominance over the military leaders in the Northern Provinces, Tuan forced the Parliament and the President into a degree of unity that had never before been achieved under the Republic. In April, 1917, the Parliament voted to dismiss Tuan as Premier, but Li hesitated until May 21 before issuing the order of dismissal.[10] The move served only to strengthen the obstinate position of Tuan and led him to assume a more threatening attitude toward the President's office. On June 9, the military leaders at Tientsin sent an ultimatum to Li threatening to attack the capital if the President did not dissolve Parliament.

Li's reaction to this threat was to call upon Chang Hsün to transfer his troops to Peking to protect the government. On the night of July 1, 1917, Chang Hsün, however, rather than moving to the defense of the Republic, seized the city and announced the restoration of the monarchy. He proceeded to move into the Forbidden City and place Henry Pu-yi upon the Throne. President Li was rescued from his protector by Japanese troops and given asylum in the Japanese legation.

THE RISE OF THE ANFU CLUB AND THE CHIHLI FACTION, JULY, 1917–JUNE, 1920

The restoration of the monarchy by Chang Hsün, even though it survived for only two weeks, radically changed the political complexion of North China.[11] Tuan Ch'i-jui was now in the position of the defender of the republic. He delayed long enough in Tientsin to build up the impression that the Restoration had been a serious threat to China and that it might have succeeded. He also emphasized the point that the policy followed by President Li had made the Restoration possible.

However, after recapturing Peking and forcing Chang Hsün to flee to the Dutch legation, Tuan Ch'i-jui found himself in the awkward position of playing the role of defender of the Republic while being confronted with the problem of a vacancy in the office of the President. It was out of the question to consider reinstating President Li, who was demanding a return to the *status quo ante*. The only alternative was to permit the Vice-President, Feng Kuo-chang, to finish out Li's term of office. However, Feng, backed by his personal following from the old Peiyang Army and his recently developed power in the Yangtze provinces, was in a position to demand from Tuan Ch'i-jui his own terms for coming to Peking to assume office. Thus, before leaving Nanking, Feng compelled Premier Tuan to accept his appointees to offices in the Yangtze area,[12] thereby assuring the retention of his power base in Central China. Only after making secure his control in this area was Feng willing to return to the North, which was under the domination of the followers of Tuan.

The division of military power that occurred with the split in the old Peiyang Army into the Tuan and Feng factions now became formalized in the conflict between the Presidency and the Premiership. This schism was further acknowledged by the establishment of the so-called Anfu Club, under the leadership of Tuan ch'i-jui, and the formation of the Chihli faction, consisting of Feng's followers.

The Anfu group was by far the better organized, but it was at best a loose association lacking a central executive organization and a fixed program. It was dominated by the personalities of Tuan Ch'i-jui and his immediate lieutenant, Hsü Shu-cheng, who was popularly known as "Little Hsü." The military power of the Anfu group rested upon Tuan's own troops and those of such *tuchüns* as Ni Ssu-ch'ung of Anhwei, Yang Shan-te of Chekiang, Li Ho-chi of Fukien, and the Commander of the Shanghai Special Area, Lu Yung-hsiang. However, the Anfu Club was not essentially an alliance of military commanders but was formed rather as a political group to dominate the Parliament and the civil bureaucracy. In so far as the conflict between Tuan Ch'i-jui and Feng Kuo-chang had not reached the point of actually resorting to military force, the struggle was fought out in terms of attempts to gain control of the institutions of government. Because the struggle was in the form of a conflict between the Presidency and the Premiership, the object of both was to gain control of the Parliament, which at this time consisted of a mass of factions, the strongest of which was the Chinputang.[13] Tuan, through the Speaker of the House Wang I-t'ang, organized the Anfu Club, which paid those members of Parliament who joined the club a monthly stipend for remaining in Peking and voting. Through this means, Tuan was assured at all times of a quorum and was thus able to thwart the efforts of Feng Kuo-chang to dissolve Parliament. Such a dissolution would have brought about a new election, which Feng hoped would result in a change in the Premiership and insure his re-election in October, 1918.

The Chihli faction, taking its name from the home province of Feng Kuo-chang and his immediate lieutenants, in the period from 1917 to 1920 was not a clearly defined group capable of united political or military action. It was made up of leaders of the old Peiyang Army who were loyal to Feng and commanders who were opposed to the power of the Premier.[14] The principal military commanders included such *tuchüns* as Wang Chan-yüan of Hupei, and Li Shun and Ch'eng Kuang-yüan of Kiangsu. The Chihli faction lacked strong leadership and a source of revenue that could be utilized for united activities. Having little influence in Parliament, and with its center of military power in Central China, the Chihli group was unable to act as an effective opposition to the Anfu group.

The Anfu members' control of the government was made secure when, in October, 1918, they were able to obtain the election of Hsü Shih-ch'ang as President to succeed Feng Kuo-chang. Hsü, former Viceroy of Manchuria, was considered a safe candidate by the Anfu group; he lacked any particular following and was regarded as an old and harmless scholar who could be easily manipulated. By the end of 1918, the Anfu group appeared to be in a position to serve as the first unifying force in China since the death of Yüan Shih-k'ai. Its control of the Peking government was undisputed, and it was backed by what appeared to be a sufficient bloc of military commanders to insure that its decisions would be effected throughout North China.

However, the Anfu Club depended for financial support upon its ability to obtain Japanese loans, and, as a result, it could not escape the accusation that it was supporting a pro-Japanese policy. Members of the Chihli faction capitalized on this already widespread popular sentiment to make numerous public statements to the effffect that the Anfu group was selling out China to a foreign power.[15] However, those in control of the Peking government appeared to be sufficiently entrenched to withstand such criticism until the summer of 1919, when the Versailles decision to give Japan the old German claims in Shantung was announced. The Anfu group now appeared, in the eyes of the more vocal of the Chinese public, unquestionably to be following a policy of permitting Japan to gain control of Chinese territory. Student groups became an active force in demanding the ousting of the Anfu clique, and student demonstrations in Peking developed into a mass assault upon certain of the more infamous Anfuites, forcing three of the cabinet members to flee to Japan.[16]

Although certain elements of the Chihli faction were quick to champion the cause of the students, the issue was not sufficient to unify all elements of the Chihli group to the point of risking any overt action against the power of Anfu. The *tuchüns* of Central China, who long had been faced with the threat that the Anfu group might turn its military power against them, fully realized the insecurity of their positions. However, so long as the Peking government refrained from taking any major punitive action against them, they preferred to follow a policy that would not provoke the government. Tuan Ch'i-jui, realizing that any direct attack on these *tuchüns* might lead to a strengthening of the rather weak ties among them, had followed a policy of attempting slowly to weaken the position of each of the area commanders separately by means of (1) economic strangulation, that is, reducing the flow of funds from the central government to the provincial areas, and (2) control of new appointments in the Central Provinces.

This latter policy was particularly effective and led to active opposition by the Chihli faction and the development of a dynamic leadership in the clique. With the appointment of Chang Ching-yao as *tuchün* of Honan, the Anfu group made a move that caused a definite stiffening of resistance on the part of the Central China *tuchüns*.[17] In particular, the appointment was interpreted by Wu P'ei-fu as a threat to his rising power in Szechwan and western Honan. The Anfu group had been forced to accelerate its program of attempting to gain greater control over the provinces because it was beginning to face serious financial problems,[18] and Japan, which was now experiencing the difficulties of postwar economic adjustment, was no longer an easy source of capital for loans of a political nature.[19] With the decision by Japan to join the Consortium,[20] the Anfu clique realized that it would now have to seek new sources of revenue.

Wu P'ei-fu's reaction to the appointment of Chang Chin-yao as *tuchün* of Honan was to seek out the support of the Chihli group and, in particular, the assistance of his old commander and tutor, Ts'ao K'un.

Ts'ao had been an officer in the Peiyang Army, but he had never clearly sided with either Tuan or Feng. However, in 1917, through the influence of Feng, he had been given the post of *tuchün* of Chihli, an office of great strategic significance, which he had been able to retain because the Anfu group sought to refrain from pushing him clearly into the Chihli faction. However, it was apparent to Ts'ao that, with the weakening of the Chihli power in Central China, the Anfu group would have little reason to tolerate his semi-independent position. Thus, when Wu P'ei-fu approached him, Ts'ao agreed to Wu's plan for a campaign against the Anfu leaders on the condition that Wu guarantee that he would be capable of building up sufficient forces to attack the center of Anfu power—Peking.[21] Wu then proceeded to call upon the *tuchüns* of Szechwan, Shensi, and Hupei, who had received little financial support from the government, to ally themselves with him against the Anfu group.[22] Thus, Wu P'ei-fu, with the support of Ts'ao K'un, was able to create a new alignment of power in North China and take over the leadership of the Chihli faction from the eastern Yangtze elements.[23]

By May 14, 1920, Wu was prepared to launch his drive into North China, and he began to move his armies up the Tientsin-Pukow Railroad line. In the meantime, he had been successful in interesting Chang Tso-lin in a campaign south of the Great Wall. The unexpected appearance of three divisions of Chang's troops moving down from Shanhaikuan caught Tuan Ch'i-jui completely unprepared. However, on June 6, 1920, Tuan ordered the Anfu troops in the capital to move to Tientsin to meet the advancing armies of Wu and Ts'ao. With the appearance of Chang's Manchurian, or, as they were more often called, Fengtien troops, the Anfu move was little more than a gesture, and the actual conflict lasted only from June 10 to June 12. The Anfu forces literally dissolved before the advancing Chihli troops, and the leaders of the Anfu group sought safety in the foreign concessions of Tientsin—Tuan Ch'i-jui himself turning to "Buddhistic studies," until he was once again called back into politics in 1924.

THE FIRST CHIHLI-FENGTIEN WAR

Wu P'ei-fu, by calling upon Chang Tso-lin to assist in the defeat of Anfu, had brought a new element into the balance of power. Previous to this time, Chang had shown little interest in developments at Peking, having followed instead a policy of consolidating his control over the three provinces of the Northeast and establishing an autonomous power center in this area.[24] However, after Wu had called in Chang to redress the balance in North China, there was no easy way to check the influence of this new power. It was soon apparent that the new coalition could find little basis for agreement, and Chang Tso-lin, distrusting the new power of Wu P'ei-fu, was willing to treat only with Ts'ao K'un. Chang made no effort to hide his dislike for Wu, referring to him as nothing more than a "divisional commander."[25] However, Chang and Ts'ao, after meeting in Tientsin, could find no easy solution to the problems of delegating the authority at the capital and appointing new officials. The problem was made more difficult because, as the result of Chang's previous autonomous program in Manchuria, he lacked the political connections and following that could easily be utilized to take over posts in Peking and other areas south of the Great Wall. The result was that, although Chang could employ delaying tactics, he could not block the expanding power of the Chihli clique, and control of the Peking government and the provincial posts gravitated to the Chihli leadership. That element had almost complete control over the petty appointments in North China, and the *tuchüns* who called Ts'ao K'un their leader steadily expanded their power.

However, Chang was able to block any changes in the offices of the President and the Premier. Thus President Hsü Shih-ch'ang, who had been able to survive the conflict between Anfu and Chihli, was now able to follow the same policy of playing off the Fengtien group against the Chihli faction to keep his own post.

This unstable balance lasted through 1921. The fact that Parliament had not been convened since the defeat of Anfu prevented the conflict between Fengtien and Chihli from emerging into the open; without Parliament, there was no need to force formal decisions on the issues of particular control between the two groups. However, Chihli was unable to forestall indefinitely a reconvening of Parliament, for not only had Chihli members claimed to be the defenders of the Republican form of government, but also, by re-establishing Parliament, they hoped to bring back to Peking the South China government. If they had been successful in accomplishing this, they would have had sufficient strength to neutralize the influence of Fengtien.

By the end of 1921, Chang Tso-lin, aware of the weakening of his own influence in Peking and counting on division within the ranks of the Chihli faction, moved to take things into his own hands and, suddenly, on December 24, 1921, proclaimed Liang Shih-i the new Premier.[26] The move caught the Chihli group off guard, and Chang made it clear that he was willing to defend his appointment by force of arms if necessary. Chang's move sharpened the break between the two groups because it compelled all the *tuchüns* to declare their allegiance openly. Wu P'ei-fu was quick to force the issue with every means at his disposal, and, in the early spring of 1922, he began to mobilize his armies, calling upon the assistance of the more powerful *tuchüns*. He sought aid particularly from Feng Yü-hsiang who was at that time *tuchün* of Shensi. Ts'ao K'un once again refused to accept the active leadership of the Chihli military campaign, although he fully supported Wu and took part in directing Wu's campaign.[27]

In April, 1922, Chang Tso-lin moved his troops south from Fengtien. Chang was so confident that Ts'ao K'un would not actively engage his troops until certain of Wu P'ei-fu's effectiveness in holding off the Fengtien armies that he was willing to leave his flank exposed to a possible attack by Ts'ao from the latter's headquarters at Paotingfu. Thus, Chang, leaving only one division at Tientsin, moved down the Chin-Pu Railroad line into Shantung. North of Chaochou the armies of Wu P'ei-fu, with the troops of Feng Yü-hsiang bearing the brunt of the fighting, checked Chang's southward movement. Chang had to make a rapid withdrawal because it now appeared that Ts'ao K'un was ready to move up from Paotingfu to cut his supply lines to his main base in Manchuria. Ts'ao however, although threatening to take decisive action, refused to move quickly enough to cause a major engagement at Tientsin. He was still uncertain of the ability of the Fengtien troops to mount a more powerful force than that which they had placed in the field at Chaochou, and he preferred to let Wu and Feng do the actual testing of Fengtien strength. Ts'ao, therefore, permitted Chang to make his escape back into Manchuria but arranged to send his troops into Peking and Tientsin at just the time when Wu's armies moved up from Shantung. Thus, Ts'ao, although not having to bear the cost and risk of a military campaign, still managed to remain in a position to claim the fruits of victory.[28]

GOVERNMENT BY THE CHIHLI FACTION

With the withdrawal of the Fengtien forces back into Manchuria, Wu P'ei-fu moved swiftly to strengthen his own position at the capital. First, he shifted Feng Yü-hsiang to Peking to act as inspector-general of the Chinese military establishment.[29] The post itself entailed little power, but it meant that Feng's troops, which were among the best in all China, would be stationed at Peking in a position to influence the political maneuvering there. Wu followed this move by launching a verbal attack against President Hsü Shih-ch'ang, who had been so successful in riding out previous storms. On June 1, 1922, Wu charged that President Hsü had been planning, with the support of Chang Tso-lin, to restore the monarchy and proceeded to oust him from office. On June 11, Wu called back into office Li Yüan-hung, who Wu claimed had been unjustly forced from the Presidency after the Chang Hsün Restoration movement of June, 1917.[30]

With these manipulations, Wu augmented his claims as a supporter of constitutional government, while, at the same time, he was insuring that the Presidential office would not be held by a man who possessed any actual military or political power. Wu's move was also intended as a gesture that might serve to bring back South China under the control of Peking. Li Yüan-hung had been acceptable to the Sun Yat-sen group, and Wu hoped that by reinstating him as President, the South would feel safe in recognizing the Peking government again. Ts'ao K'un, who was clearly understood to be Wu's superior by Wu himself as well as his followers, was willing to permit Wu to proceed with his program of establishing control over the Peking government. Ts'ao apparently reasoned that Wu would have to take the responsibilities for whatever mistakes were made, while every success of Wu's only served to heighten the prestige of his superior, Ts'ao K'un.[31]

The Chihli group now had achieved sufficient control of the situation at the capital so that, on August 1, 1922, they could take the risk of reconvening the Parliament for the first time since Chang Hsün had dissolved it in 1917.[32] With the return of Parliament to serve as a scoring device capable of reflecting the strength of various groups, the balance among the *tuchüns* became less dependent upon direct military following and strength. Thus, Wu's influence began to decline in Peking because he had few contacts and little control over its members. On the other hand, Ts'ao K'un, as the accepted leader of the Chihli group and the more experienced military-political figure, was able to direct with a surer hand the events in Peking.

Wu P'ei-fu was faced with two alternatives. On the one hand, he could attempt to enter the arena of political manipulation at the capital, where he had little experience—and, by doing so, probably changing radically the alignment in the Chihli faction, possibly even causing Ts'ao K'un to join forces with Chang Tso-lin. On the other hand, he could continue to play his role as the most efficient military leader of the Chihli party. If he could be successful in this latter course, his military position would become so secure that he would in fact become the dominant figure in the Chihli group. Also, as long as the Fengtien clique existed as a threat and continued to expand its armies, there was pressure on Wu from all elements of the Chihli faction to give his full attention to the field of military affairs. Wu, choosing to follow the latter course, withdrew from Peking and returned to his military headquarters at Loyang, where he concentrated on building up his armed forces.

The major problems confronted by the Chihli faction after it had gained control of the government were relations with President Li Yüan-Hung and the ubiquitous question of finance. The move to restore Li to the Presidency had had no effect in winning back the South, although it had augmented the new government's appearance of legitimacy and brought about a greater degree of popular acquiescence to its control than the previous regime had enjoyed. Wu's claim that he was restoring Li because he was the legitimate President had the effect of placing Li under a limited obligation to the Chihli leadership. However, Li was soon seeking to strengthen his own claim independently of the Chihli leaders, and the blocking tactics employed by the President's office once again became a critical problem for the real power-holders.

This conflict was intensified by the issues that arose over questions of finance. With the formation of the Consortium and the first defaults on foreign loans in 1921, the foreign loan market began to dry up, and Peking became less and less an easy source of finance for the military commanders.[33] The problem was further complicated by Ts'ao K'un's tactics of permitting the President to grapple with the insoluble problems of finance while he, Ts'ao, used his control over Parliament to defeat the various proposals advocated by President Li to obtain funds. It was by this technique of embarrassing the President that Ts'ao hoped to prepare the way to his own assumption of absolute power in Peking.[34] However, the lack of government funds was felt increasingly by elements of the Chihli faction, particularly those commanders who did not control definite geographic areas from which they could extract revenue. The most desperate of these commanders was Feng Yü-hsiang, who, with his troops stationed at the capital, had to depend entirely upon funds from the government coffers.

FENG's *Coup d'État* AND TS'AO K'UN'S ELECTION

Feng Yü-hsiang's financial problems soon became a threat to the stability of the Peking government. Not only was there danger that his troops might act independently in support of their demands for back pay, but also Feng himself showed signs that he would be willing to alter his allegiances if he could thereby ensure the solvency of his armies. President Li attempted to win him away from the Chihli faction primarily by playing upon Feng's sense of moral duty, but the President was neither in a position adequately to finance Feng nor was he willing to trust a man who had gained so much from the Chihli leaders.[35]

Feng, after eight meetings with Ts'ao K'un at Paotingfu, had failed to produce any acceptable financial arrangement and, on June 13, 1923, suddenly seized control of the Peking Octroi as a source of revenue for his personal armies. The Octroi, which levied a modest tax on certain items entering Peking, had been established as a direct source of funds for the President's office, and Feng's move had the intended effect of not only gaining the necessary revenues for his own troops but also destroying the President's power. The close collaboration between Feng and Ts'ao K'un in perpetrating the coup is shown not only in Feng's personal account of his activities[36] but also by the fact that, when President Li fled from Peking without relinquishing the Presidential seals, it was the troops of Ts'ao K'un that held him at Tientsin until the seals had been recovered by Feng from the President's wife, who had taken refuge in the French hospital in Peking's Legation Quarter.[37]

After Feng's initial move, he found himself in much the same position as that which Wu P'ei-fu had occupied in 1922. He had sufficient military power to destroy the Presidency, but he lacked the political allies necessary to establish even a temporary regime. Feng's actions, rather, had opened the way for his superior, Ts'ao K'un, to assume full control of the government, and, in addition, Ts'ao K'un was not burdened with the onus of having perpetrated an armed *coup d'état*.

However, the method used by Ts'ao in the assumption of formal power led to a split in the Chihli ranks. The faction under the leadership of Ts'ao K'un's younger brother, Ts'ao Ying, 'the Tientsin clique, argued that, if Ts'ao K'un were to become President, it would be essential to have full control of the Parliament, particularly when a program for the legal expansion of the sources of revenue was proposed. This faction maintained that positive control of the members of the then existing Parliament should be achieved before Ts'ao should seek election to the Presidency.[38]

The military leaders, following the lead of Wu P'ei-fu, argued that Ts'ao K'un should take direct control of the situation, oust the Parliament, establish the basis for new government, and thus clearly place himself in a position of dominance. By such direct methods, Ts'ao K'un would gain the free hand necessary to meet the financial problems and to establish a sounder government, which could act without being checked by the frictions among the Parliament, the cabinet, and the Presidency.[39]

The question was not solely one of method of approach; it also involved decisions on the appointments to desirable posts under the new administration and, hence, the problem of whether the government would be oriented toward the experts in manipulating votes in a crude parliamentary form of government or whether it would be under the control of the men who had actual military power. The Tientsin clique's approach to national politics was virtually one of investment in a cause for financial gain with no encumbering military organizations to maintain as costs. The members of this group made little effort to disguise the fact that they considered control of the Peking government as an investment opportunity, which, although entailing a degree of capital risk, might in the short run pay exceptionally good dividends.[40]

In the competition to influence Ts'ao K'un, the Tientsin clique won out as Ts'ao K'un's native cautiousness led him to favor the proposals of his brother as the plan involving the least risk. The more radical program of the *tuchün* wing of the Chihli faction would have entailed such a vast project of reorganization that it might have produced conflict among the individual *tuchüns* and exposed the whole group to attack from Fengtien. In addition, the Tientsin clique was the only group in a position to raise the immediate funds necessary to prime the pump of government. The *tuchüns* of the Chihli faction were all either in dire financial straits or were unwilling to risk a diminution of their own funds, which might weaken their military power to invest in the rather uncertain returns that might come with the control of the Peking government. Finally, there was some question as to the willingness of foreign powers to grant recognition to a government so clearly based upon military power.

The ensuing election of Ts'ao K'un was characterized by a more flagrant use of bribery than occurred during any other part of the warlord period.[41] The Tientsin clique, joining with the Speaker of the House of Representatives, first sought to make outright payments to the members of the House for each session of Parliament that they attended, much in the same manner as the Anfu Club had operated. This support of the members was extended to include promises of future subsidization depending upon the voting record of each man. On October 5, 1923, Ts'ao K'un was formally elected President and assumed office on the same day.

THE SECOND CHIHLI-FENGTIEN WAR

The election of Ts'ao K'un as President, however, did not unify Chinese politics under the Chihli faction. The actions of the Tientsin clique nearly caused an open split in the ranks of the Chihli military leadership, and Ts'ao, even if he had so desired, was not in a position to carry out a forceful policy. The situation was so serious that critical posts had to remain unfilled because of the danger of alienating those candidates who might be denied the more desirable jobs.[42] Only the threat from the outside—from Chang Tso-lin—prevented a complete rupture within the Chihli ranks. Because of this danger, Ts'ao K'un could not ignore the entreaties of the *tuchüns* upon whose military power he depended. However, at the same time, he needed the support of the Tientsin clique to keep Parliament in line. The result was a widening of the division between the capital and the provinces, with Ts'ao K'un reluctantly sanctioning a greater degree of autonomy on the part of provincial leaders.

Wu P'ei-fu continued to be the leader of the *tuchün* element of the Chihli faction. For the *tuchün* group, the center of decision-making gradually shifted from Peking to Wu's headquarters at Loyang, leading to a diminution of Ts'ao K'un's immediate control over this group. With the Peking government falling under the influence of the Tientsin clique, Wu began to speak more and more of the necessity of "unifying China by force."[43] The principal foes of Wu were Chang Tso-lin and those independent *tuchüns* who were seeking to ally themselves with the Manchurian general. The Fengtien threat consisted not only of the danger that Chang would utilize his newly reorganized armies for a sudden strike south from Manchuria but that he would be able to enlist the support of allies located to the south of the Chihli centers of power and thus force Wu into a campaign on two fronts.

This latter threat became a reality in the spring of 1924, when the *tuchün* of Chekiang, Lu Yung-hsiang, made overt moves to curry the support of Chang Tso-lin.[44] Lu Yung-hsiang was the one remaining Anfuite who had been able to survive the defeat of Tuan Ch'i-jui and keep his personal army intact. The geographic location of Lu's forces made it possible for him to gain strategic security as well as sufficient financial and political power to continue as a major leader after the defeat of Anfu. As *tuchün* of Chekiang, he was in the position to capitalize upon the strategic and economic importance of Shanghai, which was under his area of jurisdiction. In addition, the foreign interests in Shanghai served to protect the area and deter active military campaigns that might involve their holdings.[45]

Ever since the defeat of Tuan, Lu's control of Chekiang had been a constant annoyance to the Chihli faction, but it was only with the move of Lu to obtain support from Chang Tso-lin that actual plans were initiated to eliminate Lu's power. The leading protagonist for the Chihli faction in this action was a loyal subordinate of Wu P'ei-fu, Ch'i Hsieh-yüan. Ch'i, as *tuchün* of Kiangsu, had long been interested in incorporating the Special Area of Shanghai into his own sphere and, now, with the backing of Wu, felt strong enough to proceed.

Thus, the second Chihli-Fengtien conflict was launched when, on August 25, 1923, Ch'i Hsieh-yüan moved his troops out of Nanking in a drive toward Soochow and Shanghai. Wu P'ei-fu had counted on a quick victory by Ch'i, which would have meant that the threat of a combined action by Lu and Chang would be eliminated and the main Chihli forces could be kept intact for the major move against Chang. However, at the start of the actual fighting, neither Ch'i nor Lu was in a position to make rapid gains, and the danger of a costly stalemate soon developed. Wu was forced to order reinforcements from Honan and Szechwan to assist Ch'i, and finally he directed Feng Yü-hsiang to proceed to the support of the Kiangsu *tuchün*.[46] Feng, however, was well entrenched in the Peking area and for several reasons refused to comply with Wu's orders. Feng reasoned, first, that, had he assisted Ch'i to gain the victory over Lu, victory would likely still have been credited to Ch'i. It was evident to Feng that his going to the aid of Ch'i would mean giving up the security of his command in the Peking area with little hope of receiving anything in return. Feng realized, secondly, that the major conflict was to be with Chang Tso-lin and the Fengtien armies and that the political future of North China rested on the outcome of this campaign. Thus, it was to Feng's advantage to stay close to the scene of action if he hoped to improve his political and military position.[47]

Feng's refusal to join the conflict to the south was followed by Chang's declaration of war on Wu P'ei-fu and the Chihli government. Chang Tso-lin's first move was timed to reduce the pressure on Lu, who was now faced with the threat of revolt on the part of elements of his own army who perceived that Ch'i Hsieh-yüan had far greater resources at his disposal than their own leader.[48] Although Lu was defeated before Chang Tso-lin was able to move his forces south of the Wall, the un-settled conditions in Chekiang and differences over the division of the spoils among those who had fought for Ch'i served Chang's purpose in preventing the Chihli group from presenting a united front against him.[49]

The Fengtien forces advanced on three fronts. The main force under Chang himself proceeded toward Shanhaikuan and followed the Muk-den-Tientsin Railroad line. A second force struck through Jehol and had as its objective the conquest of Inner Mongolia, while the third group also moved into Jehol but then swung south to strike at Peking.

Feng's Second *Coup d'État*

Wu P'ei-fu as commander of the Chihli forces planned to meet the threat of Fengtien by moving his own armies and those of his imme-diate subordinates to the Shanhaikuan area. To check the flanking move of Chang Tso-lin, Wu, on September 23, 1924, ordered Feng Yü-hsiang and Wang Huai-ching to proceed to Jehol to meet the right wing of the Fengtien armies.

Feng, although obeying the order, made it abundantly clear that he was not satisfied with the arrangement. Not only did Feng make public statements to the effect that he doubted the probability of actual con-flict, but he left Peking without either medical supplies or the full com-plement of his combat troops.[50] Feng's position was that of a military commander who had little to gain from the campaign against Fengtien and possibly a great deal to lose. The success of the Chihli forces would mean that Wu P'ei-fu would have extended his military domination over most of North China and that Feng would be deprived of his con-trol of the capital, being left instead in charge of the less desirable area of Jehol. On the other hand, a resounding victory by Chang, who ap-peared to have great advantages in terms of preparation, equipment, and unified command, would have spelled the end of Feng's ability to maintain his independent military power.[51]

Before Feng left Peking, he had already initiated negotiations with Chang Tso-lin, but no definite commitments were made.[52] However, after the Fengtien forces entered Jehol, it was soon apparent that they would have little difficulty in continuing their drive into Inner Mongolia, and thus would be able to divert additional forces to the Shanhaikuan front.[53] Therefore, even if Feng had been able to hold back the Feng-tien armies on the center sector, he would have found himself sur-rounded if Wu was unable to hold Shanhaikuan. The best that Wu could hope for was a victory that would make it too costly for Fengtien to attempt further sorties south of the Great Wall. Such a partial vic-tory by Wu would have damaged Feng's position, because he would have had to remain in Jehol.

It is impossible to determine what factor was critical in influencing Feng in his decision to shift sides and bring about the defeat of Wu P'ei-fu.[54] However, it was after Feng had been successful in obtaining the support of Yen Hsi-shan, *tuchün* of Shansi, that he prepared to strike against Wu. Yen promised to send troops out of Shansi to Shih-chiachuang, cutting any of Wu's reinforcements that might be moved up from Central China.[55]

On the night of October 22, 1924, Feng began to move his army back to Peking from Jehol and, by means of forced marches, covered one hundred miles in thirty-six hours. He immediately took over the capital, imprisoned President Ts'ao K'un, charging him with bribery, and or-dered the arrest of the members of Parliament. Wu P'ei-fu, who at the time was in direct command of his troops at Shanhaikuan, did not react immediately to this threat to his rear. Rather, he counted on a quick victory over the Fengtien armies, which would not only check the in-vaders from the north but would demonstrate to Feng the futility of his plans.[56] However, when the Manchurian forces held back from combat and when Yen Hsi-shan's actions denied Wu the prospect of reinforce-ments from Central China, he was forced to withdraw to Tientsin, where he was able to salvage only his best divisions by removing them by ship to the Yangtze River. They were thus transported to Hankow and finally returned to Wu's old Honan headquarters at Loyang.

With the defeat of Wu and the imprisonment of Ts'ao K'un, the Chihli power collapsed. Feng appeared to be in complete control of the capital, and, on the night of November 5, he moved his troops into the Forbidden City to end the reign of the boy Emperor Hsüan-t'ung. Feng hoped that, by this move, he would be able to obtain the revenue that was being paid to the abdicated Emperor and gain control over the assets of the Palace.[57] Feng also calculated that his move would give him popular support among the elements that were strongly Republi-can and anti-Manchu in sentiment. As a further step in this direction, Feng reorganized his armies into the Kuominchün, or the National Peo-ple's Army, and proclaimed that they were the first troops in the history of the Republic to serve as a national military establishment rather than a personal army.[58] However, instead of securing the support of liberal elements, Feng's acts of treachery and the pattern and methods of his *coup d'état* frightened off most of those leaders who were desirous of seeing an end to warlordism and who interpreted his high-handed methods as merely those of one more warlord seeking personal power. The only success Feng had was that he was able, along with other leaders, to persuade Sun Yat-sen to come to Peking to take part in the formation of a new government.[59]

With the collapse of the Chihli faction, an even more tenuous balance of power emerged. Feng's position in Peking was steadily weakened by the maneuvers of Chang Tso-lin. The Fengtien commander moved his troops south from Manchuria, and, instead of stopping at Tientsin to negotiate with Feng on the future plans for the government, he first made certain of his military control of the situation by ordering his armies to proceed south on the Tientsin-Pukow Railroad. This move gave Chang control of East China from Manchuria down to the Yangtze Valley. In addition, he reached an agreement with Tuan Ch'i-jui that the old Anfu leader would have a place in the new government.[60] By taking these steps, Chang hoped to strengthen his bargaining power when it came to his meeting with Feng.

THE RETURN OF TUAN CH'I-JUI

A five-day conference took place at Tientsin from November 11 to 16, 1924, with the triumvirate of Feng Yü-hsiang, Chang Tso-lin, and Tuan Ch'i-jui plotting the future of the Chinese Government. Feng soon discovered that he had little negotiating power beyond his control of Peking, and even this was, at best, tenuous as long as Chang remained in a position to seal the trap that he had laid. Feng even found that his trump card—the promise he had obtained from Sun Yat-sen to negotiate the return of the South to the jurisdiction of the Peking government—had been stolen by Tuan and Chang, who had both established contact with Sun. The principal result of the Tientsin Conference was the agreement that Tuan Ch'i-jui would be made provisional chief executive, thus leaving the door open to Sun to continue his projected trip to Peking.[61] Feng and Chang would still hold the areas they occupied and would become chief military leaders of the new regime.

On November 24, 1924, Tuan arrived in Peking and assumed office. He immediately formed a new cabinet, which did not include a single follower of Feng. It was now apparent to the public that Feng had not only lost out at the Tientsin Conference but that he had little chance of reasserting his power in the new government. His hope for the support of unorganized public opinion was destroyed by the critical attitude of the Chinese press, which went to great extremes in pointing out the treacheries of the "Christian General."[62]

Feng responded to these developments by resigning his post as inspector general and retiring to the Western Hills, stating that in the future he would spend his time in study and travel. However, his armies still controlled Peking, and, on the night of December 2, he demonstrated this control by so maneuvering his troops that Chang Tso-lin felt it advisable to leave the city and return to Tientsin. Chang followed this step by resigning his titles in the same ostentatious, "self-effacing" manner that Feng had adopted. The result was that Tuan Ch'i-jui, though lacking military power and personally under the threat of Feng's armies, was faced with the nearly hopeless task of keeping Feng and Chang in balance while trying to establish a formal government acceptable to the foreign diplomatic corps. The death of Sun Yat-sen at this time ended the possibility that Tuan could use the return of the South as a bait to keep Feng and Chang under control.

The new government rested upon a precarious balance, which was not made more stable by the formal appointments of Feng and Chang as Defense Commissioners of the Northwest and Northeast, respectively. Feng withdrew his headquarters to Kalgan, but no obstacles lay between his forces and the capital. In Kalgan, he once again found himself situated in such a way that he could do great damage to the ruling powers but was lacking in sufficient power and following to establish a government. The control of the Northwest did not prove to be lucrative and the area could not serve as an adequate power base. However, because of his geographical location and political isolation, Feng was now in a position to accept help from a new quarter—namely, Russia. Feng's idealism and his public pronouncements on social reform had attracted the attention of radical elements, and, among his own entourage, there were several intellectual Communists. Moreover, Russia, which was concerned over Japan's increasing support of Chang Tso-lin and the growing danger that Manchuria would be absorbed by Japan, saw in Feng a possible balance against the Japanese.[63]

When Sun Yat-sen came to the North shortly before his death, he brought with him Michael Borodin, and an attempt was made at that time to arrange a meeting of Borodin and Feng while the latter was still in the Western Hills. However, Feng refused to cooperate, and only after he had withdrawn to Kalgan and preliminary negotiations had taken place in February, 1925, with other agents did Borodin and Feng meet.* The conference resulted in Feng's agreeing to permit

---

* The conference between the "Christian General" and the Soviet agent was undoubtedly one of the most bizarre incidents of the whole period of warlord politics. The meeting lasted for forty-four hours. Feng spoke at length of his many aspirations for rebuilding China and pointed to his record of establishing "model armies," "model cities," and schools, while Borodin countered with talk of building a "new society" and belittled Feng's efforts as mere "philanthropy." Feng stubbornly refused to succumb to Borodin's dialectics, insistently pointing out the black record of the Canton government and recalling its reputation of robbing the people.[64]

propagandists to enter his army in return for material support in the form of money and munitions from Russia.

Feng Yü-hsiang was now ready to prepare once again to build up his forces for a test of strength with Chang Tso-lin. In addition to organizing the Northwest as a source of revenue, Feng sought out allies. He found a willing supporter in Sun Ch'uan-fang, who had previously been allied with Wu P'ei-fu (through Ch'i Hsieh-yüan), but who felt that he had not received his deserved rewards in the Ch'i-Lu War of August, 1924. Sun was in control of part of Chekiang, but he was being threatened by the remnants of the old Chihli faction and Chang Tso-lin's new move toward the Yangtze. Political and military maneuvers were temporarily brought to a halt in the spring and early summer of 1925 as the leaders cautiously observed the developments arising from the Shanghai Incident of May 30, when British police in the International Settlement fired on demonstrating Chinese.[65]

On October 17, 1925, Sun Ch'uan-fang began his push northward, conquering Kiangsu and Anhwei as he proceeded in the direction of Shantung.[66] Feng had counted on Chang's moving his troops down from Manchuria via Tientsin, thus affording Feng the opportunity to move eastward to cut the Fengtien lines of supply and communication. However, Chang protected his flank by sending an army into Jehol, just as he had done against Wu P'ei-fu in the preceding autumn. Feng thus found that, rather than cutting Chang's line of communication, he was exposed instead to a pincer movement by Chang.

Feng, however, had discovered another vulnerable point in Chang's position: the dissatisfaction of some of his subordinate officers. In particular, Feng was able to make an agreement with Kuo Sung-ling, who was one of Chang's trusted generals and commanded some of the best of the Fengtien troops.[67] On November 27, 1925, Feng and Kuo jointly declared war on Chang Tso-lin. Kuo, at the time, was at Shanhaikuan preparing to move south to Tientsin. It was now apparent to Chang Tso-lin that the treachery of his subordinate had cut his armies in two and there was a real danger that Kuo would have little difficulty in conquering Mukden.

In any conflict in Manchuria, a critical factor was the attitude and actions of Japan. At first, the Japanese remained neutral, apparently willing to let Chang and Kuo settle their own differences,[68] but the danger that the conflict would disrupt life in Manchuria and threaten its interests in the area caused Tokyo to intervene.* The Japanese announced that they were planning to reinforce the Mukden garrison and that they were prepared to fight to maintain the neutrality of the

---

* Another factor influencing the Japanese decision was the danger that Feng, with Russian support, might replace Chang in Manchuria, thus fundamentally altering the balance in the area and threatening Japanese interests.

South Manchurian Railway zone.[69] This action by Japan forced Kuo to check his move toward Mukden and evacuate the railway sector, while Chang was given use of the railroad to bring back his troops from south of the Wall. On December 23, Kuo was defeated forty miles south of Mukden, and both he and his wife were executed.

Feng, in the meantime, had moved down from Kalgan and defeated the Fengtien garrison at Tientsin.[70] But it was an empty victory after Kuo's defeat, for most of the Fengtien troops had safely escaped north of the Great Wall. Feng found himself no stronger than before, because he still had only sufficient power to dominate the military scene around the capital, while Chang Tso-lin and his forces remained a constant threat.

The hostilities between Feng and Chang had opened the way to a new power alignment. Wu P'ei-fu, who had been quietly building up his power in Honan, now began to appear as an attractive ally, especially to Chang Tso-lin. A Wu-Chang alliance would leave Feng in an isolated position in North China with only the Northwest left as an area to which to retreat. On the other hand, it was unlikely that Feng could draw Wu into his camp because of his betrayal of Wu in 1921 and also because Wu's power was still insufficient, even if used in combination with Feng's armies, to bring about the defeat of the Fengtien forces. Wu's hopes for a return to active political influence outside of Honan depended upon his acceptance of a subordinate position to the only power capable of dominating North and Central China, namely, Chang Tso-lin.

Feng still had effective control over a small but well-trained and disciplined army. However, if he was to continue as an effective military-political figure, it would be necessary for him to ensure an increase in funds and resources. Without a well-defined area under his direct control, he would have to be dependent upon grants from the Peking government, which, if under the control of Chang and Wu, would be at best niggardly. Feng, for this reason among others, concluded that the only safe course of action would be a temporary withdrawal from active participation in the public scene. It seemed wise at this juncture to wait for a future opening, which he felt was certain to come because, according to Feng's opinion, the Chang-Wu alliance, under the stress of organizing the government, was destined to be short-lived.[71] He also felt that, if he left his troops under the command of subordinates, they would be in a far more advantageous position to obtain funds from the central government than if he himself were to make the appeals. Thus, Feng was able to confront the Peking government with a nearly insoluble problem. The government was not in a position to guarantee the Kuo-minchün, as Feng's army was now called, a steady source of revenue as it would be obliged to finance Chang's and Wu's armies first. Even if the government could afford a substantial subsidy, there was no guarantee that the Kuominchün would be loyal to Peking; instead, the subsidy might be used to build up a future threat to the new holders of power at the capital. On the other hand, with Feng loosening his direct control of his armies, the Kuominchün became a tempting prize, which might be won by the highest bidder. The weak President, Tuan Ch'i-jui, in particular, could be expected to attempt to win over the Kuominchün in an effort to strengthen his own hand. In addition, there was the constant danger that, if the best-trained army in China was not to receive any revenue, it could easily become the best-organized bandit group in the country.

Feng, leaving these problems to his subordinates and the new power-holders in Peking, turned to another possible source of power—Russia.[72] Before leaving for his year in Moscow, however, he was party to an incident that contributed to Tuan Ch'i-jui's fall from the Presidency. The Kuominchün was in control of the Taku forts, where they had been posted as defense against the Fengtien troops, and, upon being ordered to withdraw, they fired upon several Japanese gunboats and foreign merchant vessels in violation of the Boxer Protocol.[73]

The Protocol powers chose to make a major issue of the incident and, on March 16, presented an ultimatum to President Tuan demanding of the Chinese Government the cessation of preparations for hostilities in the Tientsin–Taku Bar area. The Peking government was given until noon of March 18, 1926, to reply.[74] Because Feng had already decided to withdraw, there was little possibility at the time that a campaign would be fought in the area. However, by accepting the terms of the ultimatum, Tuan lost whatever chance he had to persuade Feng to stay on and support him. Moreover, the ultimatum was interpreted as a slight to Chinese sovereignty and led to student demonstrations in Peking and Tientsin. President Tuan had the unpleasant task of suppressing the demonstrations, and his personal bodyguards, highly uneasy over the situation, appeared to have lost their heads and fired on a body of demonstrating students, killing over thirty.[75] The incident doomed any hope that the Tuan government could continue in office as it was already too weak to withstand the further challenge of an aroused populace.

After the incident, Feng delayed his withdrawal temporarily in order to see if any radical change in the situation would develop on which he might capitalize. The ultimatum, although briefly checking the movement of Chang's and Wu's troops toward the capital, made it impossible to defend the area against them. It occurred to Feng that, if he should tarry in Peking, public opinion would associate him with Tuan Ch'i-jui's actions, but, if he should openly denounce Tuan, he might only gain the unorganized support of the students and still be unable to oppose the Chang-Wu alliance.[76] Thus, on March 22, Feng withdrew the Kuo-minchün from Tientsin and moved the Eleventh Division up to Nankow Pass to the north of Peking. The last elements of the Kuominchün evacuated Peking on the first of April, and, after establishing headquarters at Kalgan, Feng traveled via Mongolia and Siberia to Moscow.

The armies of Chang and Wu arrived in the capital immediately afterward and were faced with the problem of organizing a government. Although Chang Tso-lin had supported the selection of Tuan Ch'i-jui as provisional chief executive,* it was apparent that Tuan, now under pressure of public opposition, would be incapable of establishing a stable regime, even with the full support of Chang. In addition, Wu P'ei-fu was cold to the proposal that Tuan continue since he had had no part in the original support of Tuan, and there was little likelihood that he would have much influence in a government dominated by Tuan and Chang. Wu chose, rather, to act as a champion of the dissatisfied students and the articulate public which joined in the denunciation of Tuan.[77] The latter fully recognized his impossible situation and returned to his retirement in Tientsin. Wu P'ei-fu then proceeded to release his old leader, Ts'ao K'un, from the prison in which he had been held since Feng's *coup d'état*. However, Ts'ao was no more acceptable to the public than Tuan had been. More critical was the fact that Chang Tso-lin was completely unwilling to permit the establishment of a Ts'ao-Wu regime, which might exclude his own influence.

The impasse between Wu and Chang in the selection of a suitable candidate for the formal office of President was solved by the establishment of a Committee of Public Safety with equal representation theoretically given to Wu's and Chang's followers.[78]

However, the Wu-Chang combination was not a stable balance of equals, and Chang, because of his greater military power and the resources of Manchuria to support him, was soon in a dominant position. Not only was Chang able actively to support his appointees, but it was soon apparent that at least temporary security in office depended upon receiving the support of Chang and not that of Wu. On December 2, 1926, Chang formalized his military position by declaring himself commander in chief of the reorganized Northern Armies, which were to be known as the Ankuochün, or, as it was freely translated, the Tranquillity Restoration Army. Although by this move Chang did not eliminate the armies of Wu and Feng, he was able to gain control over a major portion of the national budget for military expenditures. Thus, Chang could at last supplement his own Manchurian source of revenue with a portion of the Peking government's finances, and he was now in a position to consolidate his power and expand his area of control. However, he

---

* "Provisional" because Parliament was not available to formalize the "election" of a President.

lacked a loyal following recruited from the provinces south of the Great Wall. He had only limited influence in the Central Provinces and thus was handicapped in organizing a central government that could expect to receive a steady flow of revenue from the nonmetropolitan provinces. It was impossible for him to replace the provincial leaders with his own men, as they would be treated as outsiders by the local leaders, and Chang lacked the military power to conquer the entire North and Central areas. As Wu P'ei-fu increasingly lost control at Peking, it became harder for Chang to obtain leaders in the provinces who would acquiesce in his expansion of direct political control. Thus, as Chang consolidated his power in Peking, he was in fact bringing the Peking-Tientsin area into the Manchurian orbit of power, but he could not absorb the rest of North China. The deepening split between capital and provinces was characterized by a decisive decline in the flow of revenue and governmental expenditures between the two areas.

By June, 1927, Chang ended the sham of rule by the Committee of Public Safety and inaugurated a dictatorial military government with himself holding the post of *ta-yüan-shuai*, or "Dictator."

However, by this time, the political complex of China had been radically changed by the early successes of the Northern Expedition of the Kuomintang. The relations of the warlords to the victorious Nationalist forces will be discussed in a later chapter.

THE SEQUENCES OF STRUGGLES

There is an elementary pattern to this complex sequence of conflicts. The story of the warlords begins with the disintegration of the first attempt to create a model army in China. At first, the relations among the warlords was dominated by, for the most part, politically oriented leaders who controlled the government in Peking. This was the period when the Anfu faction stood out above all others. Its supremacy depended upon political manipulation and pretensions of legality, and the requirements of the former undercut the latter.

Consequently, Anfu quickly disintegrated during the second phase of the warlord period, when actual military power was called into play. This period saw the rise of the Chihli coalition. This phase, however, was exceedingly unstable because, once military power became an acknowledged factor in determining events, the more powerful and independent warlords began to assert themselves.

Consequently, the Chihli alliance was soon confronted with the challenge of one of its tentative members, Chang Tso-lin, who controlled all of Manchuria. The rise of Chang in turn inspired the rise of a counterforce, which emerged in the form of Wu P'ei-fu. Increasingly, Chang and Wu were seen as the principal elements in a many-faceted balance of power. This balance became relatively stable, although different actors sought in various ways to alter it by shifting their allegiances or executing coups. The manner in which this balance of power operated was essential to the basic style of warlord politics, but, before examining it, we look into the character of the individual warlord organizations and their alliances.

3. THE WARLORD ORGANIZATIONS

The basis of warlord politics was the institution of personal armies at the disposal of individual military commanders. The principal warlords were sovereign over their organizations and in their domains, and there were no formal or legal authorities that could regulate or control their actions. The autonomy of the commanders was of course limited by the realities of life and, above all, by the balance of power in which they were caught, the perpetual shortage of financial resources, the loyalty of their dependent commanders and their associate warlords, and finally their own sense of social consciousness and national idealism.

In short, both the strength and limitations of the warlords lay in their organizational structures, and therefore it is appropriate that we begin our analytical treatment of the warlord period by looking at the character of their organizations, by noting the categories of leaders, the patterns of loyalty they developed, and their use of traditional bonds and personal ties. Many of these organizational considerations involved the basic problem of modern China, the balance between technical competence and loyalty obligations that plagued every warlord and still to this day hounds Mao Tse-tung and the Chinese Communists as they grapple with the "Red and Expert" question. We shall bring together all these organizational questions in a brief case study of Feng Yü-hsiang's army, the Kuominchün, or the National People's Army, which was the first Chinese army that sought to identify itself with both the spirit of nationalism and populism. The phenomenon of personal armies has been apparent during most periods of Chinese history, and especially during the periods between dynasties. It was a major factor in the fall of the Han.[1] One of the perennial problems in the traditional pattern of Chinese government was that of the relationship of civil authority to the military during periods of both peace and war. The ambiguous feeling of the literati toward military affairs generally meant that the military commanders were relegated to a subordinate position but not one in which they were always successfully controlled by civil officials.

One of the most vulnerable aspects of the traditional system of Chinese government was this relationship between civil and military officials, and it has not been sufficiently analyzed. Not only would such a study give insight into the stability of the Imperial form of government, but it should shed considerable light on the attitudes and value orientation of the literati. The attitude of the superiority of the civil official over the military official even in military matters has already been noted in the decision to appoint civil officials to conduct the operations during the Taiping Rebellion. It should, however, be added that these were not isolated examples. A survey of the first 260 names in Arthur W. Hummel's *Eminent Chinese of the Ch'ing Period* yields the following revealing information: Only 16 were purely military leaders, whereas, of the 244 civil officials, 70 had at one time or another during their careers been called upon to raise armies and direct military operations.* This survey not only reveals the domination of the civil officials over the military, but also indicates the attitude that anyone with a general education could perform specialized skills.[2] With the overthrow of the Imperial regime in 1911, however, the military commanders who had been under effective civil control found that they were no longer bound by any responsible governmental authority. The new government did make efforts to regularize the position of the military officials by the establishment in 1912 of a Ministry of Military Affairs.[3] Although this Ministry lacked sufficient authority or adequate resources to control the military leaders, it gave formal recognition to the applications of all the military commanders under the Imperial Government for the retention of their previous ranks.[4] Thus, the previous hierarchy of rank was maintained in spite of the Revolution. Indeed, the fact that no changes in the military hierarchy occurred illustrates the weakness of the new government, which was in no position to alter the situation of the military commanders in spite of any desire it might have had to establish a new elite at the top of the military structure. The old order of rank was maintained because it was in harmony with the relative military power of each commander at the time of the Revolution. Any radical attempt to alter this order might have led to open conflict among the commanders. Thus, the new government was completely incapable of controlling or regulating the military commanders except in so far as Yüan Shih-k'ai personally was able to command the loyalty of particular leaders.

It was soon apparent to the commanders that not only were they, through the control of their armies, in a position to achieve political and

* In this survey, those of Manchu origin were excluded because their unique position as the original conquerors meant that in theory they were supreme in both military and civilian matters. It seems likely that even more Chinese civil officials might have been called upon to conduct military affairs were it not for the Banner-men.

economic power, but indeed it was absolutely essential that they maintain their power if they were to continue to be active in political life. Thus, whatever may have been the long-range objectives of the particular military commanders, they soon all found themselves prisoners of the need to maintain and expand their personal power. This need was the basic driving force behind the distinctive politics of warlordism.

In order to maintain power, the military commanders found it necessary to play a dual role. First, they had to cope with the problems inherent in the relations of any commander to his command, including the maintenance of the loyalty and control of their officers and men, the organization, training, and movement of their troops, and tactical and strategic planning. Secondly, they had to be active in the broader political arena in order to obtain financial support, political and military alliances, desirable formal appointments, and geographic areas to rule. This dual role of the leading military commanders was not unique with the Republican period. Under the Imperial structure, it had also been essential for military leaders to obtain political support of a personal nature to insure continued financial resources.[5] After the Revolution, however, the unstable nature of the governmental structure meant that the task of obtaining support in the political arena became more difficult and required a greater proportion of the energies of the military commanders. In fact, the difference was more one of kind than degree, because the political arena was no longer as clearly defined now that it centered around the relations among the military leaders rather than the relations among civilian bureaucrats and politicians.

The necessity of being active in both political and military spheres led to a crude division of labor. There were in fact three types of military commanders among the warlords. The lowest category consisted of those field commanders whose primary duties were to assume the immediate responsibilities of directing the troops and maintaining the discipline and administration of the army. These were usually men who commanded regiments and possibly divisions and, in addition, served as tactical military advisers to their superiors.

The second group consisted of those more prominent military commanders who were active in the political arena. The first group served members of this group, who devoted their main attention to critical political and economic affairs. This is not to say that the members of this group were not actively involved in the administration and handling of the troops. In spite of this crude division of labor, it is striking that the political-military commanders devoted such a great proportion of their time to the trivial duties of training troops. Feng Yü-hsiang, in his *Diary*, records that, nearly every day when he was with his troops, he devoted part of his time to the actual training and drilling of his men. Brigadier General W. D. Connor, commander of American forces in

China, reported that, on a visit to Wu P'ei-fu's headquarters in May, 1921, he was struck by the fact that Wu personally checked on such minor details as inspecting 750 new recruits and rejecting those unfit. "In this way, to Western minds, he wastes a great deal of valuable time."[6]

Although their reputation and success or failure in the political field was contingent upon the strength of their armies, these *tuchüns* found it necessary to compete with other like commanders in obtaining political and economic rewards. That there was a conscious value placed upon the skill of these commanders in gaining revenue through their political machinations can be seen from the fact that, in 1923, when Ts'ao K'un was seeking the Presidency, one of the charges made against him was that, in 1913, "[he] failed in his duties to exact payments from the government and thus had to permit his troops to loot Peking."[7] No question was raised as to the justification or desirability of military commanders' attempting to exact payments from the government as it was assumed that this was their function. When a commander had to permit looting, this was an admission of his failure in the political field.

This second category of military leaders included the leading *tuchüns*, who were engaged in building up their personal military power and who were thus active in the political scramble for power. The third category consisted of those who had been successful in this struggle and were at the time recognized as political leaders throughout the nation. They usually had some troops at their disposal, but their real power lay in the fact that they had gained the respect and loyalty of particular commanders in the second category.[8] Also, they usually were in control of administrative offices, which fact opened the way to the obtaining of the necessary financial resources to insure the continued support of the commanders of the second category. Because of the skills they developed in playing the particular brand of politics necessary in Republican China and because of the deference and respect granted them by the lesser commanders, they were the centers of power clusters and the focal point of the political-military alliances. This group of super-*tuchüns* included such men as Tuan Ch'i-jui, Ts'ao K'un, Chang Tso-lin, and, later, Feng Yü-hsiang, Wu P'ei-fu, and Sun Ch'uan-fang.

For the purpose of analyzing the role of the military leaders in the political life of modern China, the second and third categories are the critical groups. These were the men who were involved in making the decisions that affected the political and military power structure. The essential quality they possessed in common was their control of military organizations that dominated society and influenced political events. Thus, as the *tuchüns* became the arbiters of Chinese politics, their structures represented the beginnings of competitive political organizations in Chinese society.

The existence of associations of politicians and intellectuals that bore party labels during this period should not lead to the conclusion that they were effective parties. These so-called parties included such groups as the Chinputang (Progressive Party—the supporters of Yüan Shih-k'ai's imperial design and heavily conservative), Min She (People's Society—backers of Li Yüan-hung), Hsien-fa Yen-chiu Hui (Constitution-Research Association—dominated by Tuan Ch'i-jui), and other splinter groups, as well as, of course, the successor to the T'ung-meng Hui—the Kuomintang (Nationalist Party).[9] These groupings could be considered political parties only by those who had more idealistic hopes for republican institutions in China than the facts at the time warranted. They were little more than poorly organized personal cliques which sought to obtain power by permitting themselves to be exploited by the *tuchüns*. The reality of group politics lay with the *tuchüns* and their organizations and not with the so-called political parties.

To understand the basic features of warlord politics, it is necessary to appreciate the type of organizations that they developed and, in particular, the patterns of loyalty to which they gave rise. Just as the organizations were the bases of the *tuchün's* power, so were the weaknesses of these groupings a strong conditioning factor in the policies and actions of the military leaders.

THE PATTERN OF LOYALTY

The essential factor in the power structures of the *tuchüns* was the loyalty of their subordinate officers and troops. The *tuchüns* needed a body of followers whom they could fully trust, but to develop such a loyal following was no slight achievement, given the general lack of any strong ideological framework or recognized abstract political values that could serve as the basis of demands for loyalty.[11] A striking feature of the period was the fact that the soldiers themselves showed a high incidence of loyalty. Captain Anatol M. Kotenov observed that "cases of individual treachery and wilful desertion were almost unknown except when an entire unit acting under direct orders of its Commander changed its political or party allegiance and went over to the enemy."[12] He explains this situation in terms of the sense of personal honor and fair play that he felt he observed in the individual Chinese soldier. However, it would appear that other factors of possibly greater importance were involved. These included a personal loyalty to one's immediate superior officers, especially because it was they who paid the troops and supervised their immediate welfare, as well as a sense of group belonging and high morale at the company level. In addition, there was the important consideration that most of the troops came from humble peasant backgrounds and, difficult as the life of the soldier might be, it did at times give better promise of material reward and security. This was shown by the fact that, when efforts at demobilization were attempted, "the individual soldiers often were unwilling to leave the service with such an uncertain future ahead of them."[13]

Where the loyalty pattern showed its greatest weakness was at the officer level. Although it would appear that the financial factor was important in the relationship of the *tuchün* and his commanders, still it is striking that often, in spite of failure to pay subordinates, the *tuchüns* were able to continue to demand their respect and loyalty. Feng Yü-hsiang was often in arrears to his officers, and, in 1926, they were not fully paid over a period of fourteen months; yet they still remained faithful.[14] In 1924, Wu P'ei-fu had insufficient resources to pay fully his officers for nine months.[15] Proof that the relationship rested upon more than the simple economic consideration of receiving regular pay is to be found in the fact that at no time did there develop an open market for mercenary commanders who would sell their services to the highest bidder. Although there might have been strong pressure leading to such a development on the part of the subordinate officers, these were checked by the attitudes of the *tuchüns*. No *tuchün* felt that he was in such a secure position that he could guarantee a steady income to all of his subordinates, and thus he was not prepared to rely upon commanders whose obligation for loyalty lay in the payments given him. Although a *tuchün* might attempt to buy another *tuchün*'s commanders, he would not trust them to command his own troops.[16] Thus, the subordinate officers recognized that there was not an impartial and free market for their services. Although the monetary factor was often involved in the development of loyalties, the loyalty patterns which the *tuchüns* established were far more complex and cannot be explained by any theory based solely upon pecuniary motives.

Thus, although it was common in the 1920's to talk about the warlords' use of "silver bullets" and it was popular to suggest that all warlords were available if the price was right, the use of bribery was probably not that widespread in influencing actual events. Much of this popular mythology probably arose from confusion over the use of money to defeat enemies and "buy" enemy subordinates with the constant need that the warlords indeed did have for funds simply to maintain their organizations. This problem of funding did lead to extensive "informal tax collections" and the practice of demanding taxes for many years into the future. We shall return to this problem when we discuss the relationship of the warlords to the Chinese business community.

Claims for the loyalties of men may be in terms of personal and particularistic demands or they may be in the form of more impersonal and universalistic values. Given the nature of Chinese society and culture in which the personal and particularistic values dominated, the *tuchüns* had to find ways to exploit these values in order to achieve effective organizations. They needed to develop efficient organizations of men who functioned in relatively impersonal relationships without losing a sense of group obligation and loyalty.[17]

It is possible to categorize the various demands for loyalty employed by the *tuchüns* under the headings of the institutionalized loyalty structures that existed in traditional China, and to observe how these concepts were utilized by the *tuchüns*. Such an approach has the advantage of distinguishing between the traditional considerations of loyalty that the *tuchüns* supported and those which their policies tended to weaken.

FAMILY LOYALTIES

In the Chinese social setting, the strongest demands for loyalty and obligation arose from family relationships.[18] However, this tie was rarely of any importance in the relationship of the *tuchün* to his subordinates. There were only two cases in which family considerations were involved in the commander-subordinate relationship. One case was that of Chang Tso-lin and his two sons, who became commanders of divisions in the Fengtien Army. In this case, Chang was so secure in his domination of Manchuria that his pattern of control was more typical of an independent sovereign who was well on his way to establishing a family dynasty. It was possible for him to permit family considerations to outweigh the need for the best commanders, but Chang Tso-lin had to pay a relatively high price for his insistence that his sons be made divisional commanders. Tensions arose because subordinate officers, such as Kuo Sung-ling and Chang Teng-hsüan had to perform the duties of commanding the divisions nominally under the command of Chang's sons without receiving what they considered just recognition.[19] Also, the appearance of his sons in the councils of the Fengtien elite made it difficult for those leaders who held opposing views to those of Chang's sons to argue with vigor their policy proposals.[20]

The other case was that of Ts'ao K'un and his younger brother, Ts'ao Yin. However, in this instance the younger brother had also had a military career and had developed a following in the form of the Tientsin clique. Thus, it was a case of Ts'ao Ying being in a position to exploit the fact that he was Ts'ao K'un's brother rather than one in which Ts'ao K'un depended upon his brother's support to ensure his power. It would be hard to say whether it was the fact that Ts'ao Ying was the brother of Ts'ao K'un or whether it was his position of leadership in the Tientsin clique that made him such an important member in the Chihli faction. There is no doubt that at times he did serve to weaken the Chihli faction, as in the case of the first Chihli-Fengtien war, in

1924, when Wu P'ei-fu appointed him to the command of the Twenty-sixth Division—the division that permitted the Fengtien forces to break through at Chiumen. The division failed to follow Ts'ao Ying's leadership because they were still loyal to their old divisional commander.[21] All indications point to the probability that Wu was influenced in this appointment by the desire to obtain the support of the Tientsin clique, rather than by any considerations of the relationship of Ts'ao Ying to the leader of the Chihli faction.[22] On the other hand, there was no doubt, especially in 1923 when Ts'ao K'un sought the Presidency, that Ts'ao Ying became the center of attention of the politicians who desired to obtain the favor of his older brother and that they felt that the family tie was meaningful in the political arena.

Thus, although the relationship between the commander and his subordinates was modeled after that of the traditional Chinese relationships of father-son and elder brother–younger brother, actual family bonds never became important.[23] This is not to say that examples of nepotism did not exist, but it is, rather, that they were not critical in the organizations developed by the *tuchüns*. Cases of nepotism usually took the form of granting sinecures to members of one's family and even to distant relatives. Wu P'ei-fu saw that his brother was appointed director of the Peking Zoological Gardens;[24] Feng Yü-hsiang appointed a relative to a magistrate's post in Honan;[25] and Tuan Ch'i-jui secured positions in the Peking Municipal Light and Power Company for his relatives.[26] In fact, there is little doubt that these examples could be expanded indefinitely if all the records of the *tuchüns'* appointments were available and the relationships of the appointees known. However, it is noteworthy that the *tuchüns* did not employ their relatives in the important posts within their organizations and that they preferred to grant them relatively safe positions in which they would hardly be called upon to perform tasks affecting the political power of the leaders. In this era, the problems of nepotism were not so destructive of efficiency as they were in such fields as industry and business during subsequent periods. The *tuchüns* were fortunate in being in a position to control sufficient appointments so that they could, on the one hand, fulfill their obligations to relatives by appointments to relatively innocuous positions, while, on the other hand, still maintaining the efficiency of their primary organizations.

However, at times, the *tuchüns* did make use of the concepts of familial obligation in the sense that relatives were often used as mediators and negotiators. Numerous examples could be cited. Tuan Ch'i-jui used his eldest son, Tuan Chun-liang, to seek Feng Yü-hsiang's support in December, 1924.[27] In October, 1924, after Feng had betrayed Wu P'ei-fu, former Premier Chang Chin-i delegated his brother, Chang Hsiao-ch'en, to attempt to mediate between the two *tuchüns* and seek a re-establishment of the Chihli faction.[28] In May, 1925, Tuan Ch'i-jui dispatched his brother-in-law, Wu Kuan-hsin, to negotiate agreements with Sun Ch'uan-fang and Wu P'ei-fu that would strengthen the Peking government in the face of the Fengtien and Canton threats.[29] Even the Canton regime employed such practices, when it sent the son of Wu T'ing-fang, the Vice-Minister of Foreign Affairs, to Mukden, in 1922, in an attempt to negotiate an alliance between Canton and Fengtien.[30] Lu Yung-hsiang utilized his son as negotiator with Chang Tso-lin in 1924.[31] General Chang Shao-tseng, a relative of Wu P'ei-fu, was employed as mediator between Feng Yü-hsiang and the Loyang leader in 1924.[32] In these cases, the advantages were twofold: First, one could expect a high degree of loyalty and trustworthiness on the part of relatives; and, second, the other parties in the discussion would recognize that negotiations through relatives made available a more intimate and personal channel for establishing alliance relationships.[33]

In general, the stakes were too high to permit family considerations to dominate the selection of the most effective and skilled subordinates. As long as more skilled men could be trusted, it was too risky to employ individuals solely because of family connections. This point is emphasized by cases in which political considerations came into conflict with family obligations, and it was the former which dominated. In 1918, Li Ho-chi was appointed *tüchun* of Fukien by the Anfu faction. Li was a relative of Hsü Shu-cheng ("little Hsü").[34] With the defeat of Anfu in 1920, Li Ho-chi shifted his allegiance to Wu P'ei-fu, but, in the winter of 1922, "Little Hsü," seeking to return to power, obtained the assistance of Hsü Ch'ung-chih of Kwangtung and ousted his relative, Li, in a *coup d'état*.[35]

REGIONAL SENTIMENTS

Regional and provincial identification formed yet another strong sentiment of Chinese society that was manipulated by the *tuchüns*.[36] Provincial sentiments were most fully used by those *tuchüns* who were secure in their control of particular areas. The most extreme case of this kind was Yen Hsi-shan, who, in his control of Shansi province, employed only commanders who were natives of the province.[37] In order to have competent commanders, Yen followed a policy of training particularly promising young men, even sending some to Japan for their military education.[38] Chang Tso-lin also relied heavily upon natives of Manchuria and financed the training of many of his younger officers in Japanese military academies.[39] Chang's command also included many migrants from Shantung who worked with the Shantung troops in the Fengtien armies.[40] Chang was able to exploit this fact when, in 1924, the Fengtien armies conquered Shantung and he was able to place a native of the province, Chang Tsung-ch'ang, in charge of the Fengtien control of Shantung.[41] Wu P'ei-fu's subordinates included primarily natives of Honan, most of whom were products of the Honanese Army of Imperial times.[42] Although some of these men were not born in Honan, they had served for many years in armies made up of Honanese.

On the other hand, those commanders who did not have a clearly defined geographic area under their jurisdiction for long periods were forced to shift their headquarters frequently and therefore did not develop armies made up of such homogeneous bodies of natives of one area. Thus, in the case of Feng Yü-hsiang, although most of his commanders came from North China, there appeared to be no strong preference for men of any particular area, and only one of his commanders came from Feng's ancestral home of Anhwei.[43] For such organizations, the concept of sectional loyalty was of little influence in binding the upper ranks of the officer class together, but efforts were nevertheless made to ensure that at the company-level natives of the same area were brought together to strengthen morale, as well as to facilitate communication and understanding among the troops.[44]

As important as was the factor of sectional loyalty in the establishment of the *tuchüns* organization, it was dangerous for the leader to rely excessively upon this bond. In particular, it created difficulties when the *tuchün* happened to control an area of which he and his staff were not natives.* Conflicts would often develop when a *tuchün's* immediate followers were identified as representing a particular area and the *tuchün*, finding it necessary to expand the geographic base of his power, sought to incorporate commanders and men from a new area. The most striking example of this problem was the case of Lu Yung-hsiang's efforts to control Chekiang. Lu and his immediate followers were Hopei men, but he also had under his jurisdiction four divisions whose commanders and men were natives of Chekiang.[47] At the time of the Chekiang-Kiangsu war of 1924, the native troops refused to continue to follow the orders of Lu, and the revolt of these forces was critical to his defeat.[48] Of all the forces for whom Lu was financially responsible, only those under commanders who were not natives of Chekiang could be relied upon in the conflict with Ch'i Hsieh-yüan, even though the province itself stood to lose with a Kiangsu victory.† After the victory by Kiangsu, much of Chekiang was occupied by the troops of Sun Ch'uan-fang, who had pushed north from Fukien, supposedly in alliance with Ch'i Hsieh-

* Feng Yü-hsiang was faced with opposition when he became *tuchün* of Shensi in 1921 because he did not number among his staff any natives of the area, and it was necessary to incorporate local personnel into his organization in order to meet this opposition.[45] Wu P'ei-fu was so closely identified with Honan that the appearance of his troops in Chihli in 1920 and 1922 was met by local opposition.[46]

† The First and Second Divisions of the Chekiang Provincial troops went so far in attempting to subvert the authority of Lu Yung-hsiang that they maintained representatives in Peking who sought to achieve an agreement with the Chihli faction. (*China Year Book*, 1924–25. Tientsin: 1925; p. 923.)

yüan. Sun, being an outsider and having no natives of the province in his organization, soon began to have trouble in controlling Chekiang. By the autumn of 1925, the civil governor was working with the provincial troops to bring pressure on Sun to release his immediate control of Hangchou and permit the commanders of the First and Second Divisions of the Chekiang Provincial Army to control the area.[49]

TEACHER-STUDENT RELATIONSHIP

By far the most important of the traditional attitudes of obligation used by the *tuchüns* was the idealized model of the teacher-student relationship. It was on the basis of this traditional relationship that the *tuchüns* were able to build their strongest bonds of personal loyalty. The sense of obligation and indebtedness of a student to his teacher was a value fully supported by the traditional Chinese culture. The relationship also carried with it a demand for reciprocity in that the teacher was under obligation to support the interests of his protégé.

Thus, early in his career, the *tuchün* developed a following of junior officers whom he had trained, and, as the *tuchün* rose in power, these men would follow him, their careers depending to a large degree upon the success of their mentor. This pattern was initiated in the Imperial Army, where it was the custom for an officer, when given a change of command, to retain a group of immediate subordinate officers who were transferred from post to post with him.[50] As has already been pointed out in Chapter 2, the tradition for the practices of the junior officers to identify themselves with their superiors had advanced to a formally recognized and sanctioned institution during the period of the Peiyang Army and was continued when the personal army of Yuan Shih-k'ai became fragmented under the leadership of Tuan Ch'i-jui and Feng Kuo-chang. The relationship was a highly personal one, and since it extended to the relations among the dominant *tuchüns*, as well as to the members of each particular organization, it gave to all *tuchün* politics a strong personal quality.

During periods of political stability, this pattern of relations could serve admirably, as it had done under the Imperial structure, but, with the pressures of *tuchün* politics of the 1920's, it was taxed to the limit. The entire concept of the reciprocal relations of the teacher and the student was compromised when it was no longer possible for the super-*tuchüns* to continue fully to uphold the ideal in their relationships with subordinates. As the leading *tuchüns* became powers in their own right, they were often forced to pursue policies that ran counter to the previous pattern of student-teacher relations. Also, the super-*tuchüns* found it difficult to maintain an imperial attitude toward all their previous subordinate commanders that was so essential for the system to function successfully.

Thus, for example, Ts'ao K'un had five followers who were particularly close to him and who had been his students: Wu P'ei-fu, Li Shun, Ch'i Hsieh-yüan, Wang Ch'eng-pin, and Feng Yü-hsiang. When Ts'ao became the head of the Chihli faction, it was difficult for him to act impartially on behalf of all of them, so, rather than antagonizing any of them, he refused to take an active part in supporting any of them. This policy led to a decline in the close relationships that had previously existed.[51]

With the decline in the ability of the leading and older *tuchüns* to follow the pattern of behavior laid down by the dictates of the traditional teacher-student relationship, there was a general deterioration of the entire principle of such moral obligations. As long as the leaders were not living examples of the principle, it was difficult to enforce the concept on the younger officers in the organizations. Thus, over the years, as the political stresses became more intense, there was a marked decline in this traditional moral sense of obligation. There is little doubt that most critics of the period were correct in attributing this decline to the type of men active in the political arena. However, it was not so clearly recognized that the old moral precepts were intended to function in a stable social order that no longer existed. Although the older ethical rules no longer were applicable in the new political context, no clearly recognized substitute had yet been found.

The simple relationship of teacher and student was further strained by the exigencies of particular situations. That is, with the need to meet political and military crises, the *tuchün* had to depend upon the skill of his subordinates, which often meant that he must deny the favored positions of responsibility and prestige to those men who had the primary claims as being his senior protégés. The demands for efficiency became an obstacle to the strict adherence to the principle that favor should go to one's protégé of longest standing. Whether the *tuchün* selected the most skilled person or not, the very fact that he had to make decisions in respect to these competing values tended to undermine and place in a less secure position the validity of the principles of the teacher-student relationship.

The best example of these difficulties was the case of Chang Tso-lin. Chang's early career was that of a *hunghutze*, or bandit, in Manchuria, but, during the Russo-Japanese War, he assisted the Japanese armies. During the Sino-Japanese War, he supported the Imperial Government and was given a military post under Hsü Shih-ch'ang, who was then Viceroy and later President of the Republic.[52] Chang brought with him into the formal military organization many of his former bandit leaders, and these formed the nucleus of his later power structure.[53] During his early years in the Imperial Army, he added more personal followers. This early group consisted of such men as Yang Yü-t'ing, Kao Ching-ho, Wang Yung-chiang, and Chang Hsüan-hsiang.[54]

These men were personally very close to Chang and considered themselves his pupils and intimate followers. However, as Chang's power in Manchuria expanded and he became a dominant factor in the politics of North China, it was necessary for him to rely more heavily upon a new group of associates who had received more specialized training, including Japanese military education, and possessed specific skills that the earlier group lacked. This younger group included Kuo Sung-ling, Wu Chin, and Chang Teng-hsüan and was fortunate in having as a supporter Chang's eldest son, Chang Hsüeh-liang.[55] As Chang's commitments south of the Great Wall became more extensive, he tended increasingly to favor the younger group, whose members championed an active policy of expansion.[56] This led to a sharp cleavage within the ranks of the Fengtien elite, and finally culminated in the Kuo Sung-ling revolt. Kuo objected that, although Chang was giving the greater responsibilities to the younger group, he still favored the older followers in making appointments to the more desirable posts.* Chang was constantly faced with the problem of maintaining a balance between these two elements within his command.[58]

PERSONAL RELATIONS

Because of the stress of the intense political struggle, the *tuchüns* could no longer strictly adhere to the traditional concepts of their relationship with their subordinates, and, as a result, there evolved a new form of personal relations, which was ill defined and lacking in the formal sanctions of an institutionalized relationship. It was necessary to recognize the importance of skill and ability, while, at the same time, preserving the values of obligation and loyalty. Because the old traditions continued to command a degree of deference, however, the new relationship could not be based solely upon considerations of the individual's ability. The attitude of the *tuchüns* toward his subordinates continued to be highly colored by personal and specific considerations. Thus, with the decline in the importance of the strict adherence to the principles of

* At the start of the campaign of 1925, Kuo Sung-ling had been promised the post of *tuchün* of Kiangsu, which would have made him the leading Fengtien proconsul in Central China, but, after the campaign was under way, Chang decided that he should give the new post to his Chief of Staff, Yang Yü-t'ing (Department of State, 893.00/6586). Chang changed his views because of a feeling that he would have to rely upon the younger group for further military operations and thus could not afford to give their leading representative such an independent post. The position of commander in Central China would be one of great prestige for its holder, but it would have been of little importance in terms of maintaining Chang's political power in North China.[57]

obligation derived from the teacher-student relationship, there developed a new form of personal relationship, which was based upon the subordinate's expectations that he would be rewarded if the *tuchün* were successful. This relationship required that the subordinate have a high degree of confidence in the ability of the *tuchün* to achieve a position in which he would be capable of granting bigger rewards. So long as the subordinates had faith in the eventual successes of their leader and in his integrity in granting adequate rewards, they were willing to remain loyal to him.

This dependence upon personal expectations created an even more fluid situation in an already highly flexible and shifting framework. That is, the power relationship of the *tuchün* in respect to other *tuchüns* was soon reflected in the degree of loyalty he could expect from his subordinates. When it appeared that the situation favored an increase in the relative power of a leader, he found that his subordinates were very willing to comply with his demands. On the other hand, if the fortunes of the *tuchün* seemed to be declining, the loyalty pattern of the organization began to show signs of breaking. The shift to a greater reliance upon expectation of rewards was indicative of the development of *tuchün* organizations from a primarily military into a more political grouping. Rewards were to be considered in terms of political posts and commands that opened the way to greater political participation.

The consequence of this development was to make it possible for a *tuchün* to lose power rapidly after a critical defeat or to make a remarkably rapid recovery after such a defeat by creating the expectation that he had a fair chance of returning to prominence.

One of the best examples of this development was the case of Wu P'ei-fu after his defeat in September, 1924, which resulted from Feng Yü-hsiang's *coup d'état* and the victory of the Fengtien forces at Shanhaikuan. Wu was able to escape back to the Yangtze area with only his elite Third Division intact.[59] Wu's position appeared hopeless except for the fact that there was still uncertainty as to Feng's and Chang's ability to work successfully in concert.[60] As long as there was this doubtful factor, Wu's supporters, while wavering in their allegiance, hesitated to make an overt break with their leader.[61] Wu, realizing the danger and the need to restore confidence to his followers, announced, on November 14, 1924, that he was about to form a new eleven-*tuchün* alliance in Central China, which would be capable of meeting any threat from the North.[62] The announcement was successful in staving off temporarily the doubts as to Wu's powers of recovery. However, the critical question during the autumn of 1924 still remained. How successful would the Feng-Chang alliance be? When, after the Tientsin conference of November 11 to 15, it began to appear that the northern leaders would not be able to cooperate for long, Ch'i Hsieh-yüan's prospects of holding

Kiangsu seemed improved. There was a marked rise in Wu's stock when his followers began to feel that he could not be easily discounted.[63] However, with the drive into the Yangtze Valley and the defeat of Ch'i Hsieh-yüan, Wu's last remaining support began to melt away.[64] The critical blow came when the Second and Third Kuominchün, under the commands of Sun Yüeh and Hu Ching-i, respectively, commenced their drive on Loyang, and Wu had to withdraw toward Hankow.[65] It was at this point that Wu lost the support of his most trusted subordinate, Hsiao Yao-nan, who controlled Hankow at the time, and, with a group of close personal friends, had to retire from the political arena.

The telegram that Hsiao sent to Wu reflected the dilemma of a subordinate who, because of the existing situation, finds it necessary to renounce his loyalties to a superior of long standing in order to preserve his own career hopes.

> Your Excellency has at heart the desire of unifying the country, and, although you have been defeated by unforeseen mishaps, you still have not changed your attitude. Assuredly, for this, you are a hero. Now, however, the people dislike civil war, and, furthermore, you have no one to whom to entrust your commands. I, Hsiao Yao-nan, am your protégé, and, if I know of these things and do not speak of them to you, I am disloyal to my master, whereas, if I tell you other things that are not true in flattery, I am unrighteous. I therefore say that you should look upon the country with love for the people, and you should sacrifice all your possessions and offices and go into retirement. . . . All men will know you as a real hero, who has no desire to embrace selfish ambitions. I, who am only of small rank, would fain follow your footsteps and resign my office at once, but I regret that no successor to my place has yet been appointed.[66]

But, with the split between Feng and Chang and the necessity for the Fengtien troops to withdraw from the Yangtze area, the way was open for Wu to attempt a return to power.[67] Chang himself supported this movement as a means of obtaining further support against Feng and the Kuominchün and sent an emissary to seek Wu's cooperation.[68] Wu refused to commit himself definitely to the support of Fengtien, but, on October 21, 1925, when Sun Ch'uan-fang's troops replaced the Fengtien forces at Nanking, Wu made his move by suddenly returning to Hankow and stating that he was going to restore the old Chihli power with the support of Sun Ch'uan-fang.* This announcement was sufficient to cause

---

* It is impossible to determine to what extent this move had the previous support of Sun Ch'uan-fang. There are some indications that Wu's announcement caught Sun unprepared, but that Sun did not deny it because he saw the possibility that Wu's return might mean further support against the Fengtien forces. The text of Wu's announcement was carefully worded to give the impression that China was about to be unified by an alliance of leaders, and that it was necessary for Wu to return to active participation in order to insure that Hupei and Hunan would be well represented when the country was unified.

all the former commanders to return in November, 1925, and accept the leadership of Wu. Ch'i Hsüeh-yüan returned from Japan, Wu Ching-lien from Honan, and all the lesser commanders from Szechwan appeared on the scene to declare their allegiance to Wu.[69] Although Wu's power never again equaled that which he had wielded before 1924, still, he had been able to make a rapid recovery from just as sudden a decline in power.

Important as personal associations were for a warlord, they did not provide for stability in the building of political-military organizations. Indeed, the very tendency to value personal relations as essential for collective action tended to inspire jealousies among subordinates and higher conflict, not only under conditions of declining power but even more when a *tuchün* sought to expand his domain. Once a warlord had larger ambitions and sought to become a national figure, the demands on his organization exceeded the integrating adhesion of personal associations, and the deficiency of the warlord in providing an impersonal basis for his power became clear to all.

In a very fundamental sense, the limits of personal associations represented the insoluble problem of the warlords, and, in a more general sense, it may in fact be the most troublesome problem that the Chinese people have been confronted with as they have sought to change from being a Confucian society to being a modern nation-state. Personal relations have been a powerful force in building tightly integrated but relatively small-scale organizations. When the Chinese have needed larger organizations in order to meet the requirements of producing national integration and modernizing policies the force of personal ties has been inadequate because the country is so large.

As long as the warlord kept his power limited to a provincial or regional basis, he could command an organization that could optimally exploit the political and military values of traditional Chinese sentiments about the importance of respecting personal ties. Once the warlord sought to build his organization to deal with national problems, the very force of personal ties, which were so impressive in a more compact organization, tended to dissolve completely.

In the modernization of China, we find this basic dilemma plaguing all leaders and all movements. To go beyond the web of personal ties and relationships has called for an exaggerated stress on ideology that has not been consistent over time with the Chinese approach to politics. Both the Nationalists and the Communists have vacillated between an exaggerated impersonal and ideological emphasis and the recognition that personal factors are important.

In the case of the warlords, there were many examples to illustrate the fundamental principle that, once an organization sought to expand beyond the network of immediate personal ties, it was soon beset with some insoluble problems. These included such questions as: How should conquered elements be absorbed into the organization without disrupting its basic relationships? How was the warlord to decide who was to get the more desirable posts without creating disruptive jealousies? The difficulty was that, as *tuchün* organizations expanded, there emerged new centers of power, which became the nuclei of further autonomous power groups. Thus, just as the Peiyang Army spawned the leading *tuchüns*, so each of them, as they sought to become the integrating force of the nation, tended to spawn subordinates who soon felt that they had to act as independent forces because they were no longer so personally tied to their commanders.

This problem can best be analyzed in terms of a case study of a particular organization, such as can be found in the next chapter. However, before making such a study, it is necessary to mention briefly the role of political advisers in the *tuchüns'* organizations. As the military leaders became more involved in political action and their associations became less purely military organizations, it was necessary for them to incorporate into their structures men who could serve as advisers in the political arena.

POLITICAL ADVISERS

The addition of civilian advisers to the warlord organizations created problems in maintaining solidarity. The presence of these advisers and their influence upon the decisions of the warlords meant that the leaders were no longer entirely dependent upon, and at times might even disregard, the advice of their military subordinates. Chang Tso-lin, in particular, was faced with such conflicts, because, in his efforts to maintain stable administration in Manchuria, he was exposed to the conflicting opinions and advice of his military leaders, on the one hand, and the administrators and bureaucrats, on the other.

These advisers were of two types; the older form of political adviser, who was a carry-over from the Imperial times, and the younger technicians, who brought with them the skills of Western knowledge.

Chinese politics since the time of Confucius himself has always included the role of the teacher-adviser—the older—and presumably wiser philosopher-scholar who generally did not hold formal office but counseled particular figures, following them along through much of their careers. The entourages of great officials usually contained individuals who, at one time or other, had been the officials' mentors. With the disappearance of the Imperial structure, the only structures of government that the old-style mandarin could hope to influence were the *tuchüns*. Those men who had previously either functioned as advisers to officials in the Imperial government or who had been active in political affairs gravitated around the various military leaders and became important figures in the immediate followings of these men. Often their objective was simply to establish the necessary contacts in order to obtain the *tuchün's* support in winning formal appointments in the provincial or even national bureaucracy. However, although the advisers of the old school were given deference, they had only limited powers. The mandarins had lost their real function with the collapse of the Imperial bureaucratic structure, and they were now forced to assume a subordinate role to the experts in violence—once their greatest foes.

The old mandarins were still respected as the carriers of classical knowledge, which had traditionally been a part of the education of men active in political affairs. Most of the *tuchüns* did employ such men as personal instructors, and, as teachers, they were in a position to command attention whenever they sought to advise their masters. Thus, in the case of Feng Yü-hsiang, throughout the period of his political prominence, he received from time to time instruction in the *Tso Chuan, Li-Chi,* and the *I Ching* from his mandarin advisers.[70] Wu P'ei-fu was under the instruction of Pei Chien-wu and developed into a respectable calligrapher and a poet whose skill was considered more than passable.* Chang Tso-lin's instructors included men who had held official posts under the Ch'ing Government.[71]

Aside from formal instruction, the older advisers offered a real service in that they were often experts in personal politics and, as such, could assume an active role in ·the relationships of the *tuchün* with other military leaders, as well as with the more organized groups of the public. That is, their particular skill was that of a bargainer who operates in a highly personal manner, and they were thus used in negotiations with representatives of other power groups. So long as they were expected to negotiate with those who had the same traditional background and therefore thought alike and possessed the same value systems, they were relatively successful in fulfilling the functions of negotiators and adjusters.† Thus the old advisers were important in the efforts to create personal ties between *tuchüns.*

* Wu's literary skills appeared to have made Feng Yü-hsiang jealous, and caused him to criticize Wu as being too proud and without the humility of a true scholar. Feng's *Diary,* Book 2, p. 13.

† The traditional mandarin's approach to negotiations was more in the manner of a mediator or middleman. That is, he did not operate on the basis of carrying through a particular program of objectives decided upon by the decision-makers but, rather, sought to mediate between the conflicting positions of his superior and his opposite number. For a discussion of this attitude toward negotiations, see: T. F. Tsiang, "New Light on Chinese Diplomacy," *The Journal of Modern History,* III, No. 4, especially pp. 584–85; John K. Fairbank, "Chinese Diplomacy and the Treaty of Nanking," *The Journal of Modern History,* XXII, No. 1, especially pp. 19–20; C. Kuo, *A Critical Study of the First Anglo-Chinese War* (Shanghai, 1935; pp. 42–43).

However, with the increase in the violence of the period and the decline in the relative importance of personal relations, the old mandarins were of diminishing importance. Thus Pei Chien-wu, one of Wu P'ei-fu's most trusted negotiators, lost his personal influence with Wu when the Loyang Marshal decided to attempt to unify the country by force.[72] The period was replete with examples of mandarins attempting to serve as personal mediators between *tuchüns*. For example, after Ts'ao K'un's election, he sent a scholar of the old tradition, Ts'ao Yu-ku, to Chang Tso-lin in an effort to obtain the Fengtien commander's personal support of the government.[73]

Gradually, the mandarins were replaced by younger advisers, who had received elements of Western education and could serve in a technical capacity. One of the most striking anachronisms of *tuchün* politics was the presence of these Western-trained men in the entourages of the political-military leaders. Although at times they were able to serve a necessary function for their superiors, they were, neither by training nor temperament, well prepared for the type of life expected of them. The explanation of their presence is to be found mainly in the fact that the Chinese society in which they had to live was not equipped to absorb the large numbers of men who were receiving Western training. They were forced to follow the traditional path of the educated man in China, seeking employment through the political power-holders.[74] These men found that the *tuchün* organizations were, in fact, employment agencies for men desirous of serving technical or administrative roles, either in the national government or in the provincial administrations.[75]

The *tuchüns* found that, as they began to administer large areas, it was necessary to employ technicians to serve as advisers, as well as managers in such fields as communications and fiscal planning. For example, Wu P'ei-fu, during the period from 1922 to 1924, controlled the southern sector of the Peking-Hankow Railroad, and personally made all important appointments in the administration of the railway.[76] In addition, Wu attracted a large number of foreign-trained men when, in 1923, the Kiaochow territory was returned to China and Wu was in the position to appoint the important administrators of this former German- and Japanese-controlled area.[77] Feng Yü-hsiang also employed a sizable number of Western-trained experts in such capacities as administrators of his model towns and schools and educators in his own army.[78] However, Chang Tso-lin was the most active in using Western training, for, in addition to the large number of Western returned students in his administration at Mukden, Chang also employed a group of foreign advisers, who included: E. Carleton Baker, former American consul general at Mukden, as political and economic adviser; Captain F. A. Sutton, a retired British Army officer, as director of the Mukden Arsenal, with the rank of major general in the Fengtien Army; Arthur W. Hoffman, an American, as Sutton's assistant. The leading Japanese advisers included Major General Honjo and a Colonel Masuki. There were also a large number of White Russian experts in the Fengtien Army as well as in the provincial administration. All of these men, however, were important only as technical advisers and did not appear to have any appreciable influence in the making of political and military decisions.[79]

Although the appearance of the Western-trained technicians in a *tuchün*'s organization did create tensions, they were still useful and important. This was particularly true as the warlord sought to become a major political force and not just a military leader. For example, it was necessary for the major *tuchüns* to employ men who could conduct the relations with Western institutions, and especially with the diplomatic corps in Peking. For this purpose, Chang Tso-lin relied upon a trusted adviser, Wu Chin. Wu P'ei-fu employed in this capacity two men, Hsüeh Han-yu and Li Hsin-ling. Feng Yü-hsiang relied mainly upon Hsü Ch'ien and Huang Fu, but he also employed such men as H. H. Kung, C. T. Wang, and Hsüeh Tu-pi, who later were to be important figures in Chinese politics.[80] In particular, as the *tuchüns* obtained the power to command influence in the formal organs of government in Peking, it was necessary to rely upon the nonmilitary experts.

Thus it was that the warlord organizations began as armies and strived to become political groups that were a strange blend of both civil governments and political parties. They remained, throughout the period, torn between the true goals of becoming effective armies, authoritative governments, and competitive political or party structures. Confusion over these three goals was indicative of a deeper confusion in Chinese society as to whether modernization called for greater national power, more competent civil administration, or more open political competition. The fact that the warlord organizations were compelled to encompass all the pulls of Chinese society and its competing priorities explains why they were structures without clearly defined functions.

The multiple demands on the warlords' organizations greatly compromised their effectiveness, yet, as the dominant organizations, indeed almost the sole effective public organizations in the country, they were expected to perform a wide variety of functions, more certainly than any single structure could reasonably do. The entire dynamics of warlord politics was shaped by this contradiction between presumed strength and actual weakness. It encouraged the notion that the only salvation of China lay in a single warlord expanding his organization to form a new Chinese state. Warlord organizations were thus expected to have the potential of becoming the nucleus of a modernizing Chinese state but recognized as being in fact ineffectual in almost all the functions associated with a modern state.

The basic limitation of the warlords thus lay in their organizations, and in order to fully appreciate the complexity of these structures it is helpful to turn now to a more detailed case study of one such organization.

4. A CASE STUDY OF THE KUOMINCHÜN

It would be hard to make the case that any warlord organization was particularly "typical" of all such armies, for there was a fair variety among them. Chang Tso-lin was possibly the archetype of the super-*tuchün* with a secure geographical base, but Manchuria and the territory "beyond the wall" was hardly "typical" of China. The "Model Governor" of Shansi, Yen Hsi-shan, was in many respects an exemplary *tuchün*, but he was something of an isolationist and never a vigorous participant in the national political process. Possibly Wu P'ei-fu, because of the forces he built up in Honan, deserves the title of being the typical or model *tuchün*, but unfortunately his organization is not an easy subject of a case study because he left so little in the way of historical records.[1]

Although it is hardly likely that the *tuchün* who was called the "Christian General" could have been the most typical commander, we shall take Feng Yü-hsiang's experience as a guide to the range of problems that beset warlords in their attempts to create significant organizations that could shape the development of China. Feng was a man who, more than most warlords, was historically conscious, and his organization was one of the most significant factors in the complex balance of power that was at the heart of warlord politics.

For our purposes, we shall be more interested in the organization that Feng created and his policy problems than his personality and his individual style. We are fortunate that there is a remarkably insightful and historically balanced biography of Feng Yü-hsiang by James E. Sheridan.[2] Feng was an exceptional man; well over six feet tall, he exuded confidence and an openness of spirit, even when, as was his wont, he belittled himself and those about him. During his years of power, he did take some pride in his claims to Christianity; he loved the role of the pastor and preached to any available audience. He was amused that the other warlords were furious at his pretensions of religiosity, and he recognized that they felt he was cheating by making his troops into "Christian soldiers"; it was unfair, they argued, for a general to deny his men the right to smoke, drink, and whore and, at the same time, not pay them any wages. In seeking to entice men to act without regard to material incentives, Feng was the first Chinese leader to understand the practical advantages of an ideology, in this case, Christianity. He was also in the forefront in recognizing the political value of nationalism, for he was the first Chinese to take up the symbols of nationalism and democracy, as he did when he labeled his army the Kuominchün, or the National People's Army.

In his later days, when nationalism, rather than Christianity, was clearly to be the basic force for modernization in China, Feng used to dismiss the stories of his more puritan period. For example, he would laughingly remark that it could hardly have been true that he had, as commonly reported, frequently baptized his battalions by marching them under fire hoses, for, as he would say, he came from a poor part of China where they didn't even have any fire hoses.

Unquestionably, Feng was a colorful man, but, for our purposes, we must pass over his idiosyncrasies and focus on his organizational problems and his military and political record. Unfortunately, this means ignoring the qualities of mind of a man who could, on the eve of battle, orate to troops that they should put out of mind the fact that the enemy had a few airplanes, because, as he reminded them, had they ever been hit on the head by the droppings of a bird in flight? Indeed, they should consider how many more birds than airplanes filled the air of China. (Certainly, until Mao Tse-tung came along with his statements belittling the atomic bomb, these remarks of Feng must represent the high point of Chinese exaggerations about the insignificance of modern military technology.)

Feng Yü-hsiang was literally born into the tradition of the Chinese Army. His father was a petty military official under the Ch'ing. Because his father was a lieutenant, Feng was able to follow him from post to post and received special consideration in schooling. Feng admits that his father was successful in placing him on the government payroll when he was only eleven years old.[3] Although Feng was born in Hsinchichen, a small town south of Tientsin in Hopei, his father was from Anhwei, and Feng considered himself a native of that province. In 1898, when Feng was sixteen years old, he first entered the military ranks at Paotingfu, and, in 1902, with the attempt to reorganize the Huai Army (established by Li Hung-chang), Feng was assigned to this group because of his Anhwei connections.[4] However, in 1904, Feng was transferred to the new Peiyang Army and became a corporal in the new elite army the following year. It was only after the Sixth Brigade, to which he had been assigned, was transferred to Fengtien, in 1906, that he began to make rapid progress in the military ranks.

It was at this time that Feng began to show great interest in the Chinese classics and read the works of his great heroes Tso Tsung-t'ang, Tsêng Kuo-fan, and Hu Lien-i. It was also at this time that he began to apply himself as an author, writing his first book, *Shih-ping Chiao-fa* (*Methods of Training Troops*).[5] A careful analysis of Feng's personality as reflected in his *Diary* goes far in helping to explain many of his actions. He was an unabashed hero-worshiper and his Western idols included Theodore Roosevelt, Bismarck, and Gladstone.[6] Feng's heroes were very meaningful to him, because he was constantly evaluating his own life in terms of their achievements; when he found himself wanting, he was capable of deep depression. He appears to have been inclined to go through periods of contemplation and self-criticism, during which he was incapable of action. (He gives as his reason for writing his diary a need to keep a close check on his own behavior and evaluate his record of self-improvement.) However, when he did have to act, he was capable of making rapid decisions with few inhibitions. He was capable of extreme vacillations in mood, and yet, at the same time, he constantly felt himself under obligation to play a great role in the history of his country. Feng's attitudes toward religion reflected this same quality of mind. He appears to have considered religion a tool for the achievement of great things, and he was willing to spend long hours pointing out the "good and bad" points of Christianity, Buddhism, and Taoism to pastors, priests, and monks. However, at the same time, religions haunted him, because they served to remind him of his own failings.

While Feng was stationed in Manchuria, he developed the close personal ties which were later to be so critical in his climb to power, for it was at this time that he first worked with Li Ming-chung, Han Fu-chü, and Sun Yüeh.[7] These men were subordinates or junior officers who were very close to him. As a group, they continued to follow Feng throughout his career, and they served as the nucleus of his later military and political organization.

Immediately after the Revolution,[8] Feng was transferred to Nanyüan, twelve miles south of Peking and, as a battalion commander, commenced to train his own body of troops. Not only did he take with him to his new command those personal friends mentioned above, but he also added to his following a new group of personal subordinates, including Shih Yu-san, Lu Ju-min, and Sun Lien-chung. In 1913, Feng was given the command of a regiment, and further additions to his following of subordinate officers included Ch'i Hung-ch'ang and Liang Yin. This group of junior officers loyally followed Feng for as long as he had military command, and they proved themselves to be among the most professional officers, once they were integrated into the Nationalist Armies at the end of the warlord period. Ch'i Hung-ch'ang, for example, was the Chinese commander whose troops resisted the Japanese at the Marco Polo Bridge, on July 7, 1937, in the incident that triggered the Sino-Japanese War that led to the Pacific war. Sun Lien-chung was the Chinese commander at the battle of T'aierchuang, one of the few Chinese victories, or at least nondefeats, in the war. Lu Ju-min served in Chiang K'ai-shek's forces during the war, but, after Feng denounced the Nationalists and shifted his allegiance to the Communists in the spring of 1947, he followed suit.

In 1914, Feng's command was organized into the Fourteenth Brigade and, after a brief period in Honan, was transferred to Shensi in an attempt to capture the notorious bandit Pai Lang (White Wolf). While in Shensi, Feng's troops were again reorganized and became the famous Sixteenth Mixed Brigade, and it was here that Feng first met the man who was to be one of his most loyal supporters, Chang Chih-chiang.

Feng was then transferred to Szechwan and was the leading military commander at Chengtu at the time of the Yünnan revolt and the death of Yüan Shih-k'ai in 1916. Feng's eagerness to capitalize on this uprising left him a marked man after Tuan Ch'i-jui came to power at Peking.[9] Tuan attempted to separate Feng from his command and his followers by appointing him to the post of Hsün-fang Tsung-ling of southern Chihli. This was a post of nominal power to inspect and defend southern Chihli from bandit activities, but it meant that he would have to give up his military ties with his subordinates. However, Feng was only briefly deprived of his command, for, with the confusion that ensued after the Chang Hsün attempt to restore the monarch, Feng returned to his men and was welcomed back by his loyal subordinates. After Tuan regained his power at the capital, he sought to weaken Feng again by sending him to the South to oppose the Canton regime, which was just beginning to be a source of trouble. At this point, Ts'ao K'un first intervened to protect Feng and to "guarantee" him.[10] Ts'ao's act of guaranteeing him meant that Feng was now recognized as being a member of the Chihli faction and that any attack on Feng would evoke the animosity of all the members of the group. Thus Feng, in 1918, declared his allegiance to the Chihli alliance and served as the military governor of western Hunan under Wu P'ei-fu. At the time of the Anfu-Chihli War, Feng's Sixteenth Mixed Brigade moved up to the North in support of Wu's armies.

After the defeat of Anfu, Feng was sent to Shensi to replace the Anfu *tuchün* of that province, Ch'en Shu-fan.[11] As *tuchün* of Shensi, Feng was in the position to make rapid expansions in his power. Although the province was far from rich and Feng still had trouble obtaining adequate resources, he at least had a specifically defined area of control, which he could use as the base of his power. In August, 1921, Feng formed the Eleventh Division out of his old Sixteenth Mixed Brigade. With this move, he was able to give his subordinates larger commands, with Li Ming-chung taking over the Twenty-first Brigade, Chang Chih-chiang the Twenty-second Brigade, while Sun Liang-chun, Sun Chih-yüan, and Liu Yu-feng became regimental commanders.[12] This group of officers and Meng Chih-chung, the Chief of Staff of the Eleventh Division, were now recognized as Feng's most intimate followers. It was during this period that Feng was beginning to rely heavily upon his immediate subordinates to carry on both political and military negotiations with the other leaders of the Chihli alliance; Sun Lien-chung served as liaison officer with Ts'ao K'un, and Meng Chih-chung negotiated with Wu P'ei-fu.[13]

Although it was the men and officers of the Eleventh Division who served as the core of Feng's organization of power, it was as *tuchün* of Shensi that Feng was first faced with the problem of incorporating into his organization leaders who had previously developed substantial power groupings of their own. During October and November, 1921, Feng brought under his control the Shensi provincial commanders, Hu Ching-i and Yüeh Wei-chün.[14] Although Yüeh did not have sufficient power to resist the demands of Feng, Hu Ching-i attempted to preserve his autonomous power as a native Shensi leader in his home province. It was necessary for Feng to call upon the prestige and authority of Wu P'ei-fu in forcing Hu and his Twentieth Division to obey his orders,[15] and, finally, Feng had to threaten to attack the Twentieth to force its commander to comply with his wishes.[16]

With his own headquarters in Sian, and with Hu Ching-i in northern Shensi and Yüeh Wei-chün in the southern part of the province, Feng was now in a position to expand the nucleus of his organization. With the Eleventh Division still serving as the keystone of his power structure, he expanded by adding three mixed brigades, and he gave the commands of these to his close followers, Chang Chih-chiang (Seventh Mixed Brigade), Li Ming-chung (the Eighth), and Sun Chih-yüan (the Twenty-fifth).[17] With these additions, Feng was in a position to follow a policy of periodically shifting the commands of his subordinates. This was necessary in order to prevent the development of jealousies and to counteract any signs of excessive personal preferences for particular leaders.[18] It is difficult to rank his officers at this time in terms of Feng's personal preferences since he carefully endeavored to be as impartial as possible.[19] However, his closest associates were still the men who had been with him throughout his career: Han Fu-chü, Sun Lien-chung, Chang Chih-chiang, Li Min-chun, Sun Chih-yüan, Meng Chih-chung, and Lin Chi. Outside this inner circle were the commanders whom he had brought into his organization at a later date: Hu Ching-i and Yüeh

Wei-chün, whom Feng could not entirely trust but whose interests he had to support to ensure their continued loyalty.[20]

These were the followers whom Feng took with him into the second Chihli-Fengtien war of 1924, and upon whom he had to depend when he betrayed the Chihli cause and captured Peking on October 23, 1924.[21] This was a critical period for Feng, for it was at this time that he made the decision to expand his organization into a major military and political force and take on the name of Kuominchün.

According to Feng's own account, the idea of establishing such an organization as the Kuominchün came as the result of a conversation with his trusted subordinate, Sun Yüeh, on September 10, 1924. In this conversation, Sun Yüeh played upon Feng's vanity and ambitions, saying that, unless he took a positive stand and was willing to risk "great deeds," he would be remembered in history only as the "running dog of the warlords." Feng pleaded that he was too weak to be effective at that time, but Sun Yüeh argued that he could ensure the continued loyal support of Hu Ching-i if Feng was willing to make a striking move to establish an organization dedicated to opposing the other *tuchüns*.[22]

The pattern that Feng followed in establishing the Kuominchün clearly demonstrates the complex problems a *tuchün* faced when, relying upon a personal following, he attempted to make a radical expansion of his power grouping. To make any such move, it would be necessary to give many of his subordinates a greater degree of freedom than had been his custom.[23] Placing his most trusted followers in such independent positions might mean weakening the basic military organization, which was still essential to his personal power. On the other hand, if he were to permit his less dependable subordinates to have greater independence, it might lead to their breaking from him, while, at the same time, causing jealousies among the more loyal supporters, who might have felt that they had been denied opportunities to achieve positions of greater power and prestige. For Feng, the critical problem was whether he could rely upon Hu Ching-i's continued support if Hu was given greater freedom in an expanded organization. Hu had always resented the fact that Feng had taken control of Shensi from him and that Wu P'ei-fu had supported Feng in this move.[24] Feng was influenced, however, by Sun Yüeh's promise that he could personally vouch for the reliability of Hu, and Feng was finally convinced that Hu's personal hatred of Wu was so deep that he would be willing to support any movement that would eliminate the military power of the Loyang leader.[25] Feng then entered into protracted negotiations with Hu and his representatives, which extended over the period of Feng's stay in Jehol on the pretense of preparing to oppose the Fengtien group in the area.[26] Finally, feeling certain of the support of Hu and the ability of his own forces to eliminate the power of Wu P'ei-fu as long as Wu was simultaneously engaged in the conflict with Fengtien, Feng returned to Peking and, on October 26, 1924, formally announced the formation of the Kuominchün.

Feng himself was the commander in chief of the Kuominchün and concurrently the commander of the First Kuominchün Army, while Sun Yüeh had the Third Kuominchün Army.[27] The First Kuominchün was an expansion of the old Eleventh Division, Chang Chih-chiang's Seventh Mixed Brigade, Sun Chih-yüan's Twenty-fifth Mixed Brigade, and Li Ming-chung's Eighth Mixed Brigade.[28] The Third Kuominchün was formed out of the expansion of the troops that had previously been under the command of Sun Yüeh; it thus represented the granting of greater independence to a section of the previous organization, which had been under the more immediate command of Feng.[29]

The decision to label Hu Ching-i's army the Second Kuominchün was calculated to give Hu greater prestige and in this way to ensure his support.[30] Immediately after the announcement of the formation of the Kuominchün, Wu P'ei-fu sent a representative to Hu Ching-i offering him the post of inspector general of Jehol, Chahar, and Suiyüan, if he would remain loyal to the Chihli faction and break with the Kuominchün. Hu captured the representative and sent him to Feng as a display of his intended loyalty to the new organization.[31] However, in spite of this display, Feng continued to recognize that he was faced with a delicate problem, and he had serious doubts as to how far he could rely upon Hu to support the objectives of the commander in chief of the Kuominchün.

Feng encountered the difficult task of balancing the rewards that the Kuominchün could offer to the subordinates, who now, in keeping with their greater degree of independence, had higher expectations. In order to demonstrate his confidence in the immediate subordinates whom he had kept in the First Kuominchün, Feng obtained for them formal political appointments which would give them additional prestige. Chang Chih-chiang was made the *tuchün* of Jehol, Li Ming-chung was appointed the *tuchün* of Suiyüan,[32] and with these appointments went a far greater degree of independence of action than Feng had ever before permitted.[33] These positions served to compensate his most loyal followers for the greater authority that he had given to Sun Yüeh and Hu Ching-i. In this process of attempting to balance the rewards, Feng found that he was being forced into a policy of giving special consideration to Hu's interests, because he lacked confidence in Hu's readiness to comply with his orders, now that Hu had a greater degree of autonomy.[34]

Feng soon found that the establishment of the three separate armies of the Kuominchün was leading to a situation whereby he, being only in direct control of one of the armies, albeit the best one, was losing command of the balance of power within the total organization. Although Sun Yüeh was still loyal, the fact that he had independent responsibilities might lead to situations in which his own interests might not coincide with those of the commander in chief, and there would be the open temptation to join ranks with Hu in order to dominate the total organization for their own interests. To check this development, Feng went so far as to establish formally the troops under the command of Chang Chih-chiang as the Fifth Kuominchün and those under Li Ming-chung as the Sixth Kuominchün.[35] With this move, he was able to shift the formal balance in the Kuominchün so that he was absolutely certain of three of the commanders, and, with Hu and Sun in a minority position, he was also assured that Sun would not be tempted to seek further freedom.[36]

By December, 1924, Feng was faced with the threat that the newly founded Kuominchün would split apart when Hu Ching-i began to demand that a geographical area be placed under his direct jurisdiction. In particular, Hu insisted on the control of Honan, which the Second and Third Kuominchün had been in the process of conquering from the remnants of Wu P'ei-fu's troops. With both Sun and Hu seeking control of Honan, Feng refused to take a definite stand in settling their quarrel but permitted them each to obtain as much of the territory as they could conquer before he made any commitments.[37] However, when it looked as if Hu was about to achieve a dominant position in the province and possibly in Central China, Feng pushed for the appointment of Sun Yüeh as the civil governor of Honan, while leaving open the post of *tuchün* of Honan.[38] By this move, Feng hoped to restore the balance between his two subordinates by giving Sun the formal backing of the Kuominchün, while not denying the possibility that Hu could still gain a stronghold in the area.[39] However, the fact that Feng had not been in a position to give an emphatic decision in the case indicates the extent to which the Kuominchün was no longer an apparatus that Feng could manipulate to fulfill his wishes.

The impending breakup of the Kuominchün was delayed when it became apparent in January, 1925, that the general balance of power in North China was being radically altered. Until this time, Feng and the Kuominchün had been cooperating with Fengtien and the enemy had been Wu P'ei-fu and the remaining Chihli leaders. However, it was now evident that the Tientsin Conference was only the initial step in the Fengtien program of eliminating the power of Feng to obtain control of North China. Although Feng himself realized this new source of danger,[40] he was unsuccessful in convincing the Second and Third Kuominchün that they were now confronted with a new threat since they were still being tempted with the prize of capturing the areas that Wu P'ei-fu had previously dominated. To Hu Ching-i and Sun Yüeh, it was better to pursue a defeated foe than to meet a new and powerful enemy.

Feng finally decided that it was necessary to make the shocking move of withdrawing temporarily from the active scene, leaving his subordinates to adjust to the change in the common enemy.[41] By not ordering the First Kuominchün to try to block the expansion of the Fengtien forces south of the Wall, Feng allowed the Mukden armies to move into Shantung, and, with this event, it became clear to both the Second and Third Kuominchün that their disagreements over Honan were academic as long as there was the danger that the Fengtien armies would occupy all of Central China.[42] Thus Feng, rather than attempting directly to force his commands upon his recalcitrant followers, left them in a position whereby their own security could only be ensured by uniting to a greater degree under his leadership.

Sun Yüeh was the first to recognize this threat, and, in January, 1925, he moved his Third Kuominchün back into Southern Chihli and prepared to oppose the Fengtien might.[43] Hu was now left isolated in Honan, and, if he failed to assist the Kuominchün in any conflict it had with Fengtien, he would have been left to the mercy of the victor.[44] However, Hu delayed in committing his forces to any campaign against Fengtien until March, when the Third Kuominchün had several brief clashes with the Fengtien troops under Li Ching-lin in southern Chihli.[45] The threat from Fengtien had served the purpose of restoring a greater degree of unity within the Kuominchün, and Feng returned to active command of the organization.

Thus, in the early months of 1925, the ability of the Kuominchün to develop into an effective and unified factor in the politics of North China still remained in doubt. Although the Second and Third Armies were now prepared to meet the threat from Manchuria, the question of who would dominate the area that Wu P'ei-fu had controlled for so long still had not been satisfactorily resolved. The tension between Sun and Wu continued, and Sun even made a public statement to the effect that Hu was only an "opportunist."[46] At this point, Sun Yüeh unexpectedly ordered elements of the Third Kuominchün into Shensi.[47] Shensi was still considered to be within the sphere of influence of Feng and his followers, but, in particular, it represented the area that Hu Ching-i had relied upon and from which most of his troops had come.[48] This could have led to a decisive break in the Kuominchün had it not been for the sudden death of Hu Ching-i on May 10, 1924.[49] The question of who was to replace Hu might have created a serious crisis in the ranks of the Kuominchün had not Feng acted quickly to designate Yüeh Wei-chün to replace his former Shensi coprovincial as leader of the Second Kuominchün.[50]

During the summer of 1925, the Kuominchün was spared any external problems that might have provoked a crisis in maintaining the loyalties of the various groups and factions that now made up the unwieldy organization constructed by Feng in his efforts to dominate North China. However, by October, the danger of a conflict with Fengtien was more imminent, as Chang Tso-lin had ordered Chang Tsung-ch'ang to occupy Shantung, and Sun Ch'uan-fang in Chekiang was preparing to expand out of the Yangtze area.[51] Feng was again forced to try to strengthen the unity within his organization to be prepared for a major conflict with Fengtien. But he soon found that whatever attempts he made at reaching agreements with other *tuchüns* had repercussions within his own organization. Any proposal for concerted action with such leaders could be interpreted by his own subordinates as having some effect on their own standing within the total organization.

In particular, Feng at this time was faced with a split among his immediate followers. His leading political advisers, Huang Fu and Hsüan Chien, were pressing for a strong policy that included a direct alliance with Sun Ch'uan-fang and a campaign by all elements of the Kuominchün against Fengtien. These advisers felt that if the Kuominchün acted while Sun Ch'uan-fang was moving north from Chekiang, it would not be difficult to defeat Fengtien—a victory that would leave the Kuominchün in complete domination of North China. On the other hand, the military leaders of the First Kuominchün argued against such action at that time, saying that it would be best to remain neutral while Fengtien exhausted itself in a campaign in the Central Provinces. These commanders claimed that the First Kuominchün was not sufficiently trained and prepared for a major conflict at that time.[52]

Thus, although the Second and Third Kuominchün, which still had an interest in Honan and Shantung, were ready to join in concerted action, Feng found that his subordinates in the First were unconvinced that the time had arrived to move against Fengtien. Feng's task was to convince all the elements in the organization that they act together before Fengtien could secure a strong hold on Central China, and that, if Chang were permitted to continue his policies of expansion, he would become so strong that effective opposition could not exist.

It was at this point that Feng issued a circular telegram addressed to his "elder brother," Chang Tso-lin, charging that the Fengtien leader had clearly demonstrated his intentions to disturb the peace and conquer all of North China. Feng charged that Chang's support of Lu Yung-hsiang was evidence of his intentions to fight Sun Ch'uan-fang and that, unless Chang was willing to return to the spirit of the Tientsin Conference of the previous year, it would be necessary for the Kuominchün to seek to "preserve the peace."[53]

The fact that Feng had arrived at an agreement with Sun Ch'uan-fang to enter the conflict and that he had pledged himself to support Chang Tso-lin's trusted subordinate, Kuo Sung-ling, if he should revolt, indicated that Feng himself was willing to fight at the time.[54] However,

Feng still found his most trusted leaders in the First Kuominchün reluctant to commit themselves to a conflict until these allies had proved their abilities. On the other hand, the Second and Third Kuominchün, both eager to expand their power, had moved into Chihli from Honan and Shensi, respectively.[55] Only with the initial successes that came with the Kuo Sung-ling revolt and when it was apparent that Feng was now in a good position to dominate the capital did the leaders of the First join in the struggle. However, on December 28—when it still appeared that Chang would not be able to recover readily from the revolt of his subordinate—Tuan Ch'i-jui, who was still the provisional chief executive, issued a mandate appointing Sun Yüeh to the concurrent posts of civil and military governor of Chihli.[56] This was a direct blow to the officers of the First Kuominchün, and because Feng concurred in the appointment, it indicated his dissatisfaction with the way in which they had only reluctantly supported the campaign. In addition, Feng was recognizing what was practically an accomplished fact, for Sun had conquered Paotingfu as well as Tientsin.

It is uncertain as to what promises Feng may have made to his subordinates in regard to this highly desirable post. Feng's *Diary* is of little help here, as he mentions only that whoever obtained the post at this time would have a thankless task, for it would be difficult to hold such a position until the situation was more clearly defined. On the other hand, leaders of the First Kuominchün publicly stated that they had expected that Chihli would come under their jurisdiction, while Sun Yüeh was to be rewarded with Shantung. However, probably the best indication of the situation was the conversation of Feng's adviser, Han An, with members of the American legation staff. When asked if Feng had ordered the Third Kuominchün to occupy Tientsin, Han "remarked with a smile" that it was not a question of Feng's sending the Third Kuominchün to Tientsin. He thus intimated that Feng had little control over the situation and was only recognizing the independent actions of one of his subordinates.

In January, 1926, before the Fengtien forces had recovered from the effects of the Kuo Sung-ling revolt, Feng appeared to be in a position to dominate the capital. However, in the hour of temporary triumph, Feng found that the organization he had built up in order to increase his power was so divided that he could not effectively control all the elements within it. Feng was in the embarrassing position of being supported by those leaders in whom he had the least confidence. As long as his objectives coincided with their expediency demands, they would be willing to give Feng complete support, but he had no assurance that this aid would continue into the period when he would be faced with the question of granting rewards and controlling the formal organs of government.[57] On the other hand, those leaders who had been personally the closest to him, and those upon whom he would have to rely in the long run, had not been active in supporting his move against Fengtien, and as a consequence they posed a difficult question for Feng in terms of to what extent he could or should reward them.[58]

Faced with this dilemma, Feng refused to come to any decisions at this time but left it to each element in the Kuominchün to make out as best it could. However, on March 10, 1926, when the Third Kuominchün, in action against the Fengtien commander, Li Ching-lin, fired upon Japanese destroyers and merchant vessels, Feng quickly acted to disassociate himself and the Kuominchün headquarters from any responsibility in the actions of the Third Kuominchün.[59] The blunder by the Third Kuominchün had destroyed any hope that Feng might have had to establish a government in Peking which would have been acceptable to the diplomatic corps,[60] and few Peking politicians now would have been willing to serve in a regime sponsored by Feng.

Because the actions of the Second and Third Kuominchün had weakened his position, Feng attempted to reach a closer unity with the leaders of the First Kuominchün. However, he continued to find that he lacked complete control over his old subordinates. There had developed at this time a split within the ranks of the leaders of the First Kuominchün. Chang Chih-chiang, Li Ming-chung, and Liu Yu-feng were willing to support Feng in a policy of withdrawing from Chihli and permitting the Fengtien leaders to grapple with the problems of establishing a formal government at the capital.

This group argued that any attempt to establish a government in Peking would only lead to a weakening of the Kuominchün, as the symbols of the Peking government were at the time completely discredited and it would be best not to become associated with them. They felt this to be particularly true after Tuan Ch'i-jui's bodyguards had fired on the Chinese students demonstrating against the demands of the diplomatic corps for compensation for the Taku incident.

On the other hand, Lu Chung-lin, Liu Chi, and Sun Chih-yüan argued that Chihli should be held at all costs, including the sacrifice of Jehol, and that the prestige of the Kuominchün would be heightened by having the First dominate the capital and attempt to restore law and order in the area.

This group also argued that the political situation at the capital was so confused that if the First Kuominchün acted swiftly and established a government, the other groups would have to accept their leadership, and that, if this happened, the diplomatic corps would have no choice but to recognize this government. Such a government would have a fair chance of survival because the diplomatic corps would certainly bring pressure to prevent further conflicts in the Peking-Tientsin area, and, if the Kuominchün controlled the government at the time, it would mean that other groups would be unable to attack them directly. It should be noted that those who were less interested in expanding the power of the First Kuominchün in Chihli were precisely those who already had been granted control of areas in the Northwest and Jehol and that they would have been called upon to employ the resources of these areas to assist in the retention of Chihli. On the other hand, those who favored the more active policy were the subordinates who had not yet been granted any territory by Feng and could see in the conquest of Chihli the opportunity for obtaining posts for themselves.

In this controversy, Feng sided with the first group but insisted that it was essential to strengthen the Kuominchün organization so that in the future it would be prepared to take over control of the Peking government without creating any internal problems.[61]

This controversy, combined with the break between the First Kuominchün and the other two armies, could not be solved by Feng's powers of persuasion and command. The result was that Feng decided to quit the active command of the Kuominchün and force his followers to realize that he would be essential to all in the future.[62] When he went into retirement, he insured the continued loyalty of the men of the First Kuominchün by turning over to this group all his available funds and refusing to assist Sun Yüeh and the Third Kuominchün.[63] Sun soon found that he was forced to negotiate with the leaders of the First Kuominchün if he wished to receive financial assistance, and Sun finally had to give up the post of *tuchün* of Chihli in return for such aid.[64]

Thus Feng, although unable directly to order all his various associates to carry out his decisions, was still able to retain the semblance of a unified organization by forcing his reluctant commanders to recognize the logic of the situation and to realize that their best policy for individual improvement would be a policy compatible with his own general objectives. However, this meant that Feng was not in a position to initiate positive policies. Rather, the only way that he could maintain the structure of his overgrown organization was to follow a course of action that was dictated primarily by the general balance of power existing at any moment. Feng had hoped that, with the creation of the Kuominchün, he would be in command of a group capable of offsetting the power of Chang Tso-lin and Wu P'ei-fu, but, with each expansion of the organization, he lost a degree of power to command the obedience of his subordinates. Confronted with the problem of having to adjust carefully his position to the external as well as the internal balance, Feng could not proceed with any policies that would raise the issue of disproportionate sacrifice by the various subordinate leaders. The only hope for positive action came when all the subordinates discovered that all of their interests were in harmony.

At this juncture, Feng was able to find in the promise of assistance from the Soviet Union a method of further restoring unity in the Kuominchün. He argued with his subordinates that he felt certain he could obtain adequate material support from Russia to compensate all elements of the Kuominchün, and that this Soviet assistance would outweigh whatever benefits might come from risking the organization of the Kuominchün in holding Chihli and the capital.[65] In particular, the members of the First Kuominchün were willing to forgo immediate rewards in the hope that the aid from Moscow would be sufficient to guarantee adequate future power to enable them to dominate North China. Therefore, the First withdrew from the Peking area and pulled back to the Great Wall at Nankow.[66] The Second and Third Kuominchün armies were now left exposed in Chihli, and it became necessary for them also to withdraw, with the Second moving to western Honan and southern Shensi, and the Third returning to central and northern Shensi.[67]

Before leaving for Moscow in March, 1926, Feng once again reorganized the First Kuominchün and placed Chang Chih-chiang in direct command in his absence. However, he left Lu Chung-lin, Sun Chih-yüan, Ch'en Chin-shen, Meng Chih-chung, Chang Hung-yu, and Shih Yu-san each with a particular geographical area of the Northwest to control, and thus he was able to prevent Chang Chih-chiang from being able to dominate completely the organization in his absence.[68] By this move, he destroyed much of the bureaucratic character of the organization he had previously been trying to strengthen and changed the structure into a more feudal one by parceling out separate domains.

Although the relations of the *tuchüns* with foreign powers lie beyond the immediate scope of this study, it would not be out of place to note Feng's account in his diary of the Soviet efforts to propagandize him and of their treatment of him as a guest in the "vodka circuit." The pattern of the Soviet campaign unfolded while Feng and his party were making the long trip on the Trans-Siberian Railroad. At first, his Russian hosts insisted on playing phonograph records of Chinese operas, including recordings by the noted Mei Lan-fang. Feng states that he realized they were only attempting to flatter him by showing such great interest in an aspect of Chinese culture few foreigners could appreciate, but the very fact that they were doing so left him pleased. The next step was to give Feng the writings of Mahatma Gandhi to read. Feng was immensely moved not only by the spirit of Gandhi, but by the "suffering" that the people of India had undergone at the hands of the British. The Russians then quickly pointed out that all of this was the result of "imperialism," but that it was absurd for a military man like Feng even to contemplate Gandhi's ideas of nonviolence. Rather, it was Feng's duty, if he felt sincerely the sorrow of Gandhi, to dedicate himself to building up his military power to the point that he could fight British "imperialism." (Feng states that, at the time, he was so moved that he was ready to return immediately to China to call upon all the *tuchüns* to join in fighting the British.) The Russians then took up the logical question of how they might be able to assist Feng in building up his military power. Feng states that this was the first time any foreigners had appeared to be sincerely interested and willing to help him in his very real problems of command and troop training; most foreigners spoke only in terms of ideals, showed no appreciation for his problems, and even acted as if his military affairs were too sordid for them to be concerned with. After arriving in Moscow, Feng was taken on daily tours, during which his guides carefully pointed out the progress that had been made since the Revolution, while at the same time showing him many cases of backward conditions, which, his guides told him, represented the old pre-Revolutionary Russia and thus were the still unfinished aspects of the Soviet program. This "before and after" demonstration greatly impressed Feng and convinced him that China, too, could make such progress, because conditions in Russia must have been as bad, if not worse, than those existing in China. During this period of tours, Feng kept asking to be taken to see Lenin's tomb, but his hosts held him off until he had built up in his mind a great curiosity and desire to see this last sight. When at last he was permitted to view the tomb, he stated that he was completely overcome with emotion, and, at that point, he declared that he would support the Revolution in China and join the Kuomintang.

During the period of Feng's visit to Moscow, all elements of the Kuominchün were under constant pressure from Fengtien and later from the rejuvenated armies of Wu P'ei-fu.[69] The elements of the First Kuominchün under Chang Chih-chiang were responsible for defending the Nankow pass and the gateway into Inner Mongolia from the Fengtien forces moving up from Peking.[70] At the same time, the First Kuominchün was attempting to incorporate northern Shansi, and especially Ta-t'ung, into the general domain of the Kuominchün's control of the Northwest.[71] Feng, during his stay in Russia, was in constant communication with his subordinates, and they, in turn, were repeatedly pleading for his speedy return to assist in the preservation of the organization.[72] Even the Second and Third Kuominchün attempted to place themselves back into his good graces and promised that, if he would return, they would faithfully follow his orders.[73]

When Feng returned from Moscow in the early autumn of 1927 and arrived in Tat'ung, he found that the First Kuominchün had been forced back from Nankow, and there was a serious threat that it would lose control of Jehol.[74] In addition, all elements of the Kuominchün were desperately in need of funds, as they had already strained the economy of the Northwest with heavy taxes and forced loans from the local chamber of commerce.[75] On the other hand, the morale of the troops appeared to be high, and, with the expectations of greater support in munitions and funds from the Soviet Union, the various elements of the Kuominchün showed more willingness to cooperate than had been the case before Feng's departure.

It is impossible to determine the full extent of the assistance that the Soviet Union actually delivered to Feng. The raid on the Russian Embassy grounds on April 6, 1927, which was conducted by the Peking police with the approval of the diplomatic corps, produced some highly revealing documents purportedly found in the military attaché's office. According to these documents, Feng, when he was in Moscow, signed two agreements on April 15, 1926. In the first document, he agreed that he had received from the Soviet Union as of June 1, 1926, supplies worth 6,395,692 rubles. In the second document, he confirmed that he had received deliveries of supplies worth 4,501,999 rubles during the period from April 15 to July 8, 1926. In both documents, he agreed that "for all military as well as other supplies, whatever they may consist of, which I have received from the Government of the U.S.S.R. or its organs, I pledge myself to compensate their value to the Government of the U.S.S.R. at its first demand and in the manner prescribed by the Government of the U.S.S.R." No indication is given as to why there should have been two documents and why the periods overlapped. It is of interest that Feng's entry in his *Diary* on April 15, 1926, was one of the briefest, consisting only of the statement, "Rose early and went into Moscow [he was living at the time in a house outside of the city] and made preparations for returning to China."

The American consul at Kalgan did attempt to keep a record of the supplies that actually were delivered to the Kuominchün in his city. On May 13, 1926, Feng received an estimated 5 million "Mexican" dollars' worth of supplies at Kalgan, which had been delivered from Urga.[76] By Spetember 10, 1926, the American consul reported that he had seen, in addition, Russian deliveries that totaled at least 18,000 rifles and 35 million rounds of ammunition. (According to one of the documents found in the raid, the Russians had delivered to the First Kuominchün approximately the same amount of supplies except that the rifles totaled 24,970 pieces.)[77] It is to be assumed that some supplies were given to the Kuominchün, which were not delivered at Kalgan. Although Feng later claimed that the Soviets had not fulfilled their agreements completely, the supplies he did receive were sufficient to work a remarkable change in the morale of the troops under his command. It should be noted that, according to the documents found, the Russians were fully aware of the fact that their support of Feng was a risky adventure, and they were far from confident that their investment would produce all the desired results. "Supporting the Kuominchün

Armies and furthering their growth, we have in them a force that may keep Wu P'ei-fu back from making war on Canton. I say 'may keep back' because the influence of the Kuomintang on the Kuominchün Army is manifestly not strong enough to prevent it from advantageous political combinations with Wu P'ei-fu."[78]

Thus, in spite of the setbacks that the Kuominchün had suffered during Feng's absence, the organization was still intact and was more clearly united under his leadership than at any time since its inception. The difficulties his subordinates had faced when they received a greater degree of freedom of action had served to convince them that it would be more desirable to overlook many of their personal differences and attempt to function as a united organization under Feng's direct command. Feng immediately took advantage of the situation and reorganized the Kuominchün into a more compact and better-integrated structure. In particular, he reduced the size of the First Kuominchün to five divisions.[79] In addition, he reduced the independence of the Second Kuominchün by bringing Yüeh Wei-chün into the general headquarters of the Kuominchün.[80] Thus, Yüeh was no longer directly in contact with his Second Army and had to assume some of the responsibilities of the total organization.[81]

With these moves, Feng was in a better position to return to an active role in the struggle for North China. However, by this time, the balance of power in the area had been radically altered with the successes of the Northern Expedition and the capture of Central China by the Kuomintang. His strengthened organization meant that Feng was now destined to play a critical role in the final settlement of the issue of a unified China.[82] In spite of the overwhelming power of Chiang Kai-shek's armies and the unexpected revolt of Han Fu-chü,[83] Feng's organization was sufficiently united under his command to continue as an effective power grouping until 1931. Although the title of the Kuominchün was changed to the Second National Army in 1927, it continued to be the personal army of Feng. Thus, in spite of the long record of failures in establishing an organization strong enough to dominate North China, and the continued dissension within the ranks of his subordinates, it is remarkable that Feng was able to maintain his organization so far into the Nationalist period. The bonds of personal loyalty had never been sufficiently strong to serve as the cement to bind the members of the Kuominchün into a grouping that was willing to face all sacrifice together. Yet they were not so weak that they dissolved, and this peculiar mixture of personal loyalty and expectation of reward continued to be meaningful and critical even after the Nationalist triumph.

5. THE MAKING AND BREAKING OF ALLIANCES

As we have seen in the preceding chapter, the degree of cohesion in the *tuchüns'* organizations diminished with their efforts to expand their power, and, in time, these organizations lost the quality of a unified command and became what can better be termed confederations, or alliances, of leaders who recognized one man as the principal figure in the alliance. Thus, in the Kuominchün, when Feng granted greater powers of command to Sun Yüeh and Hu Ching-i, these leaders assumed an increased degree of independence. No longer was the decision-making clearly located with Feng and his staff, but rather the decisions of the Kuominchün depended upon the complex interplay of forces under the command of the separate leaders. In fact, the Kuominchün had taken on the character of an alliance.

Politics of the warlord period was not the politics of intergroup relationships but rather that of an infinitely complex web of personal relationships. Some relationships were of a pure superior-subordinate nature and others were of unqualified hostility or amity; most relationships, however, were far more mixed, and questions of superiority and inferiority, of amity and enmity, were blended. The structure of the principal *tuchün* organizations did not have clearly defined boundaries.

The difficulty of distinguishing between a single structure of authority under a leader and an alliance of *tuchüns*, goes far in indicating the nature of the alliances that prevailed during the period. Just as the *tuchün*, in his efforts to establish a strong organization, had to depend upon such factors as personal loyalty, long association, expectation of personal reward and favor, and the astute balancing of his subordinates, so, in the nation, the relations of the *tuchüns* to each other also rested upon a complex web of personal sentiment and calculations of expectations.

The tradition of basing alliances upon personal relations had its origins in the Peiyang Army and the subsequent division into the Anfu and Chihli factions. Although these alignments were initially among members who had, earlier in their careers, served under one or another of the main leaders, they assumed more concrete form during the period from 1916 to 1920 as the struggle for power between them intensified. As each individual component of the alliance became a strong power factor, a new form of alliance structure developed. Initially, the alliances were clearly under the leadership of Tuan Ch'i-jui and Feng Kuo-chang, and adherence to the alliances depended upon carrying out the objectives of these leaders and being rewarded in return.[1] However, as the two groups became more involved in the political process, they lost their quality of being personal instruments of their respective leaders. Rather, those within the factions, as they increased their power, sought to exploit the structure for their own ends.[2] Thus, the factions became apparatuses in which the members competed with one another for dominant control. But these apparatuses were so weak that, even if a leader had been able to dominate one, he could not effectively utilize it for carrying out policies. However, in spite of the decline in the power of the individual leaders and the increasing necessity for the alliances to satisfy the demands of all the members, it was nevertheless essential, in the formation of any effective grouping, that there be one prominent man who was personally identified with the alliance and could serve as figurehead and lend dignity to the enterprise. Thus, the personal factor was still important, even though individuals could no longer exercise their power in a clearly hierarchical manner.

For example, after the Feng Yü-hsiang coup of November, 1924, and the establishment of Tuan Ch'i-jui as the provisional chief executive, twenty-one military commanders in Central China sent a joint telegram to Tuan stating their opposition to the Peking government unless they were fully recognized as a united alliance.[3] This move, however, was not taken seriously, although the leaders did command substantial troops. The attempt at an alliance soon fell apart because there was no recognized leader who could either give the alliance prestige or adjust the differences of the independent leaders.

The situation was one in which the forms of personal politics were still essential, but in which personal relations were no longer completely dominant. This is clear from the fact that, whereas in the formation of the alliances the factor of personal trust and confidence was necessary, it was never strong enough to insure the functioning of the alliance. All elements were careful to adhere to the formal practices of showing deference to the leading personages, thus demonstrating their loyalty to the pact arrived at or the pact intended.

Demonstration of one's personal confidence in an alliance was often made by the observance of birthday anniversaries and the exchanging of personal gifts, reminiscent of the practices of European royalty. Examples of this include the birthday observance of Chang Tso-lin in 1925, when all the men who were in any sense allied to him made a pilgrimage to Mukden to offer their felicitations. The exodus of such officials from Peking reached such proportions that it was necessary to adjourn the Reorganization Conference, which had been in session at the time. Again, in the case of Ts'ao K'un, at the time of his birthday in 1922, all the Chihli leaders who identified themselves as being allied to Ts'ao, or who sought such an alliance, went to Paoting. It was necessary to engage two special trains to accommodate the officials who felt it advisable to offer their congratulations to the Chihli leader. Innumerable examples can be found of the exchange of personal gifts accompanying the formation of alliances or the declaration of trust in alliances. One of the more interesting examples of such personal exchanges of gifts occurred in 1923, when Ts'ao K'un presented Feng Yü-hsiang with four white horses and Feng, in turn, gave the horses to his four immediate subordinates, indicating that, just as he would be loyal to the alliance with Ts'ao K'un, so Feng also would expect them to be loyal to him. Possibly the most widely discussed exchange of gifts was the present of a bottle of distilled water that Feng sent to Wu P'ei-fu in 1923. It was generally recognized as signifying that, although Feng recognized his alliance with Wu, he disapproved of the latter's imbibing habits and that, unless the Loyang leader showed signs of altering his practices, the "Christian Marshal" would no longer feel bound by the ties of the alliance.

Thus, on the surface, there developed a body of symbolic acts and rituals, which, although performed in terms of personal relations, implied broader political behavior. For those who were keen observers of the politics of *tuchün*-ism, it was possible to interpret ceremonial acts and rituals for their implications of amity or enmity. The frame of reference for "cue-making" was a highly personal one, although the interpretation of the cues was made in terms of the broader political arena.[4] Throughout the 1920's, the cues of political action continued to be on a highly personal level, but it would appear that, by the end of the period, there was a perceptible decline in the importance of such cues and an increase in cues that possessed, in terms of symbols, a higher degree of abstraction.[5]

Just as the cues to political action were expressed in terms of personal factors and relationships, so were the symbols or language employed in making calculations of political events and consequences highly personalized. That is, political events were described in terms of individuals who were either "rising stars" or "fading lights." All of the *tuchüns* adjusted their policies according to the probable personal successes or failures of the dominant individuals. In the formation of alliances, this meant that it was necessary to have a leader to serve not only as a figurehead, but also as an individual who, in the minds of others, was likely to achieve success. For example, in the case of the Chihli alliance from December to May, 1923, it appeared that the association was about to break up into various splinter groups. Ts'ao K'un personally seemed to have little hope of achieving greater power.[6] However, with Ts'ao's move to seek the Presidency, all elements in the former alliance quickly sought to mend their differences and present a more united front.[7] When it appeared that Ts'ao would be "elected," all elements were determined to profit from the personal success of the leader of an alliance with which they were now willing to identify themselves. However, after it became apparent that Ts'ao would not be well received by the public and that there was a strong movement under way to weaken the power of the new President, various groups began to dissociate themselves from the alliance.[8]

The general tendency of the warlord period was to identify most warlords as "fading lights" and the rare individual as a "rising star" who usually only had a brief moment of potential success. The underlying logic of the culture was that any leader who sought to assert himself as a potential leader of the nation was consumed with excessive ambitions. Hence, he must be self-willed and thus self-centered, and, in Chinese culture, all self-centered people must be crass and hence corrupt, and, therefore, all aspiring warlords must, in fact, be essentially petty, corrupt politicians who could not see beyond their own self-interest.

The warlords were thus all prisoners of the basic Chinese view that, first of all, all politics rested upon a personal basis, and second, that any concern for personal ambition, which is, of course, the essence of personal politics, is tantamount to gross corruption.

In the formation of alliances, the element of personal politics was reflected in the role of individuals, both as figureheads and as clearly identifiable "rising stars" with whom others could associate or dissociate themselves. However, behind the façade of personalities, lay the realities of political and military power. Underlying the ritualistic practices of personalized cue-making and cue-taking and behind the talk of individual success and failure, was an abiding respect for "the logic of the situation." Although the "currencies" that the *tuchüns* employed as media of exchange were of a personal order, they made their calculations on the basis of a far more realistic standard. The superstructure of personal politics could serve as a rough guide to understanding the existing balance of power, but it was still necessary for each leader to evaluate the situation as he saw it. He had to determine his policies in terms of either being able to manipulate the balance if it was in his favor, or to attempt to adjust to an unfavorable situation. Although the logic of the situation was often influenced by personality factors, the real cues of actions lay in one's understanding of the current balance of power.

The cult of personalized "cue-making" did result in restricting the personal actions of the *tuchüns* in so far as they realized that their actions would constantly be viewed in terms of deeper implications. Feng Yü-hsiang once complained that any personal visit he might make with friends would be construed by other leaders as having far greater significance than he intended, and the fact that these leaders might act on their interpretation meant that he was at times forced to assume roles that he had not contemplated.[9]

Hence, the process of alliance formation was primarily a function of the power balances that emerged during the period. Basically, such alliances were attempts at collective action in the face of the threat of the rising power of other *tuchüns* or groups of *tuchüns*. Given the Chinese distrust of ambition and their association of any such demonstrations of public desires with suspicion of corruption, one is not surprised that the rhythm of alliance formation took the form of essentially defensive reactions of collective concern against the previous emergence of a threat, and not one of ambitious leaders seeking to put together an alliance that could take the initiative and govern events. Basically, the underlying logic of the warlord period was one of defensive postures and not one of bold initiatives. Even when leaders acted, they always sought to make it appear as though they were responding and not initiating, that they were reacting to public concerns, not shaping the public mind.

Although the efforts at collective action by those who were threatened were fairly simple responses to the balance of power, the problems inherent in attempting to unite were far from simple. Each group that entered the alliance on the primary grounds of seeking self-defense could still find in any proposed program of joint action possibilities of personal gain or loss. These problems can best be illustrated by the attempt of Chang Tso-lin and Lu Yung-hsiang to forge an alliance against the power of the Chihli faction.

THE CHANG-LU ALLIANCE

In June, 1920, when the forces of the Chihli faction under the leadership of Wu P'ei-fu and Ts'ao K'un defeated the Anfu troops in the outskirts of Peking, Chang Tso-lin entered the conflict at the last moment and sought to claim a major share in the victory on the grounds that his intervention had been the margin of difference between an easy victory and a prolonged conflict.[10] Initially, the Chihli leaders were willing to accept Chang's influence in the formation of the new government at Peking.[11] However, by the end of 1920, Chang realized that he was rapidly losing influence in Peking and that he would soon be isolated against a Chihli faction that seemed to be adjusting the major differences within its leadership. In Chang's effort to seek additional support against the dominant influence at the capital, he sought out the various dissident leaders in China at the time.[12]

In the spring of 1921, Chang for the first time solicited the support of Lu Yung-hsiang who was still in control of Chekiang and appeared to be the strongest remaining element of the old Anfu faction.[13] The initial response of Lu was cool toward any suggestions of an alliance that might make him the target of the all too powerful Chihli war machine. Lu chose at this time to seek to weather the storm of Chihli successes by isolating himself at Shanghai, depending upon the vested interests of the foreign, as well as native, financial and commercial groups to keep this area free from conflict.[14] Lu felt that, by playing a lone hand, he would be able to remain innocuous in the eyes of the Chihli faction and thus avoid any involvement that might have provoked their censure.[15]

Chang Tso-lin, although seeking support, was unwilling at the time to make any important concessions in return for assistance in opposing Wu and Ts'ao.[16] The Fengtien leader would welcome such support, but he was still confident enough of his own power to be unwilling to make any binding promises that might limit his freedom of action should the Chihli faction be defeated. Thus, as long as it was uncertain how much power would be required to defeat the Wu-Ts'ao coalition, Chang and those who were opposed to the Chihli faction could not agree upon terms for joint action. They were reticent to commit themselves, fearing they would pay too high a price for the defeat of the Chihli forces, and, until the cost of such an action was clearer, it was impossible to reach any agreement.

It might be noted here, as an aside, that there was a manic-depressive character to much of the communication among the warlords. At one moment, a particular group of warlords might be exchanging views about the problems that might follow upon collective success, and, then, at the next moment, they would be contemplating how they should react to disaster. Most of the time, however, they displayed a typical peasant-like suspicion that they might be paying too much for something that was benefiting someone else more than themselves.

By the winter of 1921-22, it had become obvious that Chang Tso-lin was considered a menace by the Chihli leaders, and Wu P'ei-fu made it eminently clear that he did not feel that the Mukden commander could long be tolerated as an influence in political developments south of the Wall.[17] As Chang became increasingly the focus of the combined opposition of the Loyang and Paoting commanders, he found it more and more difficult to obtain assistance for the price he was willing to pay. To Lu, it was apparent that Chang would have to fight the Chihli faction and that, in any such conflict, he could await developments before fully committing himself.[18]

Thus, in the 1922 conflict between Chang and Wu, the Fengtien forces had to fight without any direct support from the other dissident groups in China. The Fengtien defeat forced Chang to alter his policy radically. It was now apparent that he had vastly overestimated the ability of his own forces, and, although they were sufficient to ensure the security of the Manchurian fortress, they would have to be greatly strengthened if the Mukden leader was to continue as arbiter of affairs south of the Wall.[19] With his defeat and his determined efforts to rebuild his power, Chang found that he was now, oddly enough, in a better position to obtain the direct support of Lu Yung-hsiang. The Chekiang commander now felt his isolation more than ever, and there was the constant danger that, if Chang should cease to constitute a real threat to the Chihli leaders, they would no longer hesitate to attack him.[20] The sudden defeat of Chang created a great deal of concern in the Shanghai foreign community, for it was apparent to the officials there that the security of the city had long rested on the fact that the Chihli leaders would expose themselves to attack from the north if they attempted any extensive operations in the Yangtze Valley. Lu Yung-hsiang now saw in Mukden an attractive ally—one who was not so strong as to dominate any agreement that might be made, but who still was sufficiently powerful to deter the Chihli faction from seeking a war on two fronts. Thus, in March, 1923, Lu was at last willing to enter into serious negotiations with Chang with the objective of forming a mutual defense pact against the Peking government. In these negotiations, Lu relied upon his son, Lu Hsiao-chou, who remained in Mukden until the following December.[21] The mission of Lu Hsiao-chou was to obtain financial support as well as munitions from the Mukden arsenal.[22] One of the factors in Mukden's power during the entire period was its strong alliance appeal because of its sources of finance and its capacity to produce arms. Chang realized that this was the case and consequently suspected others of wanting to exploit him; therefore, he tended to distrust those who sought his assistance. He felt that they were interested only in strengthening their own forces and would not be willing in return to make equal sacrifices in times of emergency. This is one of the prime reasons that Mukden appeared always to drive such a hard bargain in negotiations.

Reports emanated from Mukden to the effect that Chang was having such success with the reorganization of the Fengtien armies that he was now prepared to enter into an alliance with Lu and Sun Yat-sen and that, to any such coalition, Tuan Ch'i-jui would be willing to give his personal support. The possibility of a return of Tuan and the personal support he could give to any movement was a constant factor influencing the calculations of the *tuchüns*. Tuan's personal prestige was so high that, even during the period when he was "studying Buddhism" in Tientsin, he was still a political factor. The possibility of a return of the

Anfu group under the auspices of Chang seemed quite real when, in April, 1924, Hsü Shu-cheng once again appeared in Mukden and had conferences with Chang.[23]

Such a grouping would have been a logical response to the balance of power that then existed. However, as the dissident powers were forced to close ranks, new problems appeared. As the possibility of an alliance became increasingly real, it was necessary to make more exact the role that each partner would play in the coalition. It was not only a question of the leadership of the alliance, but also how the costs were to be shared. At this juncture, the cleavage in the Chihli faction between the Tientsin clique and the military leaders appeared to be widening, and, because the other side appeared to be weakening, neither Lu nor Chang was willing to make the necessary concessions for a final agreement on alliance. All the leaders agreed that the time was propitious for making a move against the Chihli group, but none wanted to shoulder the financial responsibilities. As long as the Chihli faction showed signs of internal weakness, each felt that it was better to hold back before committing oneself to the cost of defeating a group that might soon pass from the scene of its own accord.

Feng Yü-hsiang's *coup d'état*, on June 13, 1923, gave both Chang and Lu further reason to hesitate in entering into a binding agreement. Uncertainty as to the consequence of the coup for the Chihli faction made each of the leaders reluctant to commit himself at the time.[24] Then the decision of Ts'ao K'un to seek the office of the Presidency further served to create a fluid situation in which it was difficult for those who did not control the Peking government to obtain agreement on a unified program. As long as it was apparent that the election of Ts'ao would result in some form of realignment within the Chihli faction, none of the anti-Chihli leaders were prepared to commit themselves to any course of action.

Feng's coup and Ts'ao's decision to become President created confusion and uncertainty not only because there were doubts as to who would emerge the dominant leader of the Chihli faction, but also because it was difficult to predict whether these actions meant a rise in the influence of the political experts or the military.

That Ts'ao K'un was seeking increased power by manipulating parliamentarians and not by directly commanding military forces indicated a major segment of the Chihli faction felt the political arena was more significant than the strictly military arena of conflict. This meant that, for the anti-Chihli groups, there could be disagreement over whether it would be best to attempt to resolve the conflict in terms of military power or by political arrangements. To Lu Yung-hsiang, the latter course seemed more desirable, especially because he felt that, through his connections with the old Anfu clique, he would find greater security than he would by becoming a junior member of a military alliance with Chang Tso-lin.[25] Chang himself was tempted to turn his back on military operations when the Tientsin clique of the Chihli group sought to obtain his support and even offered him the post of the vice-presidency.[26]

Thus, at the very time when the Chihli faction was at its low ebb of power and when any concerted action on the part of the opposing elements had the greatest possibility of success, it became even more difficult for Chang and Lu to agree upon a common course of action. As the likelihood of success appeared more real, any discussion of combined operations hinged more and more upon considerations of how the rewards of victory were to be divided.[27] The difficulty was that a policy emphasizing military operations implied that Chang Tso-lin would dominate the victorious coalition. On the other hand, a program based primarily upon utilizing politicians would leave Lu Yung-hsiang in a stronger position. This dilemma could not be resolved by the two leaders.

However, after the election of Ts'ao and the beginning of the determined policy of Wu P'ei-fu to increase his power with the object of unifying the country by force, it once again became essential for Chang and Lu to attempt to arrive at an understanding over a combined policy to meet the rising threat. By November, 1923, Chang was convinced that a military conflict was inevitable[28] and sought to convince Lu that he would be willing to grant financial assistance to the Chekiang leader if the latter would seriously prepare for military operations.[29] Chang began to grant doles to Lu at this time, but hesitated to be generous until he could be assured that Lu would actually be willing to fight, if and when the occasion arose. Lu Yung-hsiang, however, did not feel satisfied with the extent of Chang's aid and continued to seek further assistance from other quarters.[30] In addition, Lu persisted in balking at any commitments for joint military action as he still hoped to achieve security by obtaining the overt support of Tuan Ch'i-jui and the Anfu politicians.[31]

Chang Tso-lin realized that Lu's policy of seeking neutrality would mean that the Chihli faction would no longer be restrained by the danger of having to fight simultaneously in the North and in the Yangtze Valley.[32] He thus renewed his efforts to secure Lu's cooperation and to convince the Chekiang leader that he had little hope of remaining in power if he was not prepared to fight. Chang began to make public statements to the effect that developments in North China would have a critical effect on the control of the Yangtze area.[33]

As the actual conflict between Chekiang and Kiangsu neared, Lu and Chang were only committed in the vaguest manner to support each other. It was Lu now who, realizing that he could find little security in neutrality, began to plead for direct help from Chang and demanded that Fengtien attack the Chihli forces in the North to relieve the pressure on Chekiang.[34] However, for Chang, once the fighting commenced, it was only necessary that Lu tie down the Chihli reserves in the Yangtze Valley.[35] Even if the Chekiang armies were insufficient to defeat the forces of Ch'i Hsieh-yüan and Sun Ch'uan-fang, they would have served their purpose for Chang by reducing the number of reserves the Chihli leaders could order to the northern front.

Thus, although the situation had clearly pointed to the desirability of close collaboration between Mukden and Chekiang, the leaders of the two areas were unwilling to make the commitments that would have given them the initiative. The fact that they were excluded from control of the resources of the Peking government and threatened by the rising power of Chihli was not sufficient to ensure their close cooperation. Each had to make careful calculations as to what would be the cost of collaboration and what would be the marginal values to be gained by such action. Because the pattern of power was so unstable, the market in which they had to make these estimates was far too erratic for them to arrive at any binding decisions. Although both could see in Chihli a real threat, each could also envisage a defeat of the Chihli group, which would leave himself in no stronger position.

Only after the defeat of the Chekiang armies and Lu's escape to Japan did there develop any close relations between them.[36] Now Lu no longer had any bargaining power and had to accept whatever offers Chang was willing to make. Chang's request that Lu come to Mukden and his announcement that the Fengtien forces would conquer Chekiang and restore Lu to his old headquarters came as a surprise to political observers. It was impossible to determine the motives behind Chang's move to continue support of a leader who no longer had an army under his command. Speculation on Chang's actions included the following: (1) Chang felt it expedient to demonstrate that he would continue to support a former ally, even in the face of the defeat of such a collaborator; (2) Chang was responding to the pressures of Japan and, in order to ensure future support from this quarter, was willing to back all ex-Anfuites; (3) Chang realized that Lu had numerous political associates who would be invaluable if he sought to control the Peking government; (4) Chang saw in the championing of Lu a means of justifying an expansion of his area of domination just before the Tientsin Conference convened.[37] Chang appeared to be acting in good faith, when, after the Fengtien forces had driven as far south as northern Kiangsu, he appointed Lu commander of the Yangtze provinces of Kiangsu and Chekiang.[38] However, it soon became evident that Lu was helpless without the military support of the Fengtien field commanders, and he could be nothing more than a figurehead. By January, 1925, it was apparent that, regardless of what might have been the original motives of Chang, Lu was admirably serving the purposes of the Mukden leader by justifying the continued efforts of Fengtien to dominate the Yangtze area. Chang publicly stated that the Chekiang and, especially, the Shanghai communities need not feel uneasy over the entry of Fengtien armies into their area, because these forces were only seeking to restore their old leader, Lu Yung-hsiang. Chang announced further that there was an agreement with the Anfu leaders whereby Fengtien would directly control only Chihli and Shantung, while the Anfu leaders were to divide among themselves Anhwei, Kiangsu, and Chekiang.[39] However, no further evidence has been found to substantiate any such agreement. In addition, Chang appeared to be exploiting Lu in order to postpone any decision as to which of his commanders would be given control over the area to the south of Shantung, thus preventing the development of jealousies within the ranks of the Fengtien elite until the military campaigns were completed. The appointment of Chang Tsung-ch'ang to control Shantung had created tensions among the Fengtien leaders, but Chang Tso-lin had been able to justify this appointment by the fact that the notorious "Dog Meat General" was a native of the province.[40] However, jealousies persisted among the remaining Fengtien leaders for posts in the Yangtze area, and these tensions over expectations of reward culminated in the Kuo Sung-ling revolt.[41]

By now, it was eminently clear that Chang had no intention of seriously supporting the claims of Lu Yung-hsiang, and the former Chekiang defense commissioner decided to retire from politics and leave the Fengtien armies to conquer the Yangtze as best they could.[42] Only by this act could Lu strike back at his erstwhile ally, who was clearly exploiting him as a tool for Fengtien's conquests. Thus, in the end, Lu's greatest fears were realized, for the defeat of the Chihli alliance had resulted in a pattern of power that left him in an even worse position than he had previously occupied. As long as he and Chang had not been able to negotiate an alliance on equal terms to defeat a common foe, there was the danger that he would be a loser when the enemy was defeated, and now this danger had materialized.[43]

ALLIANCES OF "IN-GROUPS"

It might appear a sound postulate that the alliances formed by *tuchüns* in control of the formal instruments of government under the Peking regime had a better chance of achieving stability than those made by groups seeking to capture the powers of the legal government. In the first place, the *tuchüns* who dominated the Peking government had necessarily at one time been sufficiently united in a common policy to have achieved the positions they held; secondly, once they had secured this power, they were bound together with the common purpose of seeking to maintain whatever security they had obtained. In addition, their relations were formalized to the extent that they held specific offices and followed the conventions of operating within the structure of a legal system. Thus, in this respect, there were at least formal definitions of their relationships to each other.[44]

It was true that the existence of the formal structure of government did at times serve to stabilize the relations of those groups that had been successful in establishing control of the organs of government at Peking. Nevertheless, one of the most difficult tasks that a successful alliance had to perform was to adjust the informal relations established through the alliances to the precise structure of relationships within the formal government. Often, unsuccessful attempts to solve this problem led to the deterioration of the otherwise satisfactory arrangement among the particular *tuchüns*. An alliance had a fair expectancy of remaining in power if it was successful in assuring each of the principal members that his formal position adequately reflected what to his mind was the proper hierarchy and balance of forces within the alliance. However, this was rarely achieved, because the *tuchüns* hesitated in committing themselves to relationships that might limit the expansion of their power in the future.

Almost invariably, the relationships that developed out of the relative power positions in an alliance could not be expressed in the formal and more rigid relationships of the legal government.[45] As a result, it was often necessary to create new offices and positions. To a large degree, this explains the rapid expansion in the number of government posts during the period under study.[46]

THE CHIHLI ALLIANCE, 1920–24

When the Chihli forces defeated the Anfuites in June, 1920, the scene appeared to be set for a single group to assume control of the administration, thus furnishing to the Peking government the support of an alliance that clearly held a preponderance of power in North China.[47] Although there was some uneasiness over Chang Tso-lin's role in the new government, the fact that the Mukden *tuchün* had contributed to the final defeat of Tuan led to the belief that at least the Fengtien commander would not be in serious opposition to the new regime.

However, it was soon apparent that the Chihli alliance faced a formidable task in reorganizing the cabinet and replacing the Anfu appointments in the provinces.[48] The defeat of the Anfuites had left only Lu Yung-hsiang in a position strong enough to hope to retain his area of control. The problem of granting rewards to the leaders of the Chihli coalition, and, in particular, the assigning of provinces to their control, placed the entire alliance under a stress it proved incapable of meeting satisfactorily. The very manner in which the defeated armies of Tuan Ch'i-jui and Hsü Shu-cheng were reorganized produced tensions. Ts'ao K'un had reorganized the three best divisions of Tuan's troops and incorporated them into his armies, while Chang Tso-lin had increased his forces by four mixed brigades, which had formally been the elite troops of "Little Hsü's" Northwest Frontier Guard and which had received Japanese instruction.[49] Wu P'ei-fu, who had supplied the principal forces in the victory over Anfu, felt that he had been neglected in the apportioning of the Anfu men and supplies. Wu was able to increase his forces by approximately ten thousand men after the disbandment of the Anfu armies and turned to Hupei to obtain new recruits. Thus, the effect of the Anfu defeat and the efforts to divide the spoils was to increase the total number of men under arms in China.[50]

By August, 1920, there began to develop a split between Ts'ao K'un and Wu P'ei-fu. Ts'ao K'un found himself in an embarrassing position, because the only way in which he could give greater rewards to Wu P'ei-fu was either to deny himself the troops that he had incorporated, and thereby possibly lose his position as the leader of the Chihli alliance, or to suggest that Chang Tso-lin deny himself his portion of the spoils. The latter course would have led certainly to tensions with Mukden, and Ts'ao was not in a position to champion such a conflict at the time. Chang Tso-lin was quick to press in on Ts'ao's dilemma, suggesting that he and Ts'ao should logically dominate the Peking government and publicly stating that Wu P'ei-fu was "only a division commander" and therefore should not be consulted on political decisions.[51] The proposal that Wu P'ei-fu be made minister of war only further infuriated the Loyang commander, and Ts'ao K'un found that he was losing the confidence and support of his most trusted associate.[52]

The conflict that developed between the two principal leaders of the Chihli alliance was further aggravated by the problem of settling the new appointments in the provinces. The Chihli alliance was clearly in a position to oust most of the remaining Anfu officials, but to make changes would necessitate satisfying all elements in the Chihli group. This seemed an impossible task, particularly in view of the difference between Ts'ao and Wu.

The first of such problems appeared in Kiangsu and Anhwei. Li Shun had for a long time been the *tuchün* of Kiangsu and was considered to be a loyal member of the Chihli alliance. He had supported the plan to organize the military campaign against the Anfuites.[53] However, when the conflict came, Li failed to send troops in support of the Chihli armies, claiming that it was necessary for him to keep his armies in the Yangtze area for fear that Lu Yung-hsiang might attack Chekiang.[54] Li Shun's failure actively to enter the conflict caused Wu P'ei-fu to accuse him of seeking to expand his territory in the Yangtze area while the rest of the Chihli armies were in the North.[55] Thus, after the Anfu defeat, Li Shun found himself isolated, and, on October 12, 1920, he unexpectedly committed suicide. Although there were rumors of foul play, it appears that Li did take his own life. He was examined by a foreign physician a few weeks before his death, and the report of the examination indicated that Li was in depressed spirits.[56] He had been troubled by the loss of the support of several of his subordinates, who felt that he should have given more active support to the Chihli cause. In addition, there had been public demonstrations against him for failing to support the popular Wu P'ei-fu. The fact that such demonstrations could be engineered indicated the weakening hold of Li over his subordinates.[57] The vacancy that thus arose created further tensions within the Chihli ranks, and Wu P'ei-fu immediately gave his support to the candidacy of Ch'i Hsieh-yüan, who had been one of Li's leading subordinates as well as a former officer under the Loyang commander.[58] Ts'ao K'un hesitated to support this move and suggested that the decision of Li's successor should await the formation of the Peking government.[59] Ts'ao's reluctance to support without reservation Ch'i Hsieh-yüan led to a further split in the Chihli ranks and caused speculation as to the possibility of the appearance of a new center of power within the alliance dominated by Wu and Ch'i in the Yangtze area.[60]

Ts-ao K'un, however, by determining the new *tuchün* of Anhwei, sought to prevent any such bloc of independent Yangtze *tuchüns* from rising in the Chihli alliance. The former *tuchün* of Anhwei, Ni Ssu-ch'ung had been an active member of the Anfu Club, but, with the defeat of Tuan, Ni immediately retired without waiting for the Chihli armies to occupy the province.[61] However, Ts'ao, by attempting to operate through the Peking government, found that Chang Tso-lin had already submitted the name of the notorious and redoubtable Chang Hsün for the post.[62] Ts'ao K'un could not have supported Chang Tso-lin's appointee without further widening the breach within the Chihli ranks, but, at the same time, he found that he could not ignore Chang's suggestions and make his own appointment.[63] The result was that it was necessary to select a compromise candidate, Chang Wen-sen.[64] Although the combined backing of Ts'ao and Chang was sufficient to ensure Chang Wen-sen the post, he was so weak and lacking in followers that it meant that Anhwei would not be a threat to the other Yangtze commanders.

The Chihli alliance was further strained when it was necessary to determine who would have immediate responsibility for Shantung. The last Anfu commander in that province had been General Ma Liang, who continued to resist the power of Chihli after the defeat of Tuan's armies.[65] It was necessary for both Ts'ao and Wu to dispatch additional troops to the area before Ma was finally defeated in August, 1920.[66] Although Wu's armies had shouldered the main burden of defeating Ma, the fact that Ts'ao K'un had also dispatched armies to the area raised serious questions as to who should have the power to select the new commander in the province. Ts'ao K'un held the formal title of inspector general of Chihli and Shantung, and Wu occupied the post of assistant inspector general of the same area. This placed them both in the position of being theoretically responsible for the area.[67] However, if Ts'ao had attempted to place a strong leader in the post of *tuchün* of Shantung, it would have been interpreted as a move to undermine Wu's influence in the area. Ts'ao K'un finally was able to arrive at a compromise appointment in the person of a political and military nonentity, Hsiung Ping-chi.[68] Although Wu was in a position to dominate Hsiung, he was disappointed that he had not been free to appoint one of his own immediate subordinates to the post.[69] On the surface, both Wu and Ts'ao proceeded as though they were satisfied with the decision, but the underlying tension was demonstrated in 1922, when it was necessary to divide the administration of the province between the Tsinan *tuchün*'s headquarters and the Kiaochow Special Area. Wu was clearly in control of the latter, while Ts'ao still had recognized influence in the provincial administration.[70]

Although these problems concerning the appointments of new officials in the provinces had not resulted in a complete break in the Chihli alliance, with each decision there had been tension. As a consequence, each member of the alliance had to make fine adjustments in his relations with the other members. With Ts'ao and Wu serving as the centers of power in the alliance, all the other members had to indicate how they stood in relation to these two figures. Often this placed them under severe strain, in that, whereas they could not afford to risk the displeasure of either *tuchün*, they also had to adjust to what they considered to be either an increase or decrease in the power of either of the super-*tuchüns*.

However, at the same time, it was possible for the lesser *tuchüns* to attempt to capitalize on this division by balancing the two leaders against each other, while still remaining loyal to the concept of a Chihli alliance. Thus, for example, Wu P'ei-fu found that he was faced with a difficult problem in Honan, the province that had served as his power base. The official *tuchün* of the area was Chao Ti, who claimed to be loyal to the Chihli cause and insisted on demonstrating his sincerity by communicating directly with Ts'ao K'un and pointedly announcing his support of Ts'ao.[71] Wu P'ei-fu, in order to strengthen his control of the province, was determined to oust Chao Ti from his post.[72] Although the latter had given nominal support to Wu in the campaign against the Anfu faction,[73] he had given indications that such support was only grudgingly offered and that, in case Wu should ever be confronted with a serious threat, it was doubtful whether Chao would assist him.[74] After the Chihli victory, Chao tended to support the Ts'ao K'un wing of the coalition.[75] So, in 1921, Wu called upon Feng Yü-hsiang to eliminate Chao Ti's power. Wu indicated to Feng that, should they be successful in the operation, Feng would be made the *tuchün* of Honan.[76] Wu was able to justify his action of requesting Feng to leave Shensi and enter Honan, on the grounds that it was necessary to prepare to meet the threat of Chang Tso-lin.[77]

Thus, only as the Chihli alliance was threatened from an outside source, was it possible for Wu to strengthen his control over an area that had long been recognized as a part of his domain, without creating an issue that might have further split the alliance.

However, Feng's Eleventh Division proved to be far too powerful a tool to be applied to the elimination of the nuisance that Chao Ti had become. The result was that Wu, as he entered the conflict with Feng-tien in 1922, found that, in calling in Feng, he had, in fact, invited the proverbial camel into his tent and that Feng's control of Kaifeng would be a far greater threat to his ambitions than had been the influence of Chao Ti.[78] Wu's efforts to bolster his military power and check the dominance of Ts'ao K'un in the Chihli alliance had resulted only in decreasing his own influence in the key area of Honan.

The fact that Wu P'ei-fu had had little difficulty in defeating Chang Tso-lin in 1922 did not demonstrate that the Chihli alliance was appreciably strengthened by the victory. The successful campaign, however, had resulted in the recognition of Wu as the undisputed military leader of the alliance and had caused a subsequent decline in the prestige of Ts'ao.[79] It was at this time that the Tientsin clique within the Chihli alliance first began to become an important factor. However, by now the divisions and cleavages among the leaders had reached such extremes that the group was an alliance only in name. The decision of Ts'ao K'un to become President finally provoked the open opposition of Wu P'ei-fu.[80] All the efforts of Ts'ao to conciliate his former supporter were fruitless.[81] The alliance that had been torn by internal strife and conflict from the time it had defeated Anfu no longer had sufficient cohesion to administer the Peking government. The task of adjusting the informal relations of the alliance to the formal relations of a governmental structure had proved too difficult.

The structure of alliances in the politics of *tuchün*-ism did not become the means of ordering political and military power to the achieving of group ends. As long as the alliances were conceived in terms of personal bonds and calculations of expediency, they were not strong enough to support an alignment of power that would be sufficiently stable to give effective and meaningful ordering to the formal organs of government that they might control. The web of personal relations was so complex and intricate that it could not serve as a clearly defined premise for the building of policy objectives. It was possible to rationalize almost any course of action as being in conformity with the principles of some personal relationship or other. The calculations of expediency did not stop at the point of defining what would be best for the total alliance but, rather, were made in terms of the individual leader's expectations. Expediency calculations could serve as guides to an individual leader's behavior but had little meaning for the alliance as a whole. It was impossible to assure all members of an alliance that an investment in the form of temporary sacrifices would mean the possibility of the entire group's achieving such a position that all would receive greater dividends. This was the case because it was impossible to ensure that such a new distribution of rewards and power would not so alter the relations of the members as to leave each with the expectation that he might not be able to improve his relative power position. An increase in the absolute power of the alliance was meaningless to some, because all were operating within a frame of reference that stressed the relative power of each. Thus, the successful operation of a coalition might offer little reward, since such an operation might drastically affect one's relative power.

Although the alliances were not effective organs for the achieving of policy objectives, they still served the function of representing certain formalized relations that offered a minimum of stability in a fluid situation. To be a member of an alliance did not carry with it assurances of security, but it did alter to a slight degree the perspective that the *tuchün* employed in evaluating his relative position in the total power complex. Although leaders often violated the spirit, if not the agreements, on which the alliances were founded, such acts did carry with them a degree of risk and threat of retaliation that would not have existed without the alliances. Specifically, the lesser leaders were more effectively bound by the alliances, because only the more powerful *tuchüns* could make the overt moves to violate the bonds of a coalition. Thus, as these alignments of power assumed more formalized configurations, they did represent the most explicit limitations on the *tuchüns'* actions that existed. The need to show deference to the symbols of alliance placed restraints upon a completely cynical disregard for the relations existing among the members. The fact that the alliances rarely functioned effectively did not mean that a *tuchün* could ignore entirely the existence of such structures.

6. THE WARLORDS' BALANCE
OF POWER

That the warlord alliances served as only crude centers about which the *tuchüns* oriented their behavior indicates the complex nature of the existing balance of power. The individual leaders, concerned with the stability of their own organizations, had to make continuous calculations of the consequences of the acts of not only acknowledged opponents but also those supposedly within their coalitions. The instability and complexity of these relationships among the *tuchüns* made it extremely difficult for individual leaders to arrive at accurate evaluations of the power at the command of each of the parties in the balance. Any major move by a *tuchün* could be expected to create a situation in which some leaders would find it advantageous to support his actions, while others would react in a negative manner, but, generally, there was uncertainty as to the reactions of particular leaders.

The question arises as to whether, from this maze of relationships, one can determine any pattern of behavior that, for purposes of analysis, could be organized into a theoretical system of relations. In a sense, this would require the construction of a conceptual model based on empirical evidence, which would permit predictions of the behavior of the *tuchüns*. However, such a complete model of power relationships is beyond the scope of this study. Rather, what will be done is to explicate certain factors in the power relationships that appear critical in determining the behavior of the *tuchüns*. Using these conceptual terms, one can clarify somewhat the operation of the balance of power among the *tuchüns*.

That the warlords were so little influenced by explicit ideologies meant they represented an archetype of what might be called "Chinese political pragmatism." Quite openly they admitted that their first concern always had to be the security of their organizations, and this generally led to their second basic concern, which was to increase their power or influence. In short, their politics revolved endlessly around the issue of

94

power, its maximization for oneself, and the calculation of its relative distribution among all the others.

As far as most of the warlords were concerned, the "rules of the game" began with judgments about the relative military or organizational power of all potential friends and foes. Because this evaluation of relative power focused on the actual forces available to the command of each leader, we might usefully, for shorthand purposes in the rest of our analysis, refer to such power as the "force" that each actor possessed. Thus, the "force" a leader had in any relationship depended primarily upon the strength of his military units and his ability to maintain and expand his organizational structure. The significant factors that the *tuchüns* took into account in evaluating the "force" of another warlord would be that leader's capacity to apply military coercion, which, in turn, depended upon the loyalty and skill of his subordinates, the richness of his province, and the general effectiveness of his organization.

The balance of power among the warlords was not, however, tied to a purely military equilibrium. Much of the politics of warlordism involved stratagems, tactics, actions, and maneuvers designed to communicate threat or friendship to others, while avoiding actual military conflicts. The power balance of the *tuchüns* was thus highly responsive to another dimension of judging relative power—that which involved the capacity of a *tuchün* to act in such a manner as to cause the others to recalculate their own alignments. In some cases, this might mean an independent act, such as breaking an alliance, or executing a *coup d'état*, which might be seen by other *tuchüns* as offering opportunities to advance their own interests. In other situations, the action might compel responses, because the consequences of it might be unfavorable. Some warlords were in better positions than others to act so as to influence the realignment of others, and, in this sense, they had greater power, even though this power did not show up in the "forces" they commanded. For the purpose of our analysis we might, again for shorthand purposes, refer to this second dimension of power as the "alignment potential" of the warlord. The geographical location of a *tuchün*, the nuisance value he might have in his relations with others, or other considerations that made people recognize that a warlord had greater power than just his "force" would be the elements that made up his "alignment potential."

Generally, it was relatively easy for the warlords to calculate the balance of power in "force" terms, but great uncertainty arose over judgments about "alignment potentials." In terms of the operation of the total balance of power, this meant that a sudden change in the position of any element in the balance was followed by a period of uncertainty, even if the event did not carry with it a radical change in the relative "force" of the *tuchüns*. During this period, each *tuchün* had to make judgments as to what the change signified in terms of his interest, and this, in turn, depended upon what his new "alignment potential" would be in relation to all the other elements in the balance. During this period of hesitation, all of the *tuchüns* were attempting to calculate how they could best protect themselves or advance their interests in the new context.

This pattern—event, hesitation, and then widespread reshuffling—was related to a second characteristic of balance of power among the warlords, that of a high level of instability of relations in spite of a low level of change in objective factors. The relative stagnation of the Chinese economy at the time and the lack of technological innovations meant that there was relatively little scope for change in the objective factors that determined the relative "force" of the warlords. On the other hand, their ingrained appreciation of the scarcity of material resources made the warlords hypersensitive to the possibility that others might be profiting from any development and that one was always in danger of losing out if he did not respond cleverly to possible opportunities.

This constant concern about not missing out on short run advantages and being constantly alert to the hidden cues of opportunity was balanced by an equally strong tendency to husband one's resources carefully and avoid dangerous risks. Whenever the balance operated to create a dangerous situation, the object of every warlord was to compel some other warlord to assume the risks of coping with the danger, while seeking for himself any possible short-run advantage.

These considerations suggest that the warlord's "pragmatic" approach toward power had certain very distinctive and limiting characteristics that emerged from the ways in which they evaluated their power relations. In seeking always to be "realistic," they tended to discount the stability of the objective factors of power and react with great sensitivity to the perceived advantages of changing circumstances. The expectation that others had intentions that could be damaging to oneself was not generally balanced by an appreciation that the capabilities of the others could only change very slowly. "Realism" also seemed to require opportunism, but this search for potential advantage had to be very shortsighted, because of a conservative approach toward risk-taking.

We can best observe these general characteristics of the warlord's reactions to this balance of power situation by concentrating on three key features of the system. First, the tendency to hesitation and, then, extensive reaction based upon calculations of "alignment potentials" can be seen from the function of *coups d'état* in warlord politics. Second, the tendency to seek quick advantage can be observed in the inclination of warlords to side with strength and not weakness when forced to choose. Third, the tendency to avoid risks and seek petty advantages at times of great danger emerges dramatically from the response of the entire warlord balance-of-power system to the collective threat of the Kuomintang armies.

THE PATTERN OF *Coups d'État*

Not one of the warlords who instigated coups acted out of the belief that, by capturing the formal officers of government, he could become supreme and greatly augment his "force" level of power. The governmental apparatus was not a structure that was strong enough to guarantee to those who controlled it an effective and immediate increment of "force."[1] For the *tuchüns*, the coup was a method of seeking a readjustment in the balance, hence an increase in their "alignment potential." It was clearly not a technique for achieving a monopoly of power. It is significant that all coups were initiated by *tuchüns* who were associated with the dominant groups in the capital. Only by being identified with such a group were they in a position to station troops near enough to Peking to make a sudden move to capture the physical control of the formal offices of government. This fact did lead to the proposals that a demilitarized zone be established around the capital on the assumption that, by removing troops from the immediate environs of the city, it would be possible to eliminate *coups d'état* and reduce the pressure of the *tuchüns* on the administrative offices.[2] The coup was thus primarily a tool for dissatisfied members of a coalition who sought either to strengthen their "alignment potential" in the councils of the alliance or to establish an entirely new alignment of power, which would include other dissatisfied elements.

This function of the *coup d'état*, and the inability of the *tuchüns* to respond immediately to any abrupt change in the balance, can be observed from two examples of sudden moves to capture the Peking government by Feng Yü-hsiang. In the first instance, Feng was seeking greater recognition within the Chihli faction, whereas, in the second, he was determined to create an entirely new alignment of the *tuchüns*.

After the 1922 defeat of Fengtien by the Chihli forces and Feng Yü-hsiang's appointment as inspector-general of the Chinese Armies, Feng found that his status within the alliance was not sufficient to ensure the continued strength of his organization. In particular, he had been denied a specific area of control and would have to depend upon doles from a government under the influence of the military power of Wu P'ei-fu and Ts'ao K'un.[3] On the other hand, because his Eleventh Division was stationed at Nanyüan and he himself had offices in the capital, it was possible for him to negotiate with most of the important leaders of China. In particular, Feng met often with President Li Yüan-hung,[4] members of the Parliament and cabinet ministers,[5] as well as representatives of Chang Tso-lin, Lu Yung-hsiang, and the Canton government.[6] It is significant that, during the period immediately preceding the coup, Feng had no relations with Wu P'ei-fu, although Wu had been instrumental in bringing Feng first into the Chihli alliance and then in placing him in the office of inspector-general of the Chinese Armies.

Although meeting with the representatives of other factions, Feng sought primarily to operate within the Chihli structure. In particular, he sought to transfer his support from Wu P'ei-fu to Ts'ao K'un. From April 7 to April 15, 1923, Feng was in Paotingfu negotiating with Ts'ao K'un for further funds and for greater recognition within the Chihli councils.[7] At this time, Feng also issued a circular telegram stating that Ts'ao K'un was the leader who had the greatest interest in the welfare of the Chinese people, because, unlike Chang Tso-lin and Wu P'ei-fu, he was not interested in causing further civil strife.[8] Thus, when, on June 13, 1923, Feng ordered his troops to occupy the capital and forced President Li Yüan-hung to flee to Tientsin, he was moving to establish a new alignment of the members of the Chihli coalition. By this act, Feng not only guaranteed himself the revenues of the Peking Octroi, but also he forced a realignment of the members of the Chihli alliance.[9]

The coup was an act by which Feng had certain limited expectations of increasing his "force," but, primarily, he was seeking to change his "alignment potential" in his relations with Ts'ao K'un and Wu P'ei-fu. Previously, it was Wu who was in a position of superiority over Feng, although they shared common goals. After Wu appointed Feng inspector-general of the Chinese Armies, their relationship changed to one of greater conflict in that Feng could now hope for greater autonomy and feel frustrated by Wu's continuing claim of domination. By means of the coup, Feng sought to increase his power with respect to Wu by establishing a situation in which Ts'ao would now feel it appropriate to replace Wu as Feng's superior. Thus, through the coup, Feng had succeeded in increasing his power vis-à-vis Wu by creating a situation in which more leaders in the Chihli faction felt that their calculations of expediency demanded that they oppose Wu than had been the case before the coup.

In short, by Feng's completely independent act, he was able to indicate to all the *tuchüns* that he was now too big a man to be merely Wu P'ei-fu's subordinate. At the same time, by acknowledging that Ts'ao K'un was now his superior, Feng was able to elevate significantly the importance of Ts'ao and thus cause all the allied *tuchüns* to respond by showing that they now understood the increased importance of Ts'ao. Feng was thus able to deflate the importance of one leader and elevate another while himself avoiding the danger of being the conspicuous center of attack. Feng could insist that he was still merely a subordinate element in the larger alliance even though his actions had changed the relative power of all the others.

However, the initial reactions of the other leaders within the Chihli faction was one of uncertainty. These leaders committed themselves to support or oppose Feng only after Ts'ao K'un had ordered his troops to arrest President Li upon his arrival at Tientsin and the Paotingfu leader had issued a statement that Feng had been justified in his actions because of the "unconstitutional policies of the Office of the President."[10] Although the coup had been directed against Wu P'ei-fu's influence both in the government and in the Chihli alliance, the Loyang leader hesitated in issuing a statement, and the initiative passed to those who now sought Ts'ao K'un as the future leader for the alliance. Feng's action and the apparent support that he was receiving from Ts'ao were sufficient to alter the balance within the coalition. Although the balance among the "forces" had not perceptibly changed, the fact that Feng appeared to have succeeded in creating a situation in which Ts'ao could expect a greater realization of his objectives by acting in a coordinated manner with Feng was sufficient to cause a reordering of the "alignment potential" relations within the coalition.[11]

The *coup d'état* that Feng instigated in 1924 was of greater significance than the 1923 venture, because, this time, Feng was seeking a realignment of relations that extended beyond those of the Chihli leaders to each other. Although, in both cases, he acted to capture the same formal offices of government, the timing of the 1924 coup created a situation in which it was impossible to limit the consequences to only the relations among the Chihli leaders.

After the "election" of Ts'ao K'un to the Presidency on October 11, 1923, it was apparent that the combination of Ts'ao and Feng would be too weak to maintain a dominant position in Peking. The actions of both in 1923 had resulted in a complete rupture of relations between Chang Tso-lin and the Peking government, and there was a danger that Chang would seek, possibly with the help of Wu P'ei-fu, to re-establish his influence at the capital.[12] Ts'ao, therefore, sought a *rapprochement* with Wu P'ei-fu and promised him the full support of the government in operations against Fengtien.[13] The situation was one in which, as Ts'ao and Feng found they were losing their relative "force" in their relations with the other *tuchüns*, Wu was increasing his relative power vis-à-vis both Feng and Ts'ao. However, Ts'ao, because of his status and formal office, as well as his influence over lesser leaders of the alliance, was able to adjust this change to preserve some degree of authority over Wu. Feng, on the other hand, found that he lacked sufficient independent influence over others and thus was directly losing his relative power vis-à-vis Wu.

By spring, 1924, Feng's influence was steadily declining within the alliance, and there was a real possibility that the balance within the group would once again return to the pattern that existed before June,

1923. Feng slowly came to the realization that, as long as he was identified with the Chihli coalition, Wu's military power would overshadow his influence. Feng's disillusionment with his possibilities in the Chihli faction came about rather slowly. In January, 1924, he idealized Ts'ao K'un to his troops as an example for all soldiers to follow.[14] He even went so far as to send Wu P'ei-fu a personally inscribed scroll on the latter's birthday on March 2, 1924.[15] However, Feng was finding that his recommendations for official posts for his followers were going unheeded by Ts'ao, who had refused to consider Chou Yu-k'e for the position of director of the bureau of military affairs and Sun Yüeh for *tuchün* of Jehol.[16]

Before deciding definitely that the maintenance of his power position would require a full break with the Chihli faction, Feng sought to establish closer relations with Ts'ao and to influence the President to support his claims as the major military leader in the alliance. Just before Wu P'ei-fu arrived in Peking at the commencement of the campaign against Fengtien in the autumn of 1924, Feng had daily private conversations with Ts'ao K'un, but he was unable to alter Ts'ao's decision fully to back Wu P'ei-fu in the war against Chang Tso-lin.[17] Feng had little to offer in his negotiations with Ts'ao, because he could not guarantee sufficient "force" or "alignment potential" to defeat Fengtien and protect Peking.

It was this situation that motivated Feng to plot a second coup, which was to lead to a radical change in the balance of power that extended beyond the relations within the Chihli alliance.[18] When he suddenly returned from the Jehol front, where he had been ordered by Ts'ao and Wu, Feng succeeded in his objective of creating a drastic change in the balance of power. Only Wu P'ei-fu appears to have underestimated the effect of the coup, and he continued to prosecute his campaign against the Fengtien armies on the Shanhaikuan front.[19]

Wu's own subordinates argued with him that he should immediately act to neutralize the effect of Feng's actions in order to prevent the other *tuchüns* from joining in support of Feng in the belief that he might be successful. However, Wu rejected the suggestion on the grounds that if he ignored the coup and continued with the war against Chang, the other leaders would recognize that Feng's actions were of little significance. The problem was one of determining the correct policy to follow in order for Wu to maintain his relative "alignment potential" in his relations with the other Chihli leaders. His immediate subordinates were arguing in effect that a move of "force" in the direction of Feng would ensure Wu superior "alignment potential" with the other leaders. Wu held to the policy of continuing to concentrate on strengthening his "force" relationship over Chang Tso-lin in order to maintain his "alignment potential" over the other Chihli leaders. Wu hoped that, by ignoring Feng's coup, he could strengthen his power over all other leaders and thus force Feng again to recognize Wu's influence over him.

Feng's coup had a paralyzing effect on the other leaders in China as each one attempted to interpret its consequences in terms of his own power position. The *tuchüns* in the Yangtze Valley, who had recently given their allegiance to Wu in the expectation that he would soon be in control of North China, were now thrown into a state of uncertainty.[20] Generals Ch'i Hsieh-yüan, Sun Ch'uan-fang, Ma Lien-chia of Anhwei, Ts'ai Chun-hsün, and Chou Ying-jen of Fukien, and Admiral Tu Hsi-kuei issued a joint circular telegram, which was noncommittal, stating that the authors deplored the unhappy state of Chinese politics, with its civil wars and *coups d'état*. The telegram could be interpreted as condemning the actions of both Feng and Wu, although Feng received the greater criticism, because he was mentioned by name.[21]

Ch'i Hsieh-yüan, who had obtained the support of Wu in defeating Lu Yung-hsiang, now saw his benefactor faced with defeat but hesitated in responding to his call for assistance.[22] Sun Ch'uan-fang, who had also been assisted by Wu in the campaigns against Chekiang, likewise refused to go to his aid.[23] Wu's appeal for assistance from the provincial troops in Shantung and Honan went unheeded until it was too late and Yen Hsi-shan had decided to go to the support of Feng and Chang, dispatching troops from Shansi to intercept the reserves Wu had been attempting to bring to his assistance.[24]

In the meantime, the representatives of all the *tuchüns* in Peking were attempting to interpret the full implications of Feng's coup. The uncertainty that prevailed and the wide circulation of rumors made it extremely difficult for each leader to decide how he personally should react to the situation, and, by such hesitation, they intensified the crisis by prolonging the uncertainty.[25] During the 1920's, whenever there was a sudden change in a *tuchün's* policies, it was common to suspect foreign intrigue. The assumption was that any *tuchün* would have to have the guarantee of some foreign support before he would feel sufficiently secure to initiate a radically different policy that would incur the enmity of other leaders. Feng's decision to violate the Treaty of Abdication and take control of the Forbidden City created a clamor in the Chinese press and added to the charges that Feng was a radical. When Henry Pu-yi fled to the Japanese legation, the *Peking Leader* of February 28, 1925, commented prophetically that "other countries also want to utilize the title of Henry Pu-yi in order to carry out their aggressive plans toward China." The fact that Feng had almost daily visits with Leo Karakhan, the Russian representative of the Comintern, compounded the confusion and led to speculation that Feng was seeking to bring about a Bolshevik revolution.[26] However, there was also speculation that Feng's decision to assist Chang Tso-lin meant that Fengtien and the Kuominchün might be uniting with the active support of the Japanese Government.[27]

Out of this confusion and uncertainty, it was impossible for the various leaders to glean clues for predicting the alignments that would result from the coup. Although the disposition of the military forces was fairly well known and thus the "force" that each had under his immediate command could be evaluated, it was impossible to fathom the combinations of power that would arise or to interpret the relative "alignment potential" of each. As long as there was doubt as to the ability of Feng, Chang, and Tuan to cooperate, it was difficult for the other leaders to determine the balance of forces about which they would have to adjust their policies. Until there was some degree of certainty about this question, the other tuchüns hesitated in issuing statements that would commit them to any particular course of action. The only announcements they were willing to make were declarations to the effect that the time had arrived for the leaders of China to attempt to establish an efficient and just government and that they would be willing to support such a government.[28]

On the other hand, the leaders in the anti-Chihli movement were faced with much the same dilemma, in that they were uncertain as to how much support they could expect from the hesitating provincial leaders. Feng, in particular, found that his position was weakened by the unwillingness of the other tuchüns to commit themselves, because his own military forces were not sufficient without assistance to balance the strength of Fengtien. Feng, thus, was not realizing as rapidly as he had expected an increase in his "alignment potential." The coup had opened the way for the other tuchüns to act in such a manner in increasing their power as to strengthen Feng's position vis-à-vis Chang Tso-lin and Wu P'ei-fu, but these leaders hesitated until they could be more certain of the new alignment that would develop. Thus, neither Feng nor Chang was willing to commit himself to a binding mutual agreement until he was in a better position to evaluate his own power and that of the other tuchüns. When it was apparent that the other leaders would not move until they were convinced of the "force" possessed by the two dominant figures, Chang and Feng, each sought to increase his military establishment.[29] The only hope each had to become the leader of the new government was to increase his relative "force" vis-à-vis the other and thus to augment his "alignment potential" over the hesitating leaders. If either man could demonstrate his relative power over the other, he would be able to create a situation in which the remaining leaders would expect to increase their relative power, hence security, if they acted in such a manner as to establish that leader's relative power over the other.

Thus, Feng's dramatic and treacherous act of undercutting his new leader and implicitly cooperating with his supposed enemy failed to alter radically the alignment of *tuchüns*, because they all wanted first to determine whether Feng would indeed be fully accepted by Chang and what was to be the relative power relationship between the two. If, as was, in fact, the case, Chang could largely ignore Feng, all the others felt that they too could ignore him even though he had just demonstrated the capacity to disrupt the entire structure of *tuchün* relations.

SIDING WITH STRENGTH

The response of the *tuchüns* to a sudden change in the balance and the difficulties they faced in predicting the consequences of a *coup d'état* points to the second feature of the complex of relations within which the *tuchüns* operated, the tendency of the warlords to side with strength. The traditional and mechanistic concept of a well-functioning balance of power has as one of its basic assumptions the hypothesis that, with the increase in the relative power of one element in the balance, the other elements tend to unite and oppose the threat to the relative power of all.[30] However, in *tuchün* politics, the tendency was for the lesser leaders to join initially with the leader who demonstrated that he had potentialities of expanding his power. After any radical change in the balance, the *tuchüns* tended to hesitate in committing themselves until they could evaluate the relative power of the protagonists, and then they were inclined to side with that leader who appeared to command the greatest power. In terms of the concept of the two levels of power, this phenomenon may be described as one in which a *tuchün*, by reducing his "force" in his relations with others and directing it against a specific foe, was able to create a situation in which his "alignment potential" increased over these *tuchüns* in so far as they found it expedient to act in such a manner as to facilitate his operations against the foe. Conversely, the *tuchün* who demonstrated an inability to maintain his relative "force" relationship against the attacking *tuchün* also lost his "alignment potential" over the other leaders.

This was the case not only immediately after a sudden change, such as a *coup d'état*, but also in the early stages of any major war. The leaders tended to hesitate in committing themselves until they had some key to the probable outcome of the conflict, and then they were inclined to identify themselves with the leader they believed would be successful in the venture. In the 1922 Chihli-Fengtien War, when Wu P'ei-fu was in the process of moving his forces to the Shanhaikuan front, most of the *tuchüns* hesitated in fully committing themselves until there was some indication as to how successful Wu would be in his enterprise. However, when, in the initial encounter with the Fengtien forces, the Third Division scored a quick victory over the troops led by Chang

Ching-wei on the Tientsin-Pukow Railroad front, the hesitating leaders in Central China declared their willingness to support Wu against Mukden.[31]

This feature of the balance was indicative of the weakness of the individual *tuchüns*, because only by identifying themselves with a powerful leader did they have expectations of realizing their objectives. Although by so doing they reduced their "alignment potential" ratio vis-à-vis that leader, they were, at the same time, increasing their relative power in their relations with those who were not identified with the more powerful.

Another factor contributing to these "band-wagon" movements was the role of violence in *tuchün* politics. Given the high incidence of violence, the leaders tended to seek policies in which they would not have to oppose a leader who appeared capable of effectively applying violence. To the individual *tuchün*, it was preferable to accept an inferior "mutual alignment potential" relationship, rather than to have to prove one's inferiority in a "force" relationship. Thus, an overt threat or display of violence could be counted on to produce a situation in which the successful instigator would find his relative power increased as leaders sought to adjust their policies so as not to oppose him directly.

It is noteworthy that, at the commencement of most of the military clashes, the participants engaged in verbal combat. Not only were these propaganda efforts directed toward the objective of justifying one's own position, but also they were attempts to create the impression of superior power with the hope of attracting allies. The other *tuchüns* did not readjust their relations as a result of such statements of power but waited instead for the first test of arms before acting. However, the statements did serve to create an impression of power, which, when confirmed by the clashes of armies, caused the other warlords to act with greater dispatch.[32]

However, a necessary condition for the *tuchüns* to support the strongest figure was the expectation that, through such action, they would be able to increase their power in relation to other leaders and that they could thereby realize some of their objectives. However, this condition no longer obtained when a leader attempted to push his advantage too hard. If the leader appeared to be determined to gain an impregnable position of power, those *tuchüns* who had identified themselves with him began slowly to break away and check his power. Thus, as the leaders increased the exertions of his "force" in any particular relationship, his power over those who had initially identified themselves with him changed from the order of "mutual alignment potential" to "hostile alignment potential" as his total power began to frustrate their objectives. The *tuchüns* were willing to support a limited victory with the expectation that such action would result in an increase in their relative power over those defeated, but, if the conflict was carried to an extreme point, they found their own security threatened.

This was one factor, together with the limited power of the individual organizations, that explains why the actual conflicts were rarely pushed to a point of conclusion according to Western concepts of warfare. For a world that had just experienced a world war, the fighting among the Chinese appeared hardly to deserve the title of war. The Chinese themselves seem to have attempted to minimize the seriousness of the conflicts, expressing this sentiment in such apologetic comments as, "You forget how very civil our civil wars are." It is impossible to obtain accurate estimates of casualties in these civil wars. Lawrence Impey claimed that, in the fighting between the Kuominchün and Li Ching-lin in December, 1925, over 4,000 casualties passed through clearing stations and hospitals supervised by foreigners in the Peking area, and he also estimated that 4,000 to 5,000 more either died of wounds or did not reach the foreign hospitals.[33] In the fighting between the Kuominchün and Yen Hsi-shan in northern Shansi in June, 1926, the American consul saw between 1,500 and 2,000 casualties in the Kalgan hospitals.[34] In the Kiangsu-Chekiang War of 1924, it was estimated on the basis of the reports of foreign medical men and the Chinese Red Cross that the total casualties numbered about 13,000.[35] Relatively reliable sources indicate that during the period from 1920 to 1927, including the fighting of the Kuomintang in its Northern Expedition, a safe minimum estimate of casualties would be approximately 60,000. Because of the almost total absence of medical facilities, one might suspect there was a disproportionately high percentage of deaths in the total casualties.[36] Although individual military engagements might have been fairly intense, the available evidence would indicate that the relative weakness of the *tuchüns'* organizations and the political instability were the main factors in preventing sustained and prolonged campaigns.

With respect to the operations of the balance of power among the warlords, the process of breaking away from a powerful leader usually occurred at the point at which he called upon all forces under his immediate command to overcome his principal antagonist. The very fact that a leader had to call upon the military support of a subordinate suddenly increased the "alignment potential" of the subordinate and made him realize that he was more important than before. To call for assistance was actually to indicate weakness, and this was the cue for subordinates to look for a new alliance leader. Thus, the leader who, through his initial demonstration of initiative, had created a situation in which others identified themselves with him, found that, as he pushed his major campaign, he lost not only his relative "alignment potential" over his supporters but also his relative "force." To all of the leading *tuchüns*, this was a constant problem because none of them had enough power to conduct a major campaign and still retain a sufficient "reserve" of power to maintain their relative status with respect to those not directly attacked. The very existence of a major conflict opened the way to rapid changes in all the power relationships. The movement of the armies from one location to another created changes in the power relations, and the manner in which a defeated army was reorganized caused further alterations. As long as none of the leaders were willing to ignore the question of how such changes might affect their power, each had to seek to strengthen his position during the conflict and not defer such considerations to the end of hostilities.

The case of Sun Ch'uan-fang illustrates most clearly how the balance operated to make it possible for a *tuchün* in an inferior "alignment potential" position to rise rapidly when his leader was forced to commit his major forces to the defeat of another leader's military power. In the spring of 1924, Sun had only two divisions under his command in Fukien, but within the year he had become one of the principal poles in the balance, and, by 1926, he was one of the four most powerful super-*tuchüns* opposing the Kuomintang's Northern Expedition. Before the Chekiang-Kiangsu War of 1924, Sun was recognized as being a nominal member of the Chihli faction who had received assistance from Wu P'ei-fu in obtaining his position in Fukien. When the war between Ch'i Hsieh-yüan and Lu Yung-hsiang appeared imminent, Wu, in his efforts to support Ch'i, ordered Sun to assist him in the attack on Lu.[37]

When, on August 26, Ch'i first moved his armies out of Nanking, Sun Ch'uan-fang began his advance from the South and, on September 2, declared his intention of attacking Chekiang.[38] However, during the ensuing campaign, when it was necessary for Ch'i to apply all of his forces to the fighting at Liuho, Sun assumed a more independent role. The hard-pressed Ch'i issued three orders to Sun to direct his forces to the eastern front to relieve the pressure on the Kiangsu armies.[39] However, Sun refused to obey and engaged only the relatively weak Second Division of the Chekiang Provincial Troops.[40] Ch'i, therefore, had to support the major effort in defeating the Chekiang armies. Sun maneuvered his troops along the southern front until the Kiangsu armies had so weakened the Chekiang forces that he could move his men into the environs of Shanghai with a minimum of fighting.[41]

When the Chekiang forces finally collapsed, Ch'i found that his erstwhile ally and subordinate had occupied the Shanghai arsenal and other strategic points in Chekiang and that Sun was no longer willing to accept a subordinate position.[42] Ch'i had no alternative except to recognize the greatly expanded power of Sun, especially because, with the defeat of Wu after the Feng coup, there was a new danger that the Fengtien forces would move into the Yangtze area. Thus, the attempt of Ch'i Hsieh-yüan to apply all of his power in the achieving of a single objective had resulted in failure. His very actions had set in motion developments in the balance of power that eventually led to a thwarting of his aims.

Thus we see again that the behavior of the *tuchüns*, as they operated within the complex balance of power, indicates that none of them felt their strength sufficient to permit a decisive and positive policy in which they could consistently command the initiative. Instead, they had to seek opportunities and generally side with strength. This also meant that all the leaders had to act in hope of short-term advantages only. This need to worry about little advantages meant that the warlords' sense of pragmatism could not serve as the basis for any recognizable form of statesmanship. The *tuchün's* appreciation of the advantages of being identified with strength tended to make them at times unrealistically enthusiastic about their prospects when they felt that they could get on a "bandwagon." Indeed, on several occasions *tuchüns* tended to confuse the sensation of being on a "short-run bandwagon" with being a part of the "tide of history." That is to say, they were prone to talk at times of history and momentous long-range developments when their eyes were in fact glued to the short run.

In this respect, the warlords' pragmatic style with respect to power calculations was not so different as the approach of Chinese Communist leaders, caught up in a complex international power balance, talking a language of long-range considerations but in fact acting in terms of quite short-run, opportunistic calculations. Be this as it may, we must continue our analysis of the *tuchüns'* ways of viewing their power relationships, and particularly their ultimate tendency to so stress short-run advantages for themselves that they could not make effective sacrifices for maintaining the collective systems of which they were a part.

AVOIDING THE MAIN CHALLENGE

At no time during the period did the *tuchüns* demonstrate so unmistakably their incessant concern with short-term power considerations as they did in meeting the Northern Expedition of the Kuomintang. When, in 1926, the Kuomintang set out from Canton with the avowed objective of defeating the *tuchüns* and unifying the country under its control, the northern military leaders had before them a clear and present danger that was a manifest threat to all of them. The Kuomintang was an organization with effective military power at its command and a clearly stated policy calling for the destruction of all *tuchüns*. Furthermore, Nationalist propaganda left little hope that any *tuchün* might attempt to augment his power by identifying himself with the Kuomintang. On the surface, it would seem that the *tuchüns* had no alternative but to unite to meet this threat.

However, the behavior of the *tuchüns* indicated that none of them saw the issues in these terms. Although they issued statements attacking the Kuomintang and defining it as a threat to the Republic, none were willing to risk sacrificing their own power to take collective action. Rather, until the consequences of the Northern Expedition became clear, they engaged in a process of move and countermove in line with the balance in the North. For them, the issues were still those of maintaining their relative power in all their relations, and the defeat of the Kuomintang would be meaningless if it resulted in the damaging of one's relative power. Also, the *tuchüns* hesitated in committing themselves until the policy of the Kuomintang was actually tested and it was possible to determine precisely its effects on their power.

Both Wu P'ei-fu and Chang Tso-lin issued statements, which, although emphasizing the danger of the Kuomintang, predicted that it would be unable to maintain its unity when faced with the problems of controlling a larger territory. Wu and Chang appear to have expected that the Kuomintang, as it sought to apply all of its forces in one campaign, would meet the same difficulties the other *tuchüns* had confronted in maintaining the loyalty of subordinate and allied commander. In a sense, their predictions were correct, although they did not indicate that they foresaw an ideological rift within the Kuomintang.

At the time when the Kuomintang armies set out from Canton under the command of Chiang Kai-shek, an unstable balance existed in the North with the relations among the four super-*tuchüns* far from defined. Chang Tso-lin, secure in his Manchurian base, dominated Peking, and his subordinates Li Ching-lin and Chang Tsung-ch'ang controlled a major portion of Chihli and all of Shantung, respectively. The Kuominchün still held a portion of northern Chihli and parts of Jehol, Chahar, Shansi, and Suiyüan. Sun Ch'uan-fang was consolidating his position in Chekiang, Kiangsu, Anhwei, and Fukien. In Hupei and Honan, Wu P'ei-fu was attempting to restore his power. Sporadic fighting was taking place between the First Kuominchün and the troops of Li Ching-lin in northern Chihli. However, this was not a sufficient threat to the Fengtien position to prevent Chang Tsung-ch'ang from preparing for further conquest to the south of Shantung.[43] An armed truce existed along this front with Sun Ch'uan-fang's armies prepared to check any southern move by Chang Tsung-ch'ang and to assist the Kuominchün in case it should launch a major attack in the north.[44] However, Sun was also concerned lest Wu P'ei-fu attempt to re-establish his former power in the Yangtze Valley and extend his forces to the north. Wu appeared to be willing to seek support from Chang in order to neutralize Sun but was unwilling to risk any overt move that might provoke a direct attack on his position before Fengtien was prepared to guarantee his security.[45]

It was Chang Tso-lin who first issued a public statement calling upon the *tuchüns* to unite in order to prepare to meet the Canton armies. On

April 6, 1926, Chang proposed a major meeting of the representatives of the four *tuchüns* to be held at T'angshan.[46] Although Chang's role as arbiter of political events at the capital placed him in a logical position to call such a meeting, it was clear from his proposals that he intended to exploit the danger from the Kuomintang to expand and consolidate his own control over North China.[47] Sun Ch'uan-fang rejected all of Chang's proposals and announced that, if Wu and Chang were to collaborate for selfish reasons because of the Canton menace, he would identify himself with the Kuominchün.[48]

Thus, the first attempt to achieve unity among the *tuchüns* served only to intensify the suspicions of the various leaders, and each now adopted policies directed to strengthening his power vis-à-vis the others. Although Sun Ch'uan-fang's threat was sufficient to suspend negotiations between Wu and Chang, the former Chihli leader continued to seek out allies who could strengthen his defenses against the Kuomintang and, more important, augment his bargaining power with Sun.[49] However, when it appeared that Wu would have to increase his power before he could attract the support of the lesser *tuchüns*, the old Loyang commander changed his tactics and, on June 2, issued a circular telegram appealing to all leaders to unite under Chang Tso-lin to meet the oncoming Kuomintang.[50]

On the following day, Sun Ch'uan-fang countered by declaring the "independence" of all the provinces under his control and stating that the Peking government was failing to maintain peace and order in the country.[51] This statement not only was a direct denunciation of Chang Tso-lin but also constituted an oblique attack on Wu P'ei-fu. It even led to speculation that Sun was seeking an agreement with the Kuomintang.[52] Wu's response to Sun's action was the extraordinary step of dispatching, on June 12, two of his best divisions to assist the Fengtien armies opposing the Kuominchün in the Kalgan area. Wu calculated that assisting Chang Tso-lin in destroying the power of the Kuominchün in Chihli would contribute to the weakening of Sun Ch'uan-fang's influence.[53] On the surface, the move appeared to be a cavalier gesture of defiance of both Sun Ch'uan-fang and the Kuomintang.

Sun also indicated that he still considered critical the developments in the relations of the northern leaders. On June 3, he turned his back on the problem of contending with the Northern Expedition and chose to make a personal inspection of his northern Kiangsu forces, which were prepared to oppose the Fengtien armies in southern Shantung.[54] Just as Chang and Wu were about to initiate a final campaign to drive the Kuominchün from northern Chihli and Jehol, Sun Ch'uan-fang applied pressure on the southern lines of the Fengtien domain. There were reports that fighting could be expected at any moment between the forces of Chang Tsung-ch'ang and Sun Ch'uan-fang.[55]

However, by the end of July, after Chang Tso-lin's and Wu P'ei-fu's allied armies had driven the First Kuominchün out of Kalgan, Sun was forced to readjust his policies because it was clear that the weakening of the Kuominchün would leave him in an isolated position. For this reason, on July 24, 1926, Sun entered into negotiations with Chang Tsung-ch'ang to reduce the tension along the frontiers of their two areas.[56] In the meantime, Wu P'ei-fu discovered that the weakening of the Kuominchün had strengthened his position in negotiations with Sun Ch'uan-fang. On July 7, Wu had proposed to Sun that, if the Nationalists continued their advance, it might be advisable to cooperate in the defense of the Yangtze area.[57] However, only after the allied forces of Wu and Chang were making progress in defeating the First Kuominchün did Sun find it advantageous to enter into negotiations with Wu.[58]

Thus, by the first week in August, when the Nationalists were preparing to complete the occupation of northern Kiangsi, Sun and Wu were still able to cooperate only on an *ad hoc* basis. On August 5, the two commanders agreed that each should commit two divisions to the defense of northern Kiangsi.[59] However, it was not until August 16 that Wu P'ei fu recalled his two best divisions from the North to assist in the defense of Hankow.[60] These troops had served the function of strengthening Wu's bargaining power with Sun Ch'uan-fang. However, on August 24, when the Nationalist armies first engaged the troops directly under Wu's command, he was far from prepared for a major campaign.[61] As the fighting moved into southern Hupei, Wu found that he had lost whatever advantage he had established over Sun Ch'uan-fang. On August 27, Wu obtained a pledge of further support from Sun Ch'uan-fang, but Sun's terms required that Wu dispatch three divisions of Hunan provincial troops to Sun's assistance in defending Wuhu in Anhwei.[62]

On the same day that the above agreement was reached, the Kuomintang dramatically announced that Feng Yü-hsiang was a member of the Nationalist Party.[63] Although the Kuominchün remained silent, the announcement came as a shock to the other *tuchüns*.[64] In particular, it was a blow to Wu P'ei-fu. Wu had expected to obtain assistance from Fengtien, but, on August 28, Chang Tso-lin issued a circular telegram stating that, because the Kuomintang and the Kuominchün were now to be considered a common foe, he would have to direct all of his forces against the Kuominchün, while the Yangtze commanders should assume the responsibility of defeating the Kuomintang.[65]

On August 31, when the siege of Hankow commenced, the northern leaders were no closer to a combined policy than they had been when the Northern Expedition departed from Canton. The instability of the relations among the *tuchüns* had made it impossible for them to arrive at a united policy even when confronted with an enemy that had declared its intention to destroy them all. Even after the fall of Hankow, the *tuchüns* were unable to ignore the implications of the balance among themselves.

On September 21, after Wu had been forced to withdraw to the north bank of the Yangtze, Chang Tso-lin offered to dispatch troops to his assistance.[66] But, even though his situation appeared desperate, Wu rejected the offer, because he felt that the entry of Fengtien troops into his area of command would spell the end of his power. Instead, Wu called upon Chang Tso-lin to demonstrate his sincerity by sending him funds and munitions, claiming that his manpower was adequate.[67] Wu was proposing that Chang invest in the joint cause without obtaining in return any direct concessions in the form of an expanded area of control. When Chang Tso-lin rejected Wu's request, it was the final act destroying any hope of cooperation between the two leaders.[68]

However, as the relations between Wu and Chang deteriorated, Sun Ch'uan-fang appeared to be approaching a *rapprochement* with Fengtien. In mid-November, Sun entered into detailed negotiations with Fengtien with the objective of settling all differences between them.[69] These negotiations culminated in the announcement, on December 2, of the formation of the Ankuochün, or "Pacify the Country Army." Chang Tso-lin was the commander in chief of the new organization and Chang Tsung-ch'ang and Sun Ch'uan-fang were the two vice-commanders.

Although the formation of the Ankuochün appeared to open the way to closer cooperation among the *tuchüns*, the exclusion of Wu P'ei-fu destroyed the illusion of unity. Two days after the announcement of the formation of the Ankuochün, Chang Tso-lin dispatched an emissary to Wu to inform him that Fengtien would be willing to assist in the defeat of the Kuomintang on the following terms: (1) Wu should recognize the Ankuochün and accept the leadership of Chang Tso-lin; (2) permission should be granted the Ankuochün to enter the territories controlled by Wu in order to meet the Kuomintang; and (3) Chang Tso-lin was willing to promise in return the material and financial assistance that Wu had requested on September 24.[70] Wu P'ei-fu, although driven from Hankow and faced with the continuing threat of the Nationalists, refused to accept the offer because the terms might have meant, even if the Nationalists were defeated, the end of his influence.[71]

Wu P'ei-fu's suspicions of the use to which Chang Tso-lin would put the Ankuochün were soon confirmed, as Sun Ch'uan-fang discovered that the Fengtien leaders were not prepared to offer him the security for which he had paid so much. At the first meeting of the commanders of the Ankuochün on December 18, a deep division developed among the Fengtien leaders. One group argued for a policy of attacking the Nationalists immediately, while the other insisted on awaiting further developments and meeting the Kuomintang armies only when they attempted to push north of the Yangtze Valley.[72] Sun Ch'uan-fang was forced to recognize that, although he was formally one of the vice-commanders of the army, the real power of decision lay with the Fengtien leadership. Yang Yü-t'ing, Chang's chief of staff, was successful in arguing for the second course of action.[73] This delay in meeting the Kuomintang gave the Fengtien commanders the opportunity to reorganize the troops of Sun Ch'uan-fang into the Ankuochün so that Sun himself lost direct command over them, and the Ankuochün became clearly the tool of Fengtien policy.[74] Without the full power to direct all of his armies, Sun attempted to resist the Nationalist move into Chekiang, but by mid-January, 1927, the southern forces were threatening Hangchou, and, on February 18, the capital of the province fell.[75]

However, by this time the military and political balance in North China was radically altered by the split within the Nationalist ranks, which led to the establishment of the Nanking and Wuhan governments. The *tuchüns* now were forced to readjust their policies in line with this development.

The behavior of the *tuchüns* in meeting the initial threat of the Kuomintang clearly demonstrates the extent to which each of them felt he was the captive of the balance of power. Their behavior was particularly telling because the issue was one of maximization of power. But, even in terms of this value, not one of them felt he could ignore short-term considerations of his relative power and follow policies that might have contained hope of later, and possibly greater, expansion of power. Thus, as long as the *tuchüns* found it essential to adjust their policies to every change in the balance, it was clear that none could follow programs dedicated to realizing values that were far removed from considerations of power.

7. PUBLIC RELATIONS AND PROPAGANDA

Up to this point, our analysis has concentrated primarily upon power considerations: the organizations of the *tuchüns*, their alliances and relations with each other, and the complex balance of power in which they were involved. We have noted that their perceptions of their circumstances and their appreciation of "reality" tended to make them pragmatic political calculators who could not afford to take a long-range view.

It is appropriate now to direct our analysis to the ways in which the power realities that governed the warlords affected their relations with important segments of the civilian Chinese society. We shall begin by dealing in this chapter with the more general questions of how the warlords justified themselves to the Chinese public, what values they tried to suggest that they were most sensitive to, and what arguments they felt would impress public opinion. In the next chapter, we will examine the relations of the warlords with the Chinese civilian political class and particularly the kinds of people who served in the various cabinets. Then we shall turn to a brief review of the relations of the warlords with intellectuals and finally the business community.

It would be a gross misuse of terms to say that any *tuchün* ever had an ideological basis for his policy actions. However, with the development of the *tuchüns'* political organizations it became necessary for the military leaders to pay greater attention to the public's reaction to their rule. This process can best be described as a form of public relations work, which, in time, developed into conscious efforts at influencing the mind of the public through propaganda. Although the *tuchüns* were aware of the power of the press, there were, except for a few notable cases, few attempts at direct control over the larger native newspapers and periodicals. Foreign correspondents, of course, were completely free to report what they observed. However, the *tuchüns* usually were careful to entertain and supervise the visiting foreign correspondents in such a way as to leave a favorable impression. A noted correspondent reported that, on one occasion, this was carried to the point of making the visitor "feel like an inmate of an exclusive asylum for feeble-minded aristocrats."[1]

The media employed by the *tuchüns* to carry out their propaganda efforts were generally public proclamations, statements announcing and justifying major policy decisions, interviews, and, most important, circular telegrams. The circular telegram was a unique technique developed by the *tuchüns* and, in many ways, typified the peculiarly personal quality of most of their propaganda efforts. The circular telegram was issued by a *tuchün* or a group of *tuchüns* and addressed personally to opposing *tuchüns* or to men who held high civil office. However, copies of the telegram were released immediately to the press, and other copies were publicly posted in the areas under the influence of the *tuchüns* issuing it. The announcement was in the form of a personal communication directed to specific individuals, while the content of the telegram was written with a view to influencing a far larger audience. Even when the contents of the message related to general issues, the format of the statement preserved a distinctly personal quality.

As the *tuchüns* became more interested in the influencing of public opinion, the content of their public statements became more significant, indicating what in the minds of warlords were the most important values and concepts in Chinese society at the time. The fact that the warlords were pragmatists and not ideologically inclined gives considerable significance to the themes and appeals that they felt would put them in the best light with the Chinese people. To determine these themes I made a content analysis of the *tuchüns*' propaganda, and a similar analysis of the propaganda of the Kuomintang. As we shall shortly see, the contrasts are quite dramatic and reveal trends that have continued right into the Communist period.

It may be helpful at the outset to indicate that these trends in style and themes of propaganda appear to be related to two separate and somewhat conflicting larger trends in modern Chinese history. The first is the degree to which those involved were constrained by power relationships or were essentially dominant, or near monolithic, forces. (The warlords were the most constrained, the Kuomintang was dominant but constrained by internal rivalries, and the Communists have been the superior power with the least competition.) The second trend is the degree of modernization, or more accurately, the degree to which the Chinese politicians have been breaking from China's Confucian traditions. The progression, of course, has been in the same order, with the warlords closest to the old order and the Communists the least influenced by Confucian considerations.

Specifically the trends in propaganda that we shall be examining suggest the hypothesis that, in Chinese politics, the more complex and competitive the power relationships, the more the participants will use "pragmatic" power calculations and the more their propaganda will stress reason and modest themes and avoid excessive emotionalism. Conversely, the more that groups or individuals feel secure and seek to act as the dominant force for all of China, the more their propaganda will encompass ideological matters and stress emotional themes. In either case, there will be strong emphasis upon moralistic considerations, but those in a complex power situation tended to stress what might be called moralism of the mind, that is, a reasoned ethic, whereas those with greater sense of sovereign power will stress the moralism of the heart or the purity of emotions and hence of actions.

With respect to the trend away from Confucianism and toward some form of modernization, the effects in propaganda have been a decline in the use of reason and greater stress on emotional appeals. Thus, in the domain of political propaganda and communications, modernization for the Chinese has meant a decline in the view that authority should be rational and a rise of the concept of an emotional authority that is also emotionally demanding of the citizenry.

With these general considerations in mind, let us examine the themes in the public statements of the warlords and the Kuomintang.

A COMPARATIVE CONTENT ANALYSIS

In order to analyze quantitatively the themes employed by the *tu-chüns*, I tabulated not symbols or words but rather sentences of roughly paragraph length. This was necessary because the *tuchüns'* propaganda was not highly stylized and they did not use slogans extensively.

Table 7.1 gives a graphic representation of the results of this analysis, which was based on three hundred circular telegrams, public addresses, proclamations, and interviews. The sources employed in the compiling of the data for the table were the following: ninety-two texts from Sun Yao-pien, *Chung-hua Min-kuo Shih-k'e* (*Historical Data on the Republic of China*); sixty-three quoted texts from Chinese periodicals (*Tung-fang Tsa-chih, Kuo-wen Chou-pao, Ching-pao Fu-k'an*); seventy-seven translations of texts from the Department of State files in the National Archives; sixty-six quoted texts from English-language newspapers published in China (*North China Herald, Peking and Tientsin Times, North China Daily News,* and the *Peking Leader*).

Those entries with asterisks represent subcategories that were found to be meaningful. In this respect, it should be noted that a double listing was made of those items included in the subcategories because they were also considered under the main category appearing immediately above them. Before attempting to analyze the more significant implications of the particular themes, it should be noted that in general the *tuchüns'*

TABLE 7.1
CONTENT OF TUCHÜN PROPAGANDA

Categories	Number of Items
Personal Association (Positive)	47
Attacks on Personalities	52
Corruption, Charges of*	7
Selfishness, Charges of*	9
Treachery, Charges of*	5
Subordinates, Attacks on*	16
Moral Virtues, Appeal for	30
Republicanism (Positive)	37
Constitution, Support of	19
Antimonarchy	26
Provincial Autonomy, Demand for	11
Antimilitarism	32
Demobilization, Need for	27
Civilian Rule, Support of	10
Unification of the Country	38
Anti-Canton Regime	31
Anti-Bolshevik*	20
Anti-San-min-chu-i*	7
Pro-San-min-chu-i	6
Finances, Sound Money and Credit	31
Law and Order	37
Suppression of Bandits*	22
Reconstruction	12
Unequal Treaties	9
Treaty Revision, Moderate Demand for	15
Defense of Treaties	4
Antiforeign	8
Proforeign	7
Symbols from Ancient History	27
Symbols from Western Political Thought	12
Sympathy for the People	31
People's Rights	9
Other Concepts	39

efforts at propaganda covered a large range of topics and never reached a point of concentrating on a few limited items that were felt to be the most valuable and useful concepts. Thus, despite the high degree of uniformity in the form and temper of the public statements, they were not directed toward emphasizing and reinforcing a few specific themes as is typical of more effective propaganda.

This feature of the *tuchüns'* pronouncements is apparent when a comparison is made with the far more sophisticated propaganda of the Kuomintang during and following the Northern Expedition. Table 7.2 shows the principal themes found in one hundred samples of Kuomintang propaganda during the period from 1926 to 1929. The sources employed in compiling Table 7.2 were: eight texts from Sun Yao-pien; sixteen texts from the same Chinese periodicals employed in Table 7.1; forty-one texts from the English-language newspapers in China; and thirty-five texts from the files of the Department of State. The same procedure was used in compiling this analysis as in the first one. However, it should be noted that the task of application was far simpler because of differences in style and semantic considerations. The Kuomintang propaganda was clearly stated and unambiguous and relied heavily upon slogans and shibboleths.

The most striking feature of the *tuchüns'* propaganda, when compared with the Nationalists', is the general lack of emotional intensity of the themes and slogans. The public statements of the *tuchüns* centered on values that were recognized as valid by the vast majority of the people and that could not be safely denied by any politician. They were highly reasonable in tone and were presented in a rational form, but they were extremely weak in emotional appeal. They placed no emotional demand on the audience in terms of seeking to elicit positive action. Often they were almost analytical in character, and it would be difficult to take issue with their soundness. They were what might be termed slogans of "acceptance." On the other hand, Nationalist propaganda was far more emotional. It sought to produce on the part of those exposed to it positive reactions directed toward specific actions.

Although Nationalist propaganda was channeled directly toward

TABLE 7.2

CONTENT OF KUOMINTANG PROPAGANDA

Categories	Number of Items
Anti-imperialism	40
Unequal Treaties	28
Treaty Revision, Moderate Demand for	3
The Revolution	21
San-min-chu-i	27
Nationalism*	9
People's Livelihood*	4
Reconstruction	13
Develop the Country	23
Unification of the Country	8
Antimilitarism	19
Demobilization*	11
Political Morality	12
Eliminate Poor Officials*	9
Law and Order	4
Other Concepts	22

clearly defined objectives, the arguments were often stated in such a form as to reach all manner of biases and prejudices. For example, there is little doubt that, to the majority of Chinese, the question of "unequal treaties" was far too technical in nature to be clearly understood. However, it was obvious to all that the foreigners did live on a higher plane than the majority of the Chinese and behaved as if they were superior creatures. Thus, the phrases "unequal treaties" and "down with imperialism" became slogans that not only explained the reason for the foreigners' position but also served as symbols for the expression of real grievances as well as prejudices against them.

This difference in the two types of propaganda is illustrated in the major propaganda statement issued by Chang Tso-lin in early 1927, when the Northern Expedition of the Nationalists had conquered Central China and was threatening to move into North China. Chang, with his back literally against the Wall, issued the following public statement in order to rally support to the Peking government under his control:

"Ever since the inception of the Republic, the sovereign rights of the nation have rested with the people. The development of government of, for, and by the people should serve as the guiding principle, in pursuance of which the details of satisfactory political settlements such as preservation of national sovereign rights, restoration of law and order, spread of education, harmonious cooperation of labor and capital, extension of means of communication, and improvement of the methods of judicial administration must be solved. . . . China is suffering from poverty in spite of her immense natural wealth. The task of readjusting China's finances must be augmented by the encouragement of industrial enterprises and extensive reclamation of uncultivated lands. Secondly, unnecessary expenditures must be reduced by cutting down superfluous official posts and limitation of the size of the army. Definite and concrete financial plans can only be evolved by careful study of means of consolidating domestic and foreign loans, the installation of proper financial organization, regulation of the currency, and modification of the methods of taxation. . . . I venture, therefore, to assure the public that I shall, to the limit of my capacity, undertake to strengthen China's credit at home and abroad. . . . Equality of international treatment is the only safeguard of world peace. Our duty to foreigners residing in China is the protection of their lives and property. On the other hand, we expect the Powers to accord due respect to our public opinion and sovereign rights. . . . Frankness and mutual respect are the keynotes for effecting perpetual peace among the members of the family of nations."[2]

This statement of general policy is all the more striking when one realizes that it was issued to counteract the inflammatory statements pouring from the pen of Eugene Chen and the crusading spirit of the

National propaganda, with its short, incisive slogans of "down with imperialism" and "carry through the revolution."

The question arises as to why the *tuchüns* were reluctant to use a more forceful type of propaganda. An initial supposition might be that they were bound by a strong tendency toward inherent conservatism and that they were influenced not only by their own convictions but were also dominated by the more conservative elements in the society. There is little doubt that this was one factor in setting the tone of their public statements. However, it must be recognized, as will be shown below, that the actions and policies of the *tuchüns* were not at all times in harmony with the objectives of many of the more established interests and that they were far from being simply the political defenders of such vested groups.[3] This does not mean that the propaganda of the *tuchüns* was not often intended to pacify these interests. Although the policies of the *tuchüns* were not always directed toward the support of the conservative groups, it was still possible for the military leaders to reduce the animosity of such elements by appealing to them in propaganda statements employing symbols and slogans particularly meaningful to them.[4]

However, other reasons must be found to explain the generally passive nature of the *tuchüns'* propaganda. They were engaged in power struggles that meant their destruction if they failed to achieve success, and the game was far too costly to permit any scruples about the use of methods and slogans in which they did not sincerely believe if these techniques would mean the furthering of their power. In fact, from observing the manner in which they manipulated symbols, one finds it hard to believe that they had any strong convictions about the ideas they professed. It would also be difficult to make a case that the *tuchüns* lacked the technical capacity to produce a more emotional and dynamic form of propaganda. Within their organizations, there were young men with the education and training that would have enabled them to appreciate and produce the more modern forms of propaganda that the Kuomintang found so helpful.

It is profitable here to consider the general results of the content analysis in terms of the assumptions already arrived at about the behavior of the *tuchüns*. As we have seen, the power complex within which they operated was such that it placed serious limitations and restraints on many phases of their policies. The extreme complexity of the balance of power, combined with the relative weaknesses of the individual leaders, produced a situation in which all the *tuchüns* had to operate with extreme caution. As we have seen in the content analysis, the *tuchüns* appeared to be limited in the type of propaganda they could employ; this limitation prevented the *tuchüns* from utilizing inflammatory slogans and signs that might have left the manipulators in an exposed position. It is possible to assume, therefore, that, just as the nature of the balance of power had limited other phases of policy decision, so had it denied the *tuchüns* complete freedom of choice in their propaganda. In this manner, the results of the content analysis serve further to confirm the assumptions about the nature of the balancing process. Given the existing "tight" balance of power, the *tuchüns* found they had more to lose by employing inflammatory propaganda than by following the general practices and repeating in only modified form the broad propaganda themes of the other leaders. Had any *tuchün* tried to initiate a definite program of appealing to the more emotional symbols, he would have clearly placed himself in an isolated position, exposing himself to attack by the other leaders.[5]

Any leader who attempted to introduce a more "active" form of propaganda would not only be suspected of attempting to "violate the rules of the game" but also expose himself to the charges that he was seeking to establish relations with the Canton regime. That the statements issuing from Canton were of a more revolutionary nature meant that, if any northern leader attempted to follow such a propaganda course, he would be accused of seeking to identify himself with the Canton government. Thus, as long as the *tuchüns* saw as their main threat the power of the other *tuchüns*, it was essential not to present these leaders with a clear target for their joint opposition, such as the issue of an alliance with Canton would create.[6]

As can be observed from Table 7.1, attacks on the Canton regime were popular with the *tuchüns* and even included personal slander against Dr. Sun Yat-sen. Typical of the statements of the *tuchüns* in their efforts to discredit Canton and Dr. Sun was the utterance of President Li Yüan-hung: "The world has a false idea about Dr. Sun Yat-sen. He had nothing to do with the actual work of overthrowing the Monarchy. The Revolution was finished when he reached China. . . . If he ever provided any tangible aid to the real Revolution, I did not know of it. His reputation is largely founded on fiction."[7] Although a part of the anti-Canton propaganda was the result of sincere ideological opposition to Dr. Sun's policies, there is little doubt that much of it was stimulated by a deep distrust of any leader who broke from the web of relations upon which the Peking government rested; and thus one of the purposes of the attacks upon the southern government was to serve as a warning to any other leader who might be contemplating a similar move. The efforts to discredit the Canton government included charges that it was Bolshevik-dominated. Thus, in the propaganda of the *tuchüns*, the symbols of Bolshevism and Communism, which our analysis shows were not uncommon, came to be associated with the Canton government. The charge that any particular *tuchün* was supporting Bolshevism was interpreted to mean either that he was attempting to establish relations with the Canton government or that he was intent upon breaking with the Peking government to establish an independent regime. The term was used so freely that it lost much of its meaning, and, by 1928, it was difficult for the Nationalists to reassert the symbol of Communism as representing a real danger.[8]

It should also be noted that a program of extremely active propaganda would have made it more difficult for the *tuchün* to shift his ground and form new alliances when expediency might dictate. Issues were not forced to the point where they might create serious cleavages that would make it difficult for the participants to cooperate if the power situation so demanded. As long as the themes of the public relations material were centered on those points generally recognized as valid and did not introduce any new issues, the public statements did not serve as limiting factors conditioning the behavior of the *tuchüns*, who were free therefore to make the necessary adjustments for maintaining and expanding their power.

Thus, the very weakness of the *tuchüns* made it impossible for them to risk a more active propaganda campaign. Even if they had been able to achieve any degree of popular support from such an effort, it could not have been sufficient to counter the danger of the united opposition of all the armies to the other *tuchüns*. An excellent example of how a *tuchün* could afford a more active propaganda campaign only when he believed he was in a relatively strong power position can be seen from the shifts in the public statements of Feng Yü-hsiang. Until November, 1924, Feng was content to emphasize the general themes of personalities, moral righteousness, and respect for the Republic. However, with the formation of the Kuominchün, Feng was in a strong enough position to initiate a much more positive propaganda campaign with greater emphasis upon the themes of "unequal treaties," "nationalism," and social reform—and even Sun Yat-sen-ism. But, by February, 1925, when there was a serious threat that Chang Tso-lin would be successful in defeating the Kuominchün and Feng was seeking the support of Sun Ch'uan-fang and even Wu P'ei-fu, Feng's public statements returned to the more passive themes.[9]

The Development of Propaganda Themes

The results of the content analysis indicate that the categories with the largest number of units recorded under them were those referring to personal qualities, either in a positive or negative light. This confirms the view that *tuchün* politics was of a highly personal nature. Just as the relations of leaders to followers, as well as leaders to each other, were highly colored by personal considerations, so were *tuchün* propaganda statements replete with personalized symbols.

As long as the *tuchüns'* organizations were primarily personal groupings, the principal emphasis of their public statements was highly personal. Stress was placed on the virtues of the commander and the vices of the opposition. With the expansion of the organizations and the introductions of more generalized themes into the *tuchüns'* propaganda, there still remained the elements of personal attack and counterattack. However, there was a noticeable shift in emphasis in that often the criticism was not directed at the personality of the opposing leader, but, rather, charges were made that certain of his subordinates were unduly influencing him. Thus, as leaders gained positions of national prestige, deference could be shown them, while, at the same time, criticism could be leveled against the type of followers they attracted. The implication was that, although they might personally be admirable individuals, they had permitted themselves to be surrounded by unscrupulous characters who not only would destroy the good names of the leaders but would bring harm to the country.

Thus, when in 1926 Chang Tso-lin desired to oust Tuan Ch'i-jui from the office of provisional chief executive, he was careful to charge that

> I have always entertained a great deal of respect for Marshal Tuan and regard him as a straightforward and upright man devoid of ulterior political ambitions. But I am sorry to say that, since his coming to Peking, he has been entirely surrounded by the members of the Anfu and Chen Hsüeh [Monarchist] cliques, who are trying to utilize him as a tool for their own aggrandizement.[10]

And again, when, in December of 1925, Li Ching-lin of the Fengtien faction initiated his campaign against the Kuominchün, Tuan charged that

> The war that I am going to declare against Feng Yü-hsiang is not my original plan, as I wanted to protect the territory and to save the people from troubles. However, he lets his subordinates mislead the young men and preach Bolshevism, disrespect their superiors, defame the laws and promote evil ideas, which will spoil all moral obligations.[11]

As a result of this development, the leaders did become more immune to direct criticism, and it became possible for them to shift the responsibilities for their policies to their advisers. In 1923, when President Li Yüan-hung was forced from office by Feng Yü-hsiang and fled to Shanghai, he was able to meet the critics of some of his policies with the statement that "I was misled. . . . The true facts were not always brought to my attention."[12]

This protective shield of advisers made possible the practice of what might be termed the "politics of potentates." The leaders themselves were recognized as possessing qualities of "charismatic charm" and were considered to be superior men, but their one weakness was that they surrounded themselves with unscrupulous advisers and subordinates.[13]

This concept was meaningful and appeared to be valid to the majority of the public, because there appeared little doubt that a *tuchün*'s statements were the words of an upright individual. However, their only contact with the rule of the *tuchün* was through his lesser administrators, and here there was little doubt that a discrepancy existed between policy statements and reality. The public might, therefore, assume that the leader himself was a superior individual but that those around him were guilty of carrying out contrary and detrimental policies. The "good" leader and the "bad" advisers is a recurrent theme in the history of Chinese politics. First it was in the form of "good" emperor and the "bad" ministers and eunuchs. Later, in Nationalist China, it appeared again in the form of "Chiang Kai-shek is a sincere and devoted leader, but he has surrounded himself with reactionary followers." As long as the politics was centered primarily on a personal plane and the leaders were capable of developing charisma, it was easier to attack the advisers than the personages of the leaders.

It is difficult to say to what extent the public considered the leading *tuchüns* exceptional individuals. However, it is significant that, when the *Weekly Review of the Far East* conducted a poll in 1923 to determine the "greatest living Chinese," of the leading twelve men chosen, five were *tuchüns*. (Sun Yat-sen led the list, but by less than one hundred votes over Feng Yü-hsiang. The other men, in the order of their popularity, were Wellington Koo, Wang Ch'ung-hui, Wu P'ei-fu, Ts'ai Yüan-p'ei [President of Peking University], C. T. Wang, Chang Chien [former Hanlin scholar and at the time Director of the Huai Ho Conservancy in Shanghai], Yen Hsi-shan, David Z. T. Yin [Saint John's University], Li Yüan-hung, and Hu Shih.[14] Significantly, those questioned were Chinese students and businessmen. It might be assumed that this group would have the least respect for the *tuchüns*, and, if a more general study had been made, it probably would have resulted in an even higher rating for the military leaders. In conversations with Chinese who were observers of *tuchün* politics, the author has noted a universal spirit of condemning the entire period. But, at the same time, there was a readiness to regard particular leaders with a remarkable degree of respect.

The protective role of the advisers opened the way for the *tuchüns* to deny complete responsibility for all acts carried on by their organizations. The *tuchüns* themselves, in their public pronouncements, emphasized the point that they had only limited political responsibility; they repeatedly stated that they were only military men and that, as such, they were not qualified in terms of the traditional concepts of Chinese government to assume civil responsibilities; when such duties did fall upon them, it was only because the civil administrators had failed to perform their function.

When Ts'ao K'un assumed the Presidency, he opened his inaugural address with the statement that "Having been a military man all my life, I have had no experience in the civil branch of administration . . . but I fully recognize the responsibility of the task, and it is fortunate that the fundamental law of China has been completed just at the time when I take up office. . . . I further know that the secret of successful government is the utilization of talented men."[15] Again, when Tuan Ch'i-jui on November 24, 1924, assumed the office of provisional chief executive, his inaugural statement began, "I, Tuan Ch'i-jui, although without ability and undeserving, having been a military man all my life, do now assume office as the Chief Executive of the Republic of China."[16]

The *tuchüns* also found it advantageous at times to expand this theme to the point of championing the elimination of the entire institution of the *tuchün*-ate. The exact approach used in exploiting this topic depended upon the power position of the *tuchün* at the time. When, in 1924, Wu P'ei-fu was seeking to rally the Chihli military leaders for the campaign against Chang Tso-lin, the Loyang leader justified the move as an effort to eliminate the evils of the military government and to restore to the civil government a unified country under parliamentary rule.[17] On the other hand, the *tuchün* who found his position threatened by the rising power of other *tuchüns* often argued the principle that it was essential to do away with the office of the *tuchün* and restore the civil authorities to their rightful places.

The best example of this was the case of Lu Yung-hsiang of Chekiang. In spring, 1920, Lu realized that his position was threatened by the rising power of the Chihli faction and that his record of supporting the Anfu faction would leave him in an exposed position. In order to meet this danger, Lu sponsored a strong campaign advocating the elimination of the office of *tuchün*. Lu claimed that

> The main obstacle standing in the way of the early unification of the country is the Tuchünate. It is generally believed that the Tuchüns with their military power and wealth are in a position to dominate the situation. Such an accusation, be it justified or not, may be overlooked for the moment. But inasmuch as China is a republic, civil rule should be the fundamental principle of government. . . . Therefore, under a republican form of government such a system should not be tolerated.[18]

After the fall of the Anfu faction, Lu found himself isolated, as he had feared, and intensified his campaign for the elimination of the *tuchün*-ate.[19] In fact, Lu even went so far as to make the initial gesture by renouncing his own title of *tuchün* and assuming the less obnoxious title of defense commissioner.[20]

Thus, almost all the *tuchüns*, regardless of their power positions, could unanimously denounce the institution of the *tuchün*-ate and the dangers of military men controlling political office. Although social and political conditions had radically altered the place of the military in Chinese society, the *tuchüns* generally accepted and were willing to play upon the traditional cultural attitude of depreciating the military.[21] By assuming this attitude, they were able to exploit the traditional feelings toward the military while appearing to be defenders of the newer concepts of Republican rule. So long as the *tuchüns* professed that they were loyal to the idea of the Republic and deplored the institution of the *tuchün*-ate, they could rationalize nearly any action as being directed toward unifying the country and defending the Republic.

However, as can be seen from the content analysis, the appeal for Republicanism and the attacks upon militarism did not mean a clear championing of civilian rule. The "antimilitarism" themes were approximately three times as popular as "procivilian" rule themes. Thus, to the *tuchüns*, the need for a Republican system of government did not carry with it the demand that civilian politicians should be either respected or given power.

The recurrent attacks upon the symbols of monarchy represented further attempts by the *tuchüns* to identify themselves with the concepts of Republicanism. The abortive attempt of Chang Hsün to restore the monarchy in 1917 was often referred to by the *tuchüns* as proof that the danger of monarchism was not a dead issue.[22] In addition, issues of monarchism were exploited to challenge any leader who appeared too obviously determined to become the strong man of the country. Thus, although pro-Imperial sentiments might not be strong with the public, it was still possible to point out that any leader who achieved hegemony over the country might be in a position to re-establish a dynasty. The *tuchüns* were prepared to challenge any leader who appeared to be achieving a dominant position with the accusation that he had some such hidden ambitions.

Chang Tso-lin was most often accused of having designs of becoming Emperor or of attempting to restore the Manchus. Chang was particularly vulnerable to such charges for a variety of reasons. His unchallenged domination of Manchuria and the historic association of this area with the Manchus created suspicions. Also, in 1921, when Chang was in control of the Peking government, Prince Tuan unexpectedly appeared in the capital, returning from his place of exile in Kansu and claiming that he needed medical care. The Peking government requested the diplomatic corps to lift the order for his exile contained in Article II of the International Protocol of 1901.[23] The diplomatic corps, after insisting that the elderly prince, who had supported the Boxers in 1900, be examined by a Western physician, refused the request of the Peking government.[24] The fact that Chang's government had sought amnesty for the Manchu prince appeared to confirm the suspicions of many that

Chang still respected the imperial tradition. Also Chang Tso-lin's support of the redoubtable Chang Hsün for the position of *tuchün* of Anhwei in 1924 provoked further charges that he was seeking to follow the pattern of Yüan Shih-k'ai.

The fact that the intellectuals could and did argue that the process of achieving a republican form of government in China would be difficult and would require time,[25] only added more substance to the *tuchüns'* case that they were striving against great obstacles to achieve the generally recognized values of a republic. The need for "law and order" was an objective to which the *tuchüns* could claim they were dedicated, and they constantly stated that their policies were directed toward that end. They attempted further to identify themselves with the premise that a rule of law should be supreme by repeating, to the point of monotony, the theme that their principal task was the "suppression of bandits."

However, on the issue of how fast and how far China could go in rejecting traditional values and adopting the newer ideas from the West, the *tuchüns* usually found it expedient to refuse to take a definite position. They were constantly faced with issues arising from the changing developments in China, as Western ideas and cultural qualities were progressively adopted. In general, the *tuchüns* attempted to evade the issues, much as Ts'ao K'un did in his inaugural address, when he stated:

> Lately currents of political thought have been drifting toward newer and newer ideas. Consequently I find myself in the position of a physician who does not wish to adhere entirely to the old methods of treatment derived from the books but who at the same time dares not use his patient as a subject for experiment to ascertain the efficacy of new methods of cure.[26]

Ts'ao, after showing that he recognized the problem, shifted without interruption to safer ground, saying that:

> It is said that "Good administration does not rely upon mere words but upon deeds well done." In the administration of state affairs I will follow this principle as my guide. . . . The secret of successful government is the utilization of talented men.[27]

Thus, Ts'ao showed himself to be an adherent of the traditional Confucian concept of good government, but at the same time he left open the question of what he considered to be a "talented person."[28]

This need of appeasing both the holders of traditional attitudes and the exponents of the newer values added to the tendency of making apparently moderate and reasonable public statements. Because all statements had to be viewed in terms of their effect upon groups that held values representing both of these extremes, the only safe course was to make it appear that one's statements were based upon reason rather than upon emotion. The fact that it had been the tradition of the old literati class as rulers to appear to be operating in a rational framework made it easier for the *tuchüns* to assume the role of tempered arbiters faced with conflicting issues. This served to further the emphasis upon nonemotional symbols in the *tuchüns'* propaganda, and to increase the analytical quality of many of their statements. For example, in Tuan Ch'i-jui's statement at the time he became provisional chief executive, he made reference in the following manner to the British proposal to remit its portion of the Boxer Indemnity for educational purposes:

"Now if you ask me my opinion on the question of whether China would rather the money be applied to educational purposes or to constructive enterprises, such as railroads, I shall have no hesitation in saying that China would prefer the allocation of the money for railroad-building. It is true, China needs more educational facilities, but, as I understand it, it is proposed that the money should be devoted to the creation of more institutions of higher learning. Now the needs for higher education, I think, are met already by the existing institutions, without adding to their number. Foreign education in China, while being appreciated, tends to create differing types of Chinese who are not easily assimilable. If all the countries use their indemnity funds for higher education of the Chinese youth, we should have a conglomeration of products of dissimilar cultures. . . . We really have not progressed far enough technically and industrially to take advantage of the services of those of our countrymen who have been educated along specialist lines abroad. . . . Our main need in education today is more primary education. We require more schools in the interior, away from the industrial centers. This need can be supplied only by the Chinese and the best way to ensure it, it seems to me, is the development of communications."[*][29]

This statement of Tuan's was intended to appeal to the old values of China and at the same time appears to support the progressive development of the country. The problem of the effects of foreign education on the traditional values of Chinese culture had long been recognized by Chinese intellectuals.[30] In addition, Tuan was seeking to play upon the frustrations of the foreign-trained students who could not find in China, as it then existed, the opportunities to apply their specialized skills.[31] Tuan was thus able to handle a highly controversial subject by appearing to treat it in a clearly analytical manner.

---

[*] The reason for Tuan's interest in the development of railroads was not hard to surmise when he proposed in the same statement that the Peking-Suiyüan Railroad should be extended 7,000 miles further west into Sinkiang. This was the area that Feng Yü-hsiang was now to control, and Tuan was interested in pacifying him and emphasizing the importance of the Northwest so as to retain his support as a balance against Chang Tso-lin.

While the Nationalists had shown a readiness to appeal to emotional symbols in respect to the question of "unequal treaties" and "anti-imperialism," the *tuchüns* were nearly unanimous in adopting a moderate tone in referring to the question of treaty revision, but here again they were restrained by the need to uphold the concept of the Republic. The myth of the Republican government to a large degree depended upon the recognition of the Peking government by the diplomatic corps. The actual issues of foreign affairs were not critical problems for the *tuchüns*. Rather, it was simply a question of exploiting foreign recognition for the purposes of obtaining foreign loans or, possibly more important, of maintaining the fiction that they were all working to uphold the formal government and leading China in the direction of Republicanism. The charge against those leaders, especially Sun Yat-sen, who had broken from the arena of competition for control of Peking, was that their actions had threatened to cause the foreign governments to refuse to recognize the Republican government of China.

The only subject the *tuchüns* could embrace in their public statements that would seem contradictory to the precepts of Republicanism was the principle of "provincial autonomy." However, on this subject, the individual *tuchün* had to be extremely careful to declare himself in complete support of the principle of a central government and to indicate that he did not envisage a complete break with Peking. Rather, he had to demonstrate that he conceived of "provincial autonomy" to mean the defense of local interests within the framework of a federal system.[32]

The concept of a federal system of government for China had a great deal of appeal at the time, and the example of the United States was used to justify many of the arguments for such a development. In fact, the idea appeared to have been especially inviting to many of the intelligentsia, who felt that, through a federal system, many of the problems of China could be solved and China might actually become powerful again.[33] Given the widespread discussion of the virtues of a federal government for China and the fact that the *tuchüns'* power rested upon control of specific areas, one finds it surprising that they did not emphasize the principle of local autonomy to a greater extent than they did. However, this behavior of the *tuchüns* appears intelligible in terms of the hypothesis that the limited power of the individual leaders placed restrictions upon the policies and issues with which they could identify themselves. Given the geographic proximity of the various *tuchüns'* centers of power, the appeal to the symbols of "provincial autonomy" would represent a challenge to all the other leaders who could act together in nominal support of the principles of "unification of the country."[34]

In addition, the symbol of "provincial autonomy" could be turned against a leader if he happened to control a province of which he was not a native or if he aspired to conquer such an area. Few *tuchüns* were willing to volunteer in such a way to limit their hopes of future expansion. Finally, the idea of "provincial autonomy" could be exploited by the natives of the provinces in order to oust the *tuchün* himself or to limit the power of the *tuchün* in local affairs.

In 1922, a strong movement for "provincial autonomy" was started in Hupei with the establishment of a new provincial constitution. The object of the move was to oust the incumbent *tuchün*, Chao Heng-t'i, and indirectly weaken Wu P'ei-fu's influence in the province. However, the movement was taken over by Chao Heng-t'i and was finally suppressed when Wu reasserted his authority in the area.[35] Chao, although a native of Honan, was able to exploit with remarkable success the sentiments for local autonomy that the previous *tuchün*, Wang Chan-yüan —a native of Hupei—had inspired. His use of Honan troops to occupy the province was tempered by his announcement that, "In the consensus of opinion throughout China, the protracted period of troubles and chaos can only be terminated in this country if and when China is reorganized according to the principle of self-government in the provinces along constitutional lines. . . . Hupei should set an example of democratic self-government."

The slogan of "provincial autonomy" thus was a relatively weak symbol in the hands of the *tuchüns*. It was only during periods of uncertainty as to who would succeed in dominating at the capital and when, therefore, there were no clear "cues" to direct the other *tuchüns'* attitudes, that it was safe to utilize the concept.[36]

In effect, the story of the *tuchüns'* efforts at propaganda is the account of men attempting to establish small areas of ideological differentiation but at all times making certain that these distinctions would not too clearly isolate them from the rest of the leaders. No leader was strong enough to champion great causes and any attempt in such a direction would establish him as the foe of all the other *tuchüns*. Herein lay one of the greatest weaknesses of the *tuchüns* as leaders of the development in China of political competition based on party structures. As China outgrew the monolithic nature of her former political structure, the *tuchüns* and their organizations did constitute competing political units. However, they lacked the essential quality of most competing political parties in the sense that they could not represent clashing interests or identify themselves unmistakably with issues that were meaningful.

Harold Lasswell has proposed the hypothesis that, in the political process, groups find it necessary to compromise principles to questions of expediency and that, in the formation of parties, it is necessary first to have strong appeal to ideological issues but that, as the party gains power, these principles must be compromised because of exigencies that arise. For the *tuchün*, such a series of stages never appeared. The *tu-chüns* already had their organizations in the form of their armies when they entered the political arena, and, from the beginning, they were constantly faced with the question of expediency. These groups did not, in their initial formation, represent differing ideological principles; at the most, they represented differing personalities and groups of personal associates. Only as they became the dominant leaders in the political arena, did they find it necessary to identify themselves with questions of principle. But, in this process, issues of principle were questions of ex-pediency first and conviction only second. Ideological considerations did not serve as the basis of the organizations but were only brought in to patch up any weaknesses that might have developed in the organi-zations as they expanded. In this process, it was essential that such con-siderations not create greater stress within the organizations than had already existed, and, thus, functionally, it was necessary to dilute all questions of principle that were employed.

Not only did the historical development of the organizations limit their ability to support political principles and issues, but the fact that they were dependent on their armies placed bounds on the forms of ideo-logical competition in which they could engage. As military commanders, they depended upon the control of the resources of geographic areas. Their moves and countermoves were dictated by the need to occupy and control physical space. They were not free, as true political parties would be, to seek out and obtain the support of all like-minded individuals and groups, regardless of their location. Rather, they had to be all things to all people who occupied the areas under their control. Efforts to ap-peal to specific groups, such as students, merchants, or peasants, of the entire country would have little meaning and could not appreciably strengthen their position in the nation, while it might create dissension within the areas they did control.

As long as the issues were fought out in terms of physical violence or threats of violence, the conflicts had to take place within the frame-work of the control of, or the effort to dominate, specific geographic areas, and, within these areas, it was necessary to appeal to the minds of as large a number of people as possible. In this respect, the *tuchüns* found it nearly impossible to identify themselves clearly with recognized interest groups. Even the Nationalists, in their Northern Expedition, had to depend primarily upon military superiority, and it was only in the security they felt in the armies of Chiang Kai-shek that they were free to utilize powerful propaganda demands.[37] If a *tuchün* felt mili-tarily secure, he might feel that he could risk identification with particu-lar groups or issues, but, given the existing balance of power, few felt they could afford such a luxury.

Finally, it should be noted that the *tuchüns* were limited in the extent to which they could champion particular interests or issues by the fact that sharp cleavages had not yet divided Chinese society. Many of the old values supporting the monolithic structures of traditional society had not been destroyed. Ideas from the West were threatening the paramount position of Confucianism, but the process had not yet become a clear and definite conflict in which men had to choose sides and state their positions. The willingness to discuss Western ideas did not necessarily mean that men had renounced the concepts of Confucianism as the basis for consensus in the society. A more fractionalized society was developing in China, but it was not moving at the same pace or on the same level as were the *tuchüns* in their conflicts over political power.

Thus, although the *tuchüns* were forced to turn to elements of ideological conflict in order to strengthen their organizations and to make their rule more palatable, they could not safely assume the role of leaders in the conflict over issues. These differences had first to be fought out in the total society by such other elites as the students and the rising bourgeoisie before the *tuchüns* could identify themselves with the issues. In the struggle for political power, the leaders had to adhere closely to the borders of consensus and could not safely enter the area of opinion. In a changing society like China, only he who had great power could venture into the area of basic value conflict with assurance and conviction.

Paradoxically, the warlord, in introducing to China a politics based apparently upon violence and the use of military force, also introduced a relatively genteel and rational debater's approach to propaganda. They seemed to assume that the Chinese public could best be reached by arguments about national development that mixed reason and morality and shied away from demagogic appeals. In this respect, they had little in common with present military rulers in some of the new states who have sought to rule through the emotional appeals of nationalism. This quality of restraint of the warlords stemmed in large measure, as we have seen, from the constraints of being in a highly competitive power system.

From this examination of the political style of the warlords in dealing with the Chinese public, let us turn next to the warlords' relationships with the Chinese political elite. To do this, we shall in the next chapter focus on how the warlords influenced the making of civilian governments in Peking, the types of men that were given cabinet positions, and the general social and intellectual backgrounds of the civilian elite that emerged at the top of Chinese politics during the warlord period.

8. THE WARLORDS AND CABINET GOVERNMENT

Although the leading *tuchüns* never indicated that they considered themselves bound by the formal-legal structure of the Peking government, the very existence of such a government conditioned their behavior. As has been seen, they were on most occasions careful to show deference to the idea of Republican government, though not necessarily to particular officeholders. As long as control over and influence in the Peking government assisted the military leaders in achieving their desired goals, they were concerned with the composition of the political and bureaucratic organs of the national government. For the *tuchüns*, the key to control over the bureaucracy lay in the cabinet, and this in turn meant that the appointment of cabinet ministers was of special interest to them. Throughout the period, all cabinets had either the overt support or the tacit approval of the leading *tuchüns* of the moment.

In this sense, the development of cabinet government was at the mercy of the *tuchüns* and their policies. The composition of the cabinets and the role which they could assume depended upon the balance of power among the warlords. Although the need for the maintenance of formal cabinets served as an element in the balancing process and, as such, limited the freedom of choice of the power-holders, the cabinets were, for the most part, products of the interplay of forces of the total power complex. Thus, the nature of the balance of power among the *tuchüns* and the forms it assumed were reflected in the organization and activities of the cabinets.

Although unquestionably the phenomenon of warlordism impeded the effectiveness of civilian government, it is still important in the larger perspective of the modernization process of China to ask what kinds of civilian leaders the warlords tended to support. Did warlord politics generally support more conservative or traditional men who belonged mainly to the earlier Confucian-bureaucratic tradition? Or was the effect of the warlords one of encouraging the recognition of technical skills and modern education as the proper criteria for recruiting men to high office? Did the operations of warlord politics speed up the breakdown of the Confucian tradition and encourage the acceptance of the idea that new men were needed to manage the country? A somewhat more sophisticated question can also be raised as to whether the warlords, while championing the view that new skills were required, may in fact have set back the idea that technical competence should be an important element in legitimizing authority, because, in their insecurity over the power balance, they continually disrupted the civilian government and refused to allow the men with new skills to be effective. These are the kinds of questions we shall be asking as we examine the relationships of the *tuchüns* to the cabinets and analyze the characteristics of the civilian elite that held high office in China from 1920 to 1928.

The relationship of the *tuchüns* to the cabinets was of particular importance because it represented the focal point of the impact of *tuchün* politics upon the traditional politics of a bureaucratic order. The core of the old monolithic social and political organization of China had been the bureaucracy, which had served as the dominant feature in institutionalizing the politics and social values of the old Imperial society. In analyzing the role of the *tuchüns* in the social and political changes in modern China, one must, therefore, evaluate the impact of *tuchün* politics on what remained of the centralized bureaucratic tradition of the Imperial system.

The relationship of the *tuchüns* to the cabinet and bureaucracy represented a revolution of the most fundamental sense in the dynamic arrangements of the Chinese political system. Traditionally, the Chinese political system was largely defined by the bureaucratic structure, and there were no forces external to the mandarinate and the Imperial court that could legitimately seek to influence or control the formal institutions of government. Although it is true that the warlords did seek official titles and thus tried to encourage the fiction that they were a part of the legally established system of authority, they were, of course, recognized by everyone to be independent forces, external to the formal government, and thus, to the extent that they controlled the government, they represented a radical development in China. As leaders of organizations with power bases outside of government, the warlords were not seeking special favors from the bureaucracy but were actively engaged in a power struggle for control over formal governmental offices. Although the political process could still continue within the bureaucracy, the *tuchüns* had defined the main area of political activity as being of a broader and more informal nature. This change opened the way to the rise of political elites that were not directly connected with the bureaucracy but that had achieved positions of power and status in other areas of the society, and that, if successful in this broader power struggle, could expect to dominate the formal organs of government.

In effect, the practices of the *tuchüns* in seeking to control the bureaucracy meant that there had been a profound change in the location of the political decision-makers in the society. Under the old bureaucratic organization, there had been no clear distinction between technical experts or administrators and political practitioners for the policy-making elite.[1] Historically, the Chinese did not distinguish between the roles of administrator and politician. The institutionalized procedure was for those who sought to influence and direct government activities to identify themselves with the bureaucracy and hold official positions, regardless of what might have been their initial source of social power. With the rise of *tuchün* politics, the bureaucracy lost its freedom to make political decisions, for the power-holders were now located outside the formal organization. Although the *tuchüns* did not always participate in the decisions of the bureaucracy, their presence and their known views and demands influenced the actions of the responsible members of the bureaucracy, who were now forced to implement the wishes of individuals who did not belong to the old inner circle of officialdom.

Since the relationship of the *tuchüns* to the cabinets was not defined by law or by traditional patterns, the warlords never felt formally responsible for supporting the cabinet. Thus, on the one hand, they were in a position to dominate the cabinet, while, at the same time, they were not held accountable for the actions of the bureaucracy. Although, in the West, political parties are usually recognized as being extragovernmental organizations, which, in the political process, are formed for the purpose of competing for control of the organs of government, there are usually some forms of legal control that create a minimum degree of responsibility for those who are successful in this struggle for power. This control may be no more than periodic elections, the results of which are recognized as binding on all competing groups. However, for the *tuchüns*, there was no recognized compulsion for them to assume any form of responsibility for the actions of the formal government. This pattern of influence without responsibility contributed to the instability of the Peking government. The *tuchüns* did not have to commit themselves to the creation or support of particular cabinets and could leave this task to the civilian politicians—but the latter, without the overt support or direction of the dominant *tuchüns*, had to make decisions that they judged the *tuchüns* would approve.

In early 1926, for example, when it was clear that Chang Tso-lin had bested the Kuominchün, the Fengtien leader refused to assume an active role in the formation of the cabinet, and, during the summer and fall of 1926, the politicians attempted to form a cabinet that could meet without the opposition of Chang and might obtain his direct support.[2]

On May 13, 1926, a cabinet was formed under the direction of W. W. Yen, which contained men generally recognized as acceptable to Chang, Wu P'ei-fu, and Sun Ch'uan-fang, but Chang made it publicly known that he had not participated in the creation of the government.[3] An important factor in restraining Chang was his fear that his assuming too active a role in forming a government with Wu P'ei-fu, or his neglecting Sun Ch'uan-fang, might result in the re-establishment of the Feng-Sun alliance. He apparently concluded that control over the Peking government was not worth the risk of continuing the conflict against the forces in both Central China and the Northwest. However, without the overt support of Fengtien, the cabinet was able to function for only a little over a month. On June 22, a new cabinet was formed, headed by Admiral Tu Hsi-kuei, a supporter of Wu P'ei-fu.[4] However, Wu was far too weak to support an effective government, and, on July 6, a new cabinet was created, which included only men recognized as being loyal to Mukden. Thus, Chang Tso-lin, without directly naming the members of the cabinet, was able to force the civilian politicians to recognize that, only by creating a cabinet entirely subservient to him, would they be able to achieve his direct support of the government.

The lack of any recognized responsibility of the *tuchüns* for the cabinet stemmed in part from absence of any explicit relationship between the formal government and the holders of political power. Mechanically, there was no ready way of identifying which warlord had predominant power and thus would be held accountable for forming the government. There was no agreed way of interpreting the precise state of the balance of power among the *tuchüns* and, thus, no way in which actual power could be related to formal authority. Although in any society the political process is constantly operating, in a stable society, there are usually some institutionalized methods, such as elections, by which it is possible to establish which group or individual is in a dominant position at a specific time, and therefore should be given responsibility for conducting the government, until, by token of the same method, it is recognized that some other group or individual should replace them or him. For the *tuchüns*, physical control of Peking often carried with it certain acknowledged powers for the organization of the government. But the pattern of power which they operated was generally too fluid to make it possible to identify unambiguously those who had a clear claim to the control of, and thus the responsibilities for, the Peking government.

The absence of a regularized system of interpreting the balance of power among the *tuchüns* created a situation whereby it was possible for a leading *tuchün* to bring pressure on the cabinet even though he did not have a clear superiority over other *tuchüns*. For example, in the autumn of 1921, when Chang Tso-lin was losing influence in Peking to the Chihli faction, it was possible for the Mukden commander, by sud-

denly appearing in person in the capital on December 14, to cause a fall
of the cabinet three days later. The Chihli faction, being unwilling and
unprepared to resort to violence at this time, failed to unite behind their
previous cabinet. Therefore, the forceful demands of Chang were sufficient to bring about the establishment of a new cabinet headed by Liang
Shih-i, a strong supporter of the monarchist program of Yüan Shih-k'ai
and popularly known as the "God of Wealth." This cabinet included
members of the old Communications Clique, Yeh Kung-cho and Chang
Hu, as ministers of, respectively, communications and finance. These
men were, at the time, recognized as being willing and loyal supporters
of Chang Tso-lin's policies. Chang's only concession to the Chihli alliance was the appointment of Kao Ling-wei as minister of interior and
the promise of Wu P'ei-fu that he would receive $5 million for the pay-
ment of his troops. The latter step was probably calculated to cause further disunity among the Chihli leaders and prevent them from effectively
uniting against Chang. However, this payment would have had to come
through the ministry of war, which was under the control of Pao Kuei-
ching, the former *tuchün* of Kirin and a relative of Chang Tso-lin. Before it was possible to recapture the cabinet in June, 1922, it was necessary for the Chihli alliance to demonstrate its superiority over Fengtien
by a test of arms.

The problem of relating the balance of power of the *tuchüns* to the
formal government was further complicated by the necessity of maintaining the continuity of the cabinets and the formal government. Governments had to be formed during periods when it was difficult to predict from the balance of power who was likely to achieve the dominant
position. During such periods, when the balance of power among the
tuchüns was in doubt, the politicians in Peking hesitated in committing
themselves. An example of such a situation was the period from November, 1925, to February, 1926, when it was uncertain whether the
Kuominchün or the Fengtien forces would achieve a paramount position. Since the Tientsin Conference of November, 1924, Feng Yü-
hsiang had been denied any representation in the cabinet, but, with the
increase in tension between Chang and Feng in November, 1925, peace
talks were instituted, with the Kuominchün demanding that their representatives, Huang Fu and C. T. Wang, be included in the cabinet.
However, the negotiations for conciliation by means of cabinet appointments were discontinued with the initial successes of Sun Ch'uan-fang's
campaigns in Central China and Kuo Sung-ling's revolt of November
27, 1925. It appeared that the Kuominchün now had an excellent opportunity to eliminate the influence of Chang Tso-lin in Peking. Therefore, Tuan Ch'i-jui decided, on December 10, to resign as provisional
chief executive and to call for a return to a governing cabinet. Since
the victories of the Kuominchün were far from decisive, the problem

now was to find a cabinet willing to serve. The Kuominchün at this point indicated that the only conditions they would insist upon were the following: First, the cabinet should not be headed by Hsü Shih-ying, because he was too closely identified with Tuan; and, second, they would welcome a cabinet consisting entirely of representatives of the Kuominchün, headed by Huang Fu. However, with the continuing military conflict, the Kuominchün was unwilling to risk any dissension within its own ranks, which the efforts to designate specific cabinet members might have entailed. (There were indications that the Second Kuominchün, under Yüeh Wei-chün, was interested in making such appointments but that the First Kuominchün, which had just entered the conflict, refused to consider the question of cabinet appointments at this time.) The result was that Tuan was confronted with the task of forming a government without the active support of any of the military leaders. On December 23, Tuan succeeded in creating a cabinet with his own follower, Hsü Shih-ying, as Prime Minister and men identified with the Kuominchün in the posts of ministers of foreign affairs, interior, education, justice, and agriculture and commerce.[5] However, the sudden defeat of Kuo Sung-ling two days later placed Tuan in the embarrassing position of having moved too quickly to placate the Kuominchün. The uncertainty of the military situation forced the cabinet to reorganize, and, on December 31, a new cabinet was announced. Although representatives of Feng were named ministers of foreign affairs and of interior and an active champion of the Second Kuominchün held the ministry of agriculture and commerce, the cabinet proclaimed itself a peace cabinet, which would be willing to retire as soon as peace was achieved. However, a stable peace was not quick in coming, and, although military conflict ceased, there was no settlement of the issue between Fengtien and the Kuominchün. The result was a series of resignations of cabinet ministers, which continued until it was clear that Chang Tso-lin was in unqualified control of Peking. Tuan Ch'i-jui himself sought to escape the stigma of being associated with the precarious government by issuing a circular telegram on January 8, 1926, stating that he desired to resign as soon as a satisfactory solution could be found for maintaining the formal organs of government. He had expected to receive replies requesting that he retain his position for the good of the country, but he was disappointed; most of the leaders were unwilling to commit themselves until the difficulties were resolved between Fengtien and the Kuominchün. Only two replies were received, both asking that he remain.

Biographical Analysis of Cabinet Members

With the *tuchüns* serving as makers of cabinets, the question arises as to the types of men they considered qualified to hold such posts.

This question is particularly pertinent because the traditional bureaucracy had been given much of its distinctive quality by the fact that entrance to the rank was predicated upon the successful completion of a series of examinations based upon a classical education. Thus the members of the bureaucracy, and especially those who reached the highest posts, represented a fairly homogeneous background and training. Now that the attitudes and demands of the *tuchüns* had become the critical factor in selecting men for high posts in the bureaucracy, it might be expected that this change in itself would be reflected in the training and experience expected of candidates for cabinet positions.

During the period 1920–28, ninety-four individuals were appointed to cabinet positions.[6] Not all of these men actually accepted appointments, but they are included in the following tables because they were men considered qualified to hold cabinet offices. (Actually, there were nine who did not serve.) Table 8.1 presents the pertinent data on the background and training of these ninety-four men.[7] It should be noted that one man is frequently listed under several categories—that is, a man who had received a classical education either in a formal school or under a tutor, and who had then visited the United States and obtained a degree in an American university, was listed under both "Classical Education" and "United States." Most of the categories are self-explanatory,

TABLE 8.1

EDUCATION AND BACKGROUND OF CABINET MINISTERS, 1920–28

Education and Background	Number	Per Cent
Classical Education	52	55.32
Modern Chinese Education	9	9.57
Military Academy Education	14	14.89
Educated Abroad	51	54.26
Japan	28	29.79
Great Britain	9	9.57
United States	7	7.45
Germany	4	4.25
France	2	2.13
Russia	1	1.06
Traveled Abroad	60	63.72
Ch'ing Bureaucracy	51	54.26
Ch'ing Military Establishment	18	19.15
Business and Financial Experience	15	15.96
Legal Training and Practice	10	10.64
Professors and College Presidents	9	9.57
Editors	4	4.25
Medical Profession	2	2.13
Members of Revolutionary Groups During the Ch'ing Dynasty	18	19.15
YMCA Secretary	1	1.06

with the possible exception of "Modern Chinese Education." This term was used to define the type of education one received at a Chinese university organized along the lines of the Western academic traditions. Included in this group were foreign-sponsored institutions as well as such government-supported universities as Pei Ta (Peking National University).

As can be seen from the table, a classical education and experience in the old Ch'ing bureaucracy continued to be recognized as desirable training for careers in the governmental administration. Several of the officials had been recipients of the best of the old mandarin training: seven were former members of the Hanlin Academy and seven others had received the degree of *Chu-jen*. Although the Peking government was considered to be the product of a major revolution, the traditions of the old order were still operative. In this respect it is noteworthy that less than 20 per cent of the cabinet ministers had been identified with revolutionary groups organized to overthrow the Ch'ing Dynasty. This figure is strikingly low, especially because, after the Revolution, it was common to assert identification with previous revolutionary movements, regardless of how tenuous these claims might have been.[8]

Although the cabinet ministers did not clearly represent the rise to power of an elite identified with a revolutionary cause, they did typify a revolutionary change in the training and skills considered necessary for men holding leading positions in the administration of China. In this sense, the Peking government and the men selected by the *tuchüns* to direct it represented a marked change in the types of skills practiced by the administrative elite.

This revolution in skills is indicated by the large proportion of men who had received foreign training and had traveled abroad. In addition, other less spectacular changes had occurred in the background and training of men acceptable for the highest formal posts in the bureaucracy. The fact that fifteen men had had active experience in the fields of business and finance represents a radical change from the traditional opposition of the Chinese bureaucrats to the merchant class and the generally low esteem in which merchants were held by members of the traditional society.[9] The *tuchüns* were in this respect giving recognition to the rising class of capitalists in modern China. However, in addition, the *tuchüns* were finding that, in order to solve many of the new and complex problems, particularly fiscal problems, it was necessary to call upon those skilled in the technical fields of finance and commerce. No longer were the classically trained literati capable of mastering the complex problems of government, and gone was the day when the Confucian philosopher was recognized as the most desirable administrator. Although the change was modest, the very recognition of the need for the technician was revolutionary.

The appointment of four men with experience in editorial-writing and journalism is also significant in that it is further testimony of the increasing recognition of the importance of influencing public opinion. That two of the men with editorial experience were given cabinet posts in order to silence their extreme criticism of the government can still be considered a form of recognition of the importance of the press and public opinion. The inclusion of journalists in such important formal posts in the society also points to the extent to which Chinese society was beginning to recognize a broadening of the fields of endeavor in which an individual could receive prominence and that technical expertness of a specialized nature warranted respect.

The presence of nine men from the educational field is not surprising, but it is relevant that all these men were drawn from modern educational institutions. Although they served primarily as ministers of education, the fact that it was not considered necessary to show particular deference to men who upheld the traditional form of education indicates that the issue between the old and the new educational traditions did not particularly bother the warlords. However, the presence of ten men with advanced training and experience in the legal field is striking, since the legal structure of China was so weak that the government hardly needed the services of trained lawyers. In part, this can be explained by the fact that eight of the ten received their legal training abroad and were thus not the direct products of a society that placed great value on legal education and skills. However, of importance in the decision to select men with legal training was the fact that China was at the time struggling to remove the stigma of extraterritoriality, and the presence in the government of legal experts trained in the Western tradition could be calculated to demonstrate to the West China's determination to develop a legal system acceptable by Western standards.

Closely related are the considerations that contributed to the large number of cabinet members who had received education and training abroad. There were fifty-one men with foreign training, as well as nine who were educated in Chinese schools modeled on Western practices; hence there were sixty men who were presumably acquainted, in some degree at least, with Western knowledge.[10]

The inclusion of a large number of Western-trained men constituted a radical change in the prerequisites for membership in the administration when compared with the nearly universal classical training of the old bureaucracy. However, this change was not solely the product of the Revolution of 1911. The previous regime had initiated the program of recognizing the value of Western education, and fifteen of the men who were to hold cabinet appointments in the Republican period were actually sent abroad to study by the Ch'ing Government. However, it is doubtful that, had the Ch'ing Government continued in power, in less than ten years it would have been willing to place men with Western training in the leading offices of the bureaucracy.

Although the *tuchüns* recognized the importance of the newer technical skills, they also appreciated the critical importance in the formation of cabinets of being able to win the recognition of the Western powers. For this reason, there was a strong bias favoring the selection of men with Western training who might be expected to influence the decisions of the diplomatic corps. It is impossible to determine the comparative importance of the assumed attitudes of the diplomatic corps and the inherent prestige of Western training as factors influencing the decisions of the *tuchüns* in the appointment of men to cabinet posts. Although the constant need for the recognition of the West created a situation that enhanced the prestige of foreign training in the total society, it is uncertain to what extent such training was increasingly being accepted as a value on its own merits.

However, an indication of the rising importance of foreign-trained personnel in Chinese society of the time can be obtained from Table 8.2. This table is based on a sample of the returned students and indicates the fields of endeavor in which they engaged.[11] A great deal of care must be taken in making generalizations from the table, because we know so little about the size of the universe from which the sample was taken, and the sources of the biographer undoubtedly had certain biases. It would be safe to assume, for example, that the government served as the largest single employer of returned students, but the relative proportion, as shown in the table, is probably inaccurate because a man employed in the government service would probably have a greater likelihood of being included in the listings than would, say, an individual engaged as a junior executive in a private firm or a young man in the medical or educational field. A person in government service would be more likely to be considered of general news value.

Another necessary qualification is that it would be inadvisable to use the information in the table to generalize about the relative efficacy of American, European, and Japanese educational methods in preparing an individual for service in the Chinese cultural and social complex. Certain qualified conclusions might be drawn from the fact that students returned from America and Europe found the greatest opportunities for employment in technical capacities, whereas the Japanese-educated students were far more successful in the fields of policy-making and political action. However, it would be dangerous to attribute this entirely to the difference in educational emphasis and cultural attributes of the West and Japan. An important factor contributing to the radical difference in the employment of returned students was the fact, as has been mentioned above, that most of the students who traveled to America and Europe found themselves relatively isolated, and, at best, living in

TABLE 8.2
PROFESSIONS OF RETURNED STUDENTS

Professions	Japan	Returned from United States	Europe
Politics[a]	21	6	2
Bureaucracy			
Policy-Makers[b]	42	12	4
Technicians	10	27	14
Ministry of Foreign Affairs[c]	9	28	23
Army	32	3	4
Navy	2	0	5
Legal	12	8	4
Education and Religion	8	21	10
Business and Finance	4	11	5
Medicine	1	6	3
Journalism and Publishing	6	5	1

Notes—Table 8.2

a. These represent men engaged in the formation of the political cliques and factions that were seeking the support of the *tuchüns* and also those men who served as advisers or assistants to the *tuchüns*.

b. An effort was made to distinguish between men employed in a technical capacity as experts with specific skills and those who were employed as general administrators and policy advisers. However, the distinction was often based on highly impressionistic criteria because of the limited information available. A man was listed as a technician if he was employed over a long period in an office presumably requiring specific skills. For example, a man who served regularly in such bureaus as the mint or the railroad maintenance department was considered to be a technician. Those engaged in policy activities included men who had had a highly varied career in the bureaucracy and whose particular skill appeared to be in the field of administration and in winning the friendships of influential men.

c. The men employed in the Ministry of Foreign Affairs were listed separately because of the high incidence of returned students in this ministry as compared with the other members of the bureaucracy.

small communities of their compatriots while abroad. They were unable to establish associations that would ensure political appointments when they returned to China. On the other hand, the student who went to Japan found a large community of Chinese who were effectively organized into political groups and could thus establish personal relations with a large number of individuals who later assisted each other in finding employment.[12]

However, the table does indicate that there were possibilities for men to receive recognition in many new fields previously nonexistent in China and that the *tuchüns* and the government did, in fact, recognize that Western skills were meaningful and important in the conduct of the government. Apparently, then, Western-trained specialists had become increasingly important and were appointed not solely to gain the recognition of the diplomatic corps or of foreign countries. Thus, although there was a definite change in the general qualifications of ministers of state, the change appears to have been consistent with changes in Chinese society at the time.

The appreciation of Western technical skills also brought about the acceptance of a wider range of educational backgrounds and greater diversity in the elite. The previous Ch'ing bureaucracy had been characterized by men with the same general backgrounds and skills in all offices. Apparently the *tuchüns*, in their role as arbiters of cabinet appointments, did attempt to distinguish among the particular qualifications of the candidates for the separate ministries. During the entire period under study, there were thirty-one occasions in which decisions were made about the appointments of all the members of the cabinet. This does not mean that at each time there was a complete change in the composition of the cabinet, but, rather, that on thirty-one occasions changes did take place that required those making the decision to consider the desirability of either changing or retaining the holder of each portfolio. In addition, there were numerous cases in which individual cabinet ministers were changed but the change did not affect the status of the other members of the cabinet. Since the dominant *tuchüns* were involved in all these decisions, we can note from the qualification of the candidates for each of the ten posts in the ministries the criteria of specialization that the warlords appeared to be applying.

Table 8.3 shows the educational and professional backgrounds of the cabinet ministers according to the various positions.[13] As might be expected, a classical education and experience in the Ch'ing bureaucracy were still considered desirable qualifications for officeholders, regardless of what kind of office they were to administer. However, it is striking that, at one time or another, men with military training and experience held all of the cabinet positions except those of justice and finance.[14] This would suggest that, during the 1920's, the power and prestige of the military were increasing in China and soldiers were becoming the general all-purpose administrators that Confucian scholars had once been. Just as, previously, skill in command of the written language and knowledge of the classical tradition qualified a man for any and all specialized tasks, so now there was the tendency to treat those skilled in the military field in the same manner. This change is not surprising; the practitioners of the military arts were at the time the arbiters of power, and there was considerable violence in the political arena. However, it does show that the traditional aversion to employing military men in civilian and government positions was decreasing and members of the military profession were considered publicly acceptable for such appointments. The warlords thus set in motion the trend toward giving greater prestige to men in uniform that has continued to this day in China. After the warlords had established the precedent, it was no longer surprising during the Nationalist or Communist periods to have

TABLE 8.3

EDUCATIONAL AND PROFESSIONAL BACKGROUNDS OF CABINET MINISTERS, BY OFFICE

	Classical Education	Ch'ing Bureaucracy	Modern Chinese Education	Japanese Education	Western Education	Military	Business and Finance	Law	Journalism and Publishing	Professional Educators	Member of Revolutionary Groups	Average Age	Average Age Rank by Ministries
Prime Minister	9	8	0	2	2	2	1	0	0	0	1	54	8.69
Foreign Affairs	2	4	1	2	8	2	0	0	0	0	0	43	1.73
Interior	13	12	1	2	3	2	3	1	1	1	1	51	7.31
War	4	3	0	5	0	7	0	0	0	0	2	52	6.13
Navy	1	2	0	2	2	4	1	0	0	0	0	60	9.08
Agriculture & Commerce	7	6	1	6	1	2	2	1	0	1	1	50	5.54
Finance	12	11	3	5	6	0	10	1	0	1	1	49	3.23
Communications	5	5	1	1	3	2	4	1	0	1	2	47	3.84
Education	3	4	2	8	2	1	1	4	4	4	7	44	4.46
Justice	8	7	1	8	4	0	0	6	4	1	3	45	3.13

military men in civilian offices. What is possibly more surprising is that the warlords did not go further in filling civilian posts with soldiers, especially when we consider how readily both the Nationalists and Communists have used soldiers for civilian tasks.

Another significant conclusion to be drawn from Table 8.3 is that, taken as a body, the members of the cabinets appeared to have been relatively young. This would suggest that the traditional prestige of age was giving way to the necessity for more specialized persons to occupy the strategic positions in the society.[15] This hypothesis is confirmed by the fact that the ministries administering the more technical and modern aspects of government had, on the average, younger men and proportionately fewer classically trained mandarins. This can be seen from the column giving the "Average Age Rank of Ministers," in which the lower figures represent the younger men.[16] Such offices as ministers of foreign affairs, of finance, and of communications, which required technical skills of a more modern order, were filled for the most part by the younger men in each cabinet. On the other hand, the posts of Prime Minister, minister of the interior, and minister of war were occupied by the older members.[17]

The tendency of the *tuchüns* to recognize that some forms of specialization were desirable in the selection of candidates for the various posts points to another feature of the relations of the *tuchüns* to the cabinets and the resulting effects on the development of cabinet government in China. The *tuchüns* did not conceive of the cabinet as a unified decision-making body that could be held responsible for the conduct of the government.[18] For the *tuchüns*, control of the cabinet meant, in effect, control of the individual cabinet offices and the exploiting of these heads of government departments for the qualities and skills they offered. The cabinet as a whole was only expected upon occasion to give formal approval to the political acts of the *tuchüns* in order to maintain order and the appearance of legality. This was important not only for propaganda purposes but also because Peking was the source of all legitimate wars. Thus, the Kuominchün, on February 22, 1926, was able to force Tuan Ch'i-jui to issue a mandate that Wu P'ei-fu was "disturbing the peace" and that Yüeh Wei-chün was acting in the name of the government in opposing him. However, when the Kuominchün was driven from the capital, Chang Tso-lin and Wu P'ei-fu exacted a similar statement from the new cabinet, which termed the Kuominchün rebel forces. In addition, such claims of legitimacy were important because the diplomatic corps tended to adhere closely to conventional concepts of international law and identify the conflicting groups as being either government armies or rebel forces.

In the main, however, the *tuchüns* saw little value in strengthening the position of the cabinet as a unit but recognized that the individual members controlled important offices. For the cabinets this attitude meant that there were no strong pressures forcing them to seek unity, yet their only power was the threat to resign as a body.

The most outstanding example of this tactic was the Chang Shao-tseng cabinet, formed on January 4, 1923, which periodically threatened to resign in an effort to demand a more coherent program of support from the Chihli military alliance. Because the *tuchüns* were wholly engrossed in the developments that finally led to the election of Ts'ao K'un to the Presidency, none were willing to assume responsibility for assisting the cabinet to solve the administrative problems that confronted it. On March 8, 1923, the cabinet submitted its resignation as a body after Wu P'ei-fu had demanded that the cabinet formally appoint Sun Ch'uan-fang and Shen Hung-lien as *tuchüns* of Fukien and Kwantung, respectively. This threat was sufficient to cause Wu to promise to assist the cabinet in meeting the problem of administrative expenses, whereupon the cabinet approved the appointments on March 21, 1923. However, on June 6, 1923, the Chang Shao-tseng cabinet was again forced to employ the tactic of submitting its resignation to obtain the assistance of the Chihli leaders in meeting the financial problems associated with the Dragon Boat Festival.

The failure of the cabinet to serve as an organized body meant that, in attempting to relate the balance of power among the *tuchüns* to the formal organs of government, it was impossible to utilize the cabinet as an institution that could serve as a quantitative index of the *tuchüns'* relative power. Because the body did not act together in making decisions affecting the bureaucracy, it was meaningless numerically to divide the offices among the *tuchüns* according to their relative power. For this reason, the cabinet could not serve as a "scoring device" that might have reduced the need for threats or acts of violence to regularize any change in the power complex. The critical problem was not how many votes a *tuchün* could command in the cabinet but, rather, which ministers he controlled.

The great differences in the relative importance of the respective cabinet posts created further problems for the *tuchüns*. Because control of a given number of ministries did not imply a proportionate control over what might be extracted from the formal government, it was difficult to use the cabinet posts as units in bargaining for the organization of coalitions. Because there were only a limited number of desirable offices, it was almost impossible to achieve a satisfactory division of the Peking government, which would appeal to all the leaders who might join in such a coalition. Also, because such a premium was placed on the control of certain ministries, whenever an alliance controlled Peking, it was usually under a great strain in assigning control over these key ministries.

An example of these problems can be seen in the developments of 1920 after the defeat of the Anfu faction. The Chihli leaders had devoted their main attention to problems of the military conflict and had neither reached agreements among themselves as to how they should reorganize the cabinet nor established working relations with the candidates for such offices. The result was that, although the Anfu cabinet fell and the more notorious Anfu Club members fled the capital, the victorious military leaders were unprepared to offer a new slate of ministers. Thus, there resulted one of the few cases in which, after a radical change in the military balance of power, there was no immediate change in the appointment of the Prime Minister.[19] The Chihli leaders, uncertain even of their relations with each other, hesitated in suggesting a new Prime Minister for fear of creating tensions in the alliance. Therefore Chang Tso-lin, who had cooperated in the final stages of the defeat of the Anfu group, was free to engage in the selection of the new cabinet ministers. When the new cabinet was formed on August 11, 1920, it contained only one member, Tung K'ung, who could be safely called a supporter of the Chihli alliance, and he held the relatively unimportant ministry of justice.[20] The rest of the cabinet consisted either of such semi-independent figures as W. W. Yen, minister of foreign affairs, and Sa Chen-ping, minister of the navy, or supporters of the Fengtien leader.

Chang Tso-lin's success was due not only to the inability of the Chihli leaders to reach an agreement among themselves as to the appointment of the cabinet officials; Chang also found assistance from an unexpected source, President Hsü Shih-ch'ang. This was possibly the last time that the President of China was to play an important role in the developments at the capital. With the Chihli leaders undecided, Hsü sought the backing of Chang in appointing new cabinet members. President Hsü had, through his long service in the bureaucracy under the Manchus, developed a large personal following. Particularly during the period when he was viceroy of Manchuria, he had been active in supporting the careers of men who were later to hold high office. Because many of these men were natives of the area that Chang Tso-lin now dominated, it was easy to obtain his support at this time. As a result, these men who had initially received office through the influence of Hsü now moved into Chang's direct orbit as the office of the Presidency declined. This was particularly true of Chang Chih-t'an, the new minister of interior, and Wang Nai-p'ing, minister of agriculture and commerce.

Another factor that strengthened Chang's influence in the Peking government was that the old Communications Clique, seeking to return to power and finding the Chihli leaders disunited, turned to Chang Tso-lin and offered him their experience and services in return for support in obtaining cabinet posts. This group, led by Yeh Kung-chou (who was made the new minister of communications) and Chang Hu, had been exceedingly influential in the ministry of communications during the period of Yüan Shih-k'ai's power, but they had lost much of their power during the Anfu regime.

The result was that the first cabinet formed after the fall of both Tuan Ch'i-jui and the Anfu faction was one whose main support came from Chang Tso-lin, while the real power in North China was in the hands of the Chihli leaders. This led not only to a rapid decline in the prestige of the cabinet but also to increased tensions between the Fengtien and Chihli leaders. In May, 1921, the Chihli leaders were sufficiently united to seek further control of the cabinet. Through the influence of Ts'ao K'un, Li Shih-hui was made the minister of finance and Ch'i Yao-shan replaced Chang Chih-t'an as minister of interior. However, Ts'ao also removed Yeh Kung-chou as minister of communications and replaced him with Chang Chih-t'an, who, although considered to be. a supporter of the Fengtien leader, was not a member of the Communications Clique. This move was calculated to place Chang Tso-lin in a difficult position if he should openly attempt to oppose the change, because opposition would mean that he would have to repudiate a man he had supported, although for a different post. Chang would thus be forced to decide between outright support of the Communications Clique or continued reliance upon the men he had gained through President Hsü.[21]

Although this change did give the Chihli leaders control over the cabinet commensurate with their military power, it also meant that Chang Tso-lin had lost control over the important ministries of finance and communications. There was no possibility of achieving a coalition government that would adequately represent the respective powers of the two groups, and the efforts at control over the Peking government led only to further tension between them.

The tendency to recognize a functional difference in the various cabinet offices also led to the acceptance of certain posts as being primarily important for what might be termed the "ceremonial function." Although the cabinets did not operate as a body, it was nevertheless important for them to appear as an organization possessing formal importance and prestige. The fiction of a Republican government was too important in the politics of the *tuchüns* for them to overlook the need of giving the cabinet some degree of prestige. Not only were the cabinets expected to serve as respectable fronts for the actions of the *tuchüns* but also as targets of public criticism, thereby reducing the vulnerability of the actual power-holders to such attack. Because respectability and ability to rule were synonymous in the public mind, the more respectable the members of the cabinet, the greater the public expectation that they would have power of their own. Thus, when disappointments came, the cabinet would have to share public criticism with the dominant *tuchüns*.

The practice developed whereby those posts that did not produce material rewards for the controlling *tuchün* could be treated primarily as ceremonial offices lending respectability to the total cabinet. The criterion for the appointment of a man to such a post was mainly his ability as a respected individual to contribute to the acceptability of the entire cabinet. Aside from the need to ensure that the appointments could be exploited for patronage purposes, the *tuchüns* were relatively free to seek out the most respectable candidates available.

The question of patronage appears to have been present with each major change in the control of the ministries. It is impossible to obtain figures on the exact extent of these turnovers, and it is doubtful whether careful records were ever kept on the personnel of all the ministries. However, some indication of the extent of the changes can be seen from the statements of incoming ministers who, in the name of economy, removed men from the bureaucracy only to replace them later. On January 1, 1922, when Chang Hu was made minister of finance in the Liang Shih-i cabinet, he announced that he had ousted 500 of the more than 1,200 employees in the Peking offices of the ministry and that he would replace them with more efficient workers.[22] With the victory of the Chihli alliance in June and the fall of the Liang cabinet, the new minister of communications, Kao En-hung, announced that, during his first week in office, he had discovered nearly 4,000 employees who could be removed from office and replaced with more efficient workers at a saving of nearly $25,000,000 (Mexican) a year.[23] However, Kao also gave the traditional rationalization for the practices of patronage—they are bad, and we are good—when he stated that, "General Wu has driven the robbers out of the country, and I am going to drive them out of the government."[24]

The trend toward vesting certain cabinet posts with a primarily honorific character was exhibited in the type of men selected for the offices of Prime Minister and minister of interior. Both of these offices were, in theory, posts of great power and importance, but in practice their functions were limited by the power of the military leaders. During the entire period, there was no Prime Minister who wielded the power expected of such an office. After Tuan Ch'i-jui resigned as Premier in 1918, no further attempts were made by the actual holders of power to assume that office, and, with the military leaders preferring to engage in political action without benefit of formal office, there was a sharp decline in the power associated with this position. On the other hand, it was still essential to find men with sufficient prestige for the post in order to lend dignity to the entire cabinet.

In searching for persons with the desired qualifications but without real power to fill these posts, the *tuchüns* relied heavily upon men with classical training and experience in the Ch'ing Government. All except four of the eighteen men who were formally appointed Prime Minister or Acting Prime Minister were the products of a classical education and resembled the traditional mandarin in experience.[25] Each of these fourteen men had held respected posts under the Ch'ing and five had been Hanlin academicians. The two Prime Ministers who had received only Western training were in office for a total period of just six months and were officially designated as Acting Prime Ministers. Two of the Prime Ministers, Chin Yün-p'eng and Chang Shao-tseng, had had careers in the field of military affairs.[26] These men, through their personal associations with the leading *tuchüns* and because they lacked military power to threaten the position of any of the *tuchüns*, managed to maintain the most stable cabinets for the longest periods of any of the Prime Ministers. The relative success of these men as compared with the mandarins served further to discredit the old tradition and contribute to the rising prestige of the military.

In theory, the minister of interior was a member of the cabinet whose power should have been noteworthy. Under the Constitution, the ministry of interior was responsible for the appointments of all civil governors and indirectly in charge of the appointments of all local magistrates and civil officials. However, with the *tuchüns* in control of the provinces, the only function of the ministry was to give formal sanction to the appointments the *tuchüns* made. Of the nineteen different ministers of interior, the vast majority were typical of the old bureaucracy. The three Western-trained men who held the office served for a total period of only five months, whereas the two ministers who had studied in Japan were military leaders who had never had strong armies under their command.

Another post carrying ceremonial functions was that of minister of war. Theoretically, this ministry was responsible for not only the promotion of all officers in the military establishment but also the size and financing of all the *tuchüns'* armies and the ordering and transferring of these officers and organizations. In practice, the ministry did little more than regularize accomplished facts and support the will of the *tuchüns* who currently controlled the government. However, the minister of war also functioned as an important negotiator and mediator between the military leaders. For example, Wu Kuan-hsin, as minister of war in the autumn of 1925, in a cabinet under the control of Chang Tso-lin, spent considerable effort attempting to mediate between Fengtien, Sun Ch'uan-fang, Feng Yü-hsiang, and Wu P'ei-fu. In September, he attempted to reach a negotiated settlement between Wu P'ei-fu and his surviving followers, Tu Shih-chu and Hsiao Yao-nan, on the one side, and Yüeh Wei-chün and the Kuominchün, on the other. During October and November, he attempted to mediate a settlement between Fengtien and Sun Ch'uan-fang. In addition, after a military campaign, the minister of war was on occasion expected to negotiate the final terms between the victor and the vanquished. These functions placed a premium on selecting men for the post who were personally respected by most of the prominent *tuchüns* and who had little in the way of military power themselves.

The tendency of the *tuchüns* to select men with a classical background to hold offices of only ceremonial importance indicates that, as a group, they were still prepared to show deference to tradition and to exploit the prestige of the mandarins. However, the *tuchüns'* insistence that the mandarin class serve in honorific positions directly contributed to an acceleration in the decline of the status of the old bureaucratic class. The *tuchüns*, by supporting the appointments of these officials but, at the same time, denying them effective power, forced them into an impossible position whereby they rapidly lost the respect of the public. Although the trend away from the traditional mandarin was inescapable, the *tuchüns* directly contributed to their downfall by preventing them from functioning as effectively as they might, given any degree of real power.

On the other hand, the need to exploit certain ministries for the achievement of material values contributed, either directly or indirectly, to the recognition of the role of Westernized specialists in Chinese society. Control over a ministry meant nothing unless that ministry was capable of functioning efficiently enough to produce some returns that were of positive value to the *tuchüns*. The two ministries that were of particular importance to the *tuchüns* and that offered the greatest opportunities for financial reward and power were the ministries of finance and of communications.[27] Although some men appointed to these ministries had previous experience in the Ch'ing government or had received a classical education, the vast majority had also received foreign training as well or had pursued careers in business and commerce. Thus, in general, to fill these offices, the *tuchüns* sought men recognized as possessing special skills in fields related to the problems of these ministries.[28] Although twelve of the twenty-one men who at various times during the period were in charge of the ministry of finance had received traditional educations, all except three had gone on to further training in foreign institutions or had had successful careers in private business. Of the nine men who had shared in directing the ministry of communications during the period, seven had either foreign training or experience in private enterprise or both.

Above all, the *tuchüns'* treatment of the ministry of foreign affairs enhanced the prestige of the modern specialist. Although the *tuchüns* did not lack interest in foreign relations (all foreign loans depended in the first instance on the maintenance of acceptable diplomatic relations with the Western powers), they rarely attempted to intervene directly in the operations of the ministry of foreign affairs. Rather, they permitted the foreign ministers to function as best they could as nearly independent experts on foreign relations.[29] The result was the development of a group under the leadership of Wellington Koo, Alfred Sze, and W. W. Yen, which might be called the foreign-affairs clique. These men and the other ministers of foreign affairs were the most successful civilian leaders in China, and, through their adroit exploiting of the international balance of power and current world sympathies, they were able to achieve results completely out of proportion to the power of China. So, by refraining from hampering the actions of the ministry of foreign affairs, the *tuchüns* contributed to the respectability of a ministry that was almost entirely under the control of modern specialists. Of the ten men who served as ministers of foreign affairs, all except two had received training abroad, and the two classically educated individuals had both served in the foreign service of the Ch'ing Government and had lived abroad most of their adult lives.

Thus, the *tuchüns*, either through conscious policy or indirectly through the consequences of the type of politics in which they engaged, positively contributed to the decline of the old bureaucracy and the rise in prestige of Westernized specialization. As the *tuchüns* carried the political struggle outside of the recognized structure of the bureaucracy, they were destroying the essential quality of the old monolithic society. However, as competing groups, they lacked coherent programs, and they were incapable of serving as a force that could integrate on a new plane the performance of government. As long as violence was the key to the political arena, the *tuchüns* placed high value on only limited aspects of formal government, and they were unable to serve as potential political parties or groups capable of integrating all aspects of the formal government. Thus, although they had introduced a new dimension to Chinese politics, they were incapable of regularizing this new quality to produce a form of competitive politics in which the multiplicity of values of a changing Chinese society could be expressed.

Although the activities of the *tuchüns* in controlling the cabinets and the government led to a decline in the prestige of the old bureaucracy, other factors were also contributing to the lowered efficiency and the decline in status of this bulwark of the old society. Changes were also taking place in the character and the magnitude of the problems with which the bureaucracy was expected to deal. The task of administering a traditional agrarian society can hardly be compared with the difficulties of giving unified direction to a modernizing society. For example, the administration of the railway services and telegraphic and postal communications of modern China was a more complex problem than directing the systems of communication and transportation under the Imperial system. As the bureaucracy found itself increasingly incapable of dealing efficiently with the problems of modernization, there was a decline in the prestige of the civil servant in the eyes of the rest of the community.

As the bureaucracy lost its former prestige through its lack of political power and its inability to function efficiently in the solving of new problems, there was a concomitant rise in the prestige of other forms of endeavor. Honors and status could be sought in such relatively new fields as commerce, journalism, medicine, and the modern form of education, which was not directly concerned with the training of civil servants. No longer were the highest honors of the society to be gained through government service as had been the case in previous periods, and, as the society became more diversified, the bureaucracy had to expect to find greater competition from other interests in the procurement of capable and intelligent recruits. However, in the midst of these social forces that were active in weakening the old order, the *tuchüns* and their form of politics were a catalytic agent accelerating the decline of the bureaucracy.

9. INTELLECTUALS AND BUSINESSMEN

As we have seen, the warlords, ensnared in the constraints of competitive power, adopted a reasoned approach in appealing to the Chinese public, and, in supporting civilians for high office, they tended to balance competence in the foreign office with more traditional concepts of prestige for the office of Prime Minister. These were not unreasonable tendencies in furthering the modernization of China. Yet, at the time, the Chinese public tended to see the warlords as an antimodern force, and, in particular, they saw the competition among the warlords as being destructive of progress.

This appeared to be the case especially in the eyes of the two groups who were the most important nongovernmental elements of Chinese society, the intellectuals and the business community. The *tuchüns'* relations to the intellectuals and businessmen were of critical importance because the former had been a dominant elite in traditional China and the latter would be decisive in providing the thrust necessary for the economic development essential for further modernization. With respect to the intellectuals, the workings of warlord politics probably destroyed any possibility that Chinese modernization would proceed under their leadership and caused the Chinese educated classes to become so alienated from competitive politics that they would thereafter seek only to identify themselves with monolithic authorities. On the other hand, the consequence of warlordism on the financial and commercial communities was less harsh but still damaging because it resulted in divisions that discouraged a coherent approach toward economic development.

In general terms, *tuchün* politics not only constituted a direct assault upon the monolithic structure of the traditional society but also, in its indirect consequences, served to undermine the position of those who might have sought to preserve the old. As the *tuchün* organizations developed into political associations competing for power, they succeeded in denying political power to other groups in the society. That no single *tuchün* could effectively direct his power to the realization of broad political objectives and policies served further to weaken the influence of other segments of the society. These groups could not find in the *tuchün* organizations the political power necessary for the achieving of their aims, and, as a result, they tended to withdraw from the political arena. The problem was not solely one of what values should be propounded in the political field; rather, the difficulty was the impossibility of obtaining sufficient political power to further any particular goals of development. As long as political power revolved around the question of ability to apply violence and the practitioners of violence found that they were bound by the dictates of a complex balance of power, there was little opportunity for the conduct of effective political programs.

In examining the consequences of this dilemma of power in the *tuchüns'* relations with the intellectuals and business communities, we cannot review the complete role of these two groups in the Republican period. Much has already been written about the fate of the modern Chinese intellectuals, and the full range of problems of Chinese economic development lie well beyond the scope of this study. Our concern can only be with the more limited question of the ways in which the operations of the balance of power among the warlords affected these two elements in Chinese society.

The *Tuchüns* and the Intellectuals

For a society that traditionally was highly deferential to the intellectual and in which the scholar was formally recognized as having a superior social and political status, the development of *tuchün* politics represented a radical change. Although the ideal of the scholar was by no means dead and, in the minds of the people, the man of letters was still a superior individual, it was clear to the intellectuals that they had lost their power. No longer could they expect to exercise control over political events in China, although they could continue to exist as an elite body in the society. Skill in violence had forced out the power of enlightenment. The political arena was now one in which not only was there a high incidence of violence but also the ultimate test of all issues was in terms of violence. In tradition and temperament, the scholar was not suited for such an arena and was ill equipped to counteract the power of those engaged in it. The traditional literati class had previously been able to maintain an unstable balance of superiority over the military through the monolithic structure of the society and the need of maintaining the bureaucracy. But now, with the destruction of the monolithic society, the intellectuals found that they lacked a framework in which they could effectively maintain power in the society. Even the symbols of Republican government had been usurped by the *tuchüns*.

For the intellectuals there was little alternative but to divorce their activities from the political scene and to follow more private pursuits. A letter written by Huang Yüan-yung, one of the leading publicists and intellectuals of the period, to Chang Shih-chao indicates the general reaction of the intelligentsia to the political scene. "In my humble opinion, politics is in such confusion that I am at a loss to know what to talk about. Ideal schemes will have to be buried for future generations to unearth. . . . As for fundamental salvation, I believe its beginning must be sought in the promotion of a new literature. In short we must endeavor to bring Chinese thought into direct contact with the contemporary thought of the world, thereby to accelerate its radical awakening."[1]

The problem was far more serious than merely a withdrawal from violence and strife. In fact, many of the students and intellectuals were called upon to demonstrate real physical courage in the mass demonstrations they were frequently capable of producing.[2] Even if the students had attempted to enter the political arena by identifying themselves with one or another of the *tuchün* organizations, they would have had little power.[3] As we have seen, individual *tuchüns* often welcomed such recruits in their organizations, because the latter could sometimes offer real services. However, the intellectuals could not function as they desired, for, once they had accepted the *tuchün* organizations as a means of realizing their values, they discovered that these organizations were not sufficiently powerful to carry out the programs they were capable of formulating. Just as the *tuchüns* found that the balance of power forced them to sacrifice all to the prime goal of maximizing power, so the intellectuals found that the military leaders lacked sufficient strength to dominate the state and carry out effective policies. The power of the *tuchüns* as a group was sufficient to usurp basic power in the society and to leave impotent the intellectuals. But, in terms of their relative power, none was in a position effectively to administer programs that the intellectuals found meaningful. Therefore it was necessary for the intellectuals who did enter the political arena to leave behind the schemes and ideals of the intellectual world and accept the dictates of a world of power calculations.

As the political scene frustrated the intellectuals and drove them back into a self-sufficient world of their own, this world flourished and produced one of the most intense and stimulating periods of intellectual ferment known in Chinese history. The Chinese renaissance, which touched all fields of intellectual activity, was kindled by Western ideals and fanned into flame by the scholars' forced withdrawal from the political scene. To a degree, the intellectual life became a safe haven from the violence and impotence of the political world. On the other hand, the intellectuals, disgusted with the developments in Chinese politics, found it possible to justify their intellectual activities as the only hope for the reconstruction of China. Thus, the Chinese renaissance was a combination of frustration and withdrawal from the real world of political action and a belief that, through intellectual pursuits, China might be saved. This gave to the entire movement a quality of missionary zeal and the intellectuals freely identified themselves as the future saviors of China.

This fervor was further stimulated by the comments of both foreign and Chinese leaders that, out of such a movement, would come China's salvation. These praises increased the expectations of the new student bodies that they could serve a meaningful function in the society. The difficulty was that, while the students were stimulated by what might be termed a continuous series of "commencement addresses," they also found that there was lacking a "placement bureau" in the background that could give practical application to their ambitions. For this reason, many of the intellectuals, driven into intensive study by frustration, found that, even though increasing their intellectual skills, they were still frustrated, because the society could not absorb the products of the new learning.

In the rhetoric of the 1920's, it was common for both Chinese and foreigners to suggest that, as more Chinese received modern professional training, China would have the benefits of these professions. This belief that Western knowledge could be directly transferred to China with results comparable to the West led Y. S. T'ao to argue that an analysis of the fields of specialty of Chinese who had received foreign training might suggest the pattern of the future Chinese society.[4] We have used Dr. T'ao's data and the *Who's Who in China* of 1925 to construct Table 9.1, in which we have sought to distinguish between those who, in their subsequent careers, appear to have applied their specialized training, partially applied it, or not applied it professionally.[5]

Although the evidence is not clear cut, the results of this tabulation

TABLE 9.1
USE OF SKILLS AFTER GRADUATION, BY FIELD OF STUDY

Field of Study	Applied	Partially Applied	Not Applied
Engineering	79	30	40
Political Science	17	4	5
Psychology and Philosophy	10	1	1
Law	3	2	7
Education	19	8	8
Business	25	2	8
Agriculture and Botany	11	6	8
Medicine	12	0	1
Journalism	2	0	1
Mathematics and Architecture	7	3	1

seem to suggest that, where the specialized training led to academic roles, there was a relatively higher utilization of the skill, but, where the skill called for careers outside of academic life, there was less chance of applying it. Thus, the skills that called for the most direct involvement in the economy and society tended to produce the highest likelihood of frustration, aside from careers in business.

This is not to say that the Chinese renaissance movement was without substance. The efforts to simplify the Chinese written language were lasting and constituted a positive contribution to Chinese learning, drastically raising the potential for reducing illiteracy in the country. Also, a body of intellectuals who could accept, challenge, and be stimulated by such leading Western thinkers as Bertrand Russell and John Dewey, both of whom spent time in China during the 1920's, cannot be dismissed as lacking in real ability. In spite of obstacles of language and culture, many of the Chinese intellectuals were able to compete favorably with the best students in the West.

However, underlying the entire movement, was a certain quality of unrelatedness to the China scene. Large numbers of the intellectuals, while discovering a stimulus in Western concepts, could find in these new ideas little that was relevant to the immediate problems of China. They apparently found fascination in and eagerly accepted the latest ideas of the West, which might have had significance in an Occidental setting, but they were incapable of reformulating these ideas to be meaningful in terms of Chinese social and political problems.

Some of the intellectuals were driven to the point where they looked with disdain upon Chinese society and sought to mimic Western customs and attitudes. This attitude widened the gap between the world of the scholar and the realm of practical politics. The already existing inclination of the intellectual to seek out purely theoretical problems was intensified, and there was often little relation between the intellectual problems of the scholar and the immediate social and political questions of China. One of the striking ironies of much of the intellectual movement was that the pragmatist John Dewey and the idealist Bertrand Russell were recognized as the philosophers to be followed, while, at the same time, many of their "followers" were unable to practice the teachings of these leaders. A striking number of the intellectuals appeared to find satisfaction in expounding the pragmatic point of view, because, by doing so, they were able to claim, in theory at least, that they were devoting their energies to the practical problems of bettering society. Yet many of the discussions of the works of John Dewey seem to have resulted in reformulating pragmatism into a highly idealized philosophy that showed little relation to the spirit of Dewey.[6]

The consequence of these developments was to reduce the intellectual's interest in the operational aspect of politics. When political expression was necessary, it came through student movements, which, although intensely emotional and capable of great power, never were sufficiently organized and sustained to lead to concrete programs in the political field. For the intellectuals, there was little opportunity to organize for political action. Not only were the scholars too divided in their positions on theory to unite as a single body for political purposes, but such unity would require an organizational structure capable of competing for power, which the intellectuals could not construct.[7]

In the intellectuals' groping for influence, they tended to place their hope in some single structure of power that would be able to dominate the society and effectively enforce policy decisions. This structure would have to carry the "democratic" label and profess the values associated with this concept. However, they had little confidence in the concept of a democratic society as being one in which various groups would have the opportunity to compete freely for control of the government without threat of coercion. Thus, although the ideal of universal suffrage was important to them, the Chinese intellectuals showed little interest in the concept of competing political parties that could give expression to the popular will.[8]

The inability of the *tuchüns* to serve as competing political associations that could effectively command power caused the intellectuals to search for a new single structure of power capable of dominating the politics of China. In this sense, they were emotionally and intellectually prepared for the concept of one-party rule by the Kuomintang. Any form of politics that placed a premium on compromise and adjustment was repugnant to the Chinese intellectuals, and the ability to achieve defined objectives increased the appeal of single-party government.

From this brief review of the intellectuals' reactions to warlordism, it is clear that, in the 1920's, Westernized intellectuals in China experienced many of the frustrations and problems of finding a satisfying role in society that were later to bedevil intellectuals in the postcolonial world. It would seem, therefore, that the source of their problems extended well beyond just the phenomenon of warlordism. They shared, for example, many of the feelings and attitudes that present-day Indian intellectuals manifest in a democratic setting devoid of military domination.

On the other hand, while intellectuals were excluded from an elite role in politics, the operation of the warlord system still left them free to develop in their own sphere. Consequently, China did during that period produce many intellectuals who were highly skilled in their own fields. Technical talent was thus built up, and the Chinese steadily increased their pool of professionally competent men who later did have opportunities to contribute to their nation's development.

At the same time, however, *tuchün*ism decisively broke the old tradition that the best-educated people should dominate government and established the new pattern of intellectuals as technical subordinates of the political class. Thereafter, during both the Nationalist and Communist eras, the Chinese political class has tended to discount the influence of intellectuals and even to be openly anti-intellectual. Possibly the trend was inevitable, for it is doubtful that in any form of modernized China an intellectual class could have ever recaptured the extreme elite role that intellectuals had under the Confucian system. Yet clearly the warlords made a harsher and more decisive break than mere social evolution would have required. They also left the intellectuals more disillusioned about politics than most intellectuals have been in the new states and, hence, more prone to sell their allegiances to one-party rule.

WARLORDS AND THE WORLD OF FINANCE

Whereas the intellectuals had once been the elite in traditional China, the merchant class had always been placed near the bottom of the social hierarchy. But the Western impact had been steadily working to give a greater role to those engaged in commerce and finance. The impact of the Treaty Ports, the demands for industrializing the country, and the obvious problems of stabilizing the economy and raising the standard of living of a traditionally agrarian society had all combined to heighten the prestige of the merchant class.

It is noteworthy that, in the early Republican period, there was a tendency for the scholar and official class to drop many of their old prejudices against the merchants and to recognize that the rising *bourgeoisie* might be a possible ally in the modernization of China. Even the early Communists and radical intellectuals tended to see this group of "national *bourgeoisie*" who had adopted Western practices as a possibly progressive force in the struggle against outmoded traditions.

For these considerations, it is therefore important to review briefly how warlord politics affected the financial world and those who might have played a critical role in the economic development and modernization of China. Again we must add the qualifying note that we shall not attempt a detailed study of the problems of economic development in Republican China but will examine how the system of warlord politics impinged upon the merchant and financial classes.

The financial class could not withdraw from the area of political activity as easily as the intellectuals, because questions of political stability directly affected the conduct of their activities. On the other hand, just as with the intellectuals, their form of power was neither sufficient nor of the right form to operate within a pattern of politics in which violence was prevalent. The dilemma of the merchants was that, possibly even more than the intellectuals, they required peace and stability in order to achieve their objectives, while the only way in which they could effectively influence political developments was to contribute to the military operations of particular *tuchüns*. Thus, the merchant class also found that they were relatively impotent in the field of direct political action.

This impotence was harshly criticized by the foreign business community, which continually insisted that, if only the Chinese merchants would seek to influence political events, China would achieve stability and the country would be conducted in terms of "good business practices." These criticisms rarely recognized the difficulties of the businessman who attempted to operate within the context of the politics of contemporary China and usually assumed that the Chinese merchant was at fault in not seeking to assert the influence he was presumed to possess. The following excerpt from an editorial in the *Peking and Tientsin Times* summarizes the prevailing attitude of the foreign business community:

> It must be considered unfortunate that the Chinese merchant class, while capable of remarkable perseverance in the conduct of trade and industry under the most adverse conditions, does not display the same qualities in politics. . . . The merchants submit without any serious attempt at resistance to the exactions and oppressions of the militarists, year after year. They permit themselves to be blackmailed into making huge and illegal "contributions" towards the support of armies which they know, only too well, constitute a serious menace to their interests. . . . As an organized body they have hitherto abstained from entering into politics, leaving the field clear to the professional politicians. . . . The passivity of the Chinese merchant class is the most discouraging feature of the present situation. . . . Individually they are shrewd but collectively they are incapable of effective or constructive effort. . . . They almost invariably prefer indirect and therefore unsatisfactory means of working for their particular ends.[9]

In general, this appears to be a valid statement of the merchant's position in respect to the political scene, but it overlooks several important aspects of the role of the merchants. The difficulties the modern merchants faced in attempting to unite were more than just temperamental and traditional antipathy toward political action.[10] It should be recognized that not all of them were affected in the same manner by the politics of the *tuchüns*, and the reasons for their attitudes therefore differed. In particular, the Chinese business class of the period can be divided into two separate groups. On the one hand, there were those engaged in trade and commerce along Western lines who had close associations with the foreign firms in the Treaty Ports. These men were developing a modern structure of business and financial relations closely modeled after Western practices, and they depended upon developments in the foreign trade field. These might be called the new commercial

elite. On the other hand, there were the traditional merchants and banking groups, which tended to adhere to the old Chinese practices.

For the first group, *tuchün* politics had little immediate effect. They
operated in terms of the exchange value of the Chinese silver dollar and
the general condition of international trade. It is significant that the
fluctuations of the exchange value of the Chinese *yuan* showed little
correlation with the activities of the *tuchüns* and, even during the serious fighting near Shanghai in 1924, the Chinese dollar remained amaz-
ingly strong.[11] Instead, the value of the Chinese dollar showed a far
closer correlation to the fluctuation in the world price of silver and the
economic activities of the United States and Great Britain.[12]

These businessmen were remarkably immune to the vicissitudes of
Chinese politics, and they found in the world silver market an impersonal
force permitting them to operate on a level quite removed from that of
the *tuchüns*. That both the commercial community and the political
power-holders agreed that, in general, the value of the Chinese dollar in
foreign exchange should be protected from the tampering of political
action further served to divorce these two fields.[13]

The one principal complaint of the modern merchant group was that
the conflicts of the *tuchüns* disrupted transportation and interfered with
commercial transactions. This resulted in impeding the movement of
exports to the port cities and forced the distributors to refuse to purchase
imports for transshipment into the interior.[14] Although this did lead to
temporary disruptions of business activities, it did not provoke any
general decline with long-run effects. In fact, most of the modern Chinese business firms followed a policy of hedging against such crises by
moving goods and raw materials to storage centers near the industrial
areas when conflicts appeared imminent.[15] In fact, the expansion of
Chinese international trade during this period would tend to indicate
that *tuchün* politics had not seriously hampered the operations of this
phase of Chinese economic life.[16] Although not all members of the new
economic elite were engaged directly in foreign trade, all were closely
associated with the structure of finance, which depended upon foreign
commerce.

The difficulties confronted by these groups were far more fundamental than the immediate issue of *tuchün* politics. The problem for
them was not so much the need for a stable government, as the necessity for a complete transformation of Chinese society, which would
be capable of supporting a far more diversified and industrialized program. The new economic elite could expect substantial assistance from
the politicians only if there was a sweeping change in Chinese politics
and the establishment of an effective government, with the maintenance
of "favorable" commercial treaties with foreign powers and the raising
of the general standard of living among its objectives. Since this was

patently out of the question, these groups sought by and large to remove themselves from the political arena.

The only political area in which this commercial elite was of critical importance was that of the conduct of financial administration. Here this group served as technicians in the ministry of finance and in such semigovernmental institutions as the Bank of China and the Bank of Agriculture and Commerce. So long as the *tuchüns* were able to obtain what they considered sufficient returns from these institutions, they were willing to grant a high degree of independence to the new financial elite. However, this arrangement created a situation in which the new economic elite, although frequently serving in the government, was generally aloof from the major political developments. They were not called upon to identify themselves personally with any particular leader and, therefore, were not drawn into the political process. When they assumed public office, they did so as administrators with limited authority in the fields with which they were particularly concerned and not as individuals who had broader interest in political developments. Although the members of this elite were relatively capable and respected administrators, they did not constitute a political check on the power of the *tuchüns*.

In sharp contrast, the second group of businessmen, composed of those elements of the commercial community who still followed traditional business practices and constituted the vast majority of merchants and businessmen, found that they could not escape so easily from the consequences of warlord politics. These merchants lacked the advantage of operating in terms of a currency that was above political manipulation. Rather, they utilized in their businesses local provincial currencies and various forms of bank credits. It has been estimated that there were over twenty-six major types of paper currency in circulation in China during the 1920's, and, in addition, there were innumerable forms of bank notes issued by the native banks employed in local commerce.[17]

These currencies were far from sound even before the advent of warlordism.[18] Chinese bankers had traditionally preferred to operate on the basis of personal relations rather than in terms of an impersonal money market. This feature of personal relations in Chinese business was similar to the personal form of politics characteristic of the traditional society. The difficulty was that, with the development of *tuchün* politics, it was impossible for the merchants to function as they traditionally had done. The system of independent bank-note issues placed the local bankers under the pressure of the *tuchüns* who could force them to issue unbacked notes for the maintenance of the armies.

The result was that those merchants who operated primarily in terms of local currencies found that they were at the mercy of the *tuchüns*. Not only did the demands of the military leaders affect the value of the currencies, but the political policies and the successes and failures of the individual leaders could cause wide fluctuations in the value of the provincial currencies. In June, 1926, when Wu P'ei-fu's political power appeared to be declining, because of the increase in the Fengtien influence in the Yangtze area, the value of the currency within Wu's area of jurisdiction dropped more than 30 per cent.[19] When the Anfu faction was defeated in 1920, the currency Hsü Shu-cheng ("Little Hsü") had backed declined in value as much as 90 per cent.[20] Possibly one of the strongest of the provincial currencies was the *feng piao*, used in Manchuria.[21] However, even this currency fluctuated with the policies of Chang Tso-lin, declining in value with each major campaign.[22]

The dilemma of the local merchants had two aspects: On the one hand, the *tuchüns* were their largest debtors, and the businessmen therefore had a vested interest in the successes of the particular leader who controlled the area; on the other hand, the policies the *tuchüns* were forced to follow to maintain their power caused a severe drain on the resources of the small merchants. Thus, the merchant groups found that they were being forced to pay exorbitant rates to the *tuchüns* while not obtaining genuine security in return.

The merchant groups reacted to this situation by entering into closer associations with each other, and this increased the importance of such organizations as the chambers of commerce and local guilds. In their efforts to organize for political action, the merchants had varying degrees of success, and it is impossible to generalize about the developments in all sections of China. In some areas, the efforts to unite the merchants made it easier for the local *tuchün* to apply pressure on the entire group, because he now could present his demands to a single organization representing all of the merchants. This appears to have been particularly true of the chamber of commerce in Hankow, which Wu P'ei-fu had little difficulty in controlling. Even after its effort to strengthen its political influence during the temporary decline of Wu in 1924, Wu, upon his return to politics, easily regained his domination. Also, after the defeat of Chao Ti, the local chambers of commerce and the trade guilds in Kaifeng (Honan) joined together to increase their political power, but, when Feng Yü-hsiang assumed control of the province, he found that this reorganization of the local merchants made it relatively easy for him to apply effective pressure on the local commercial community.

In other areas, the merchant groups began to exert a greater degree of direct and organized pressure on political events than at any previous time. These groups not only established offices in Peking but also were active in provincial politics. Frequently they served as mediators in the conflicts among the *tuchüns* of the area. The Kiangsu guilds and chambers of commerce appear to have been particularly effective. In March, 1921, these organizations expanded their representation at Peking and sought to enter directly into the political conflicts at the capital. The

Anhwei gentry organized itself into the Anhwei Self-Government Association and sought not only to influence developments in Peking and Shanghai, but also engaged in a policy of seeking to persuade other provincial merchant groups to organize for political action. There were two main chambers of commerce for the Shanghai area. One represented the larger, modern commercial groups, and the other supported the interests of the native merchants. These groups, when they united, managed to influence the policies of all the leaders who controlled Shanghai and were particularly successful in keeping conflicts from the environs of Shanghai.

Thus, just as the politics of the *tuchüns* had driven both the intellectuals and the modern commercial elite out of the arena of politics, it forced the merchant elements to attempt to organize in self-defense and to enter the political arena. What is particularly significant is that not all of these efforts by the merchant groups to influence political events followed the traditional pattern of seeking only "favors" from those in power but included actual efforts to assume power themselves. This was particularly evident in their attempts to dominate the provincial assemblies and thus to attempt to control the formal offices of government.

The *North China Herald*, of December 18, 1925, observed in an editorial that there had been a striking change in the memberships of most of the provincial assemblies. Most of the members of these assemblies now consisted of representatives of organized chambers of commerce or guilds, whereas previously the delegates had primarily been either members of the old bureaucracy or individuals with personal prestige and wealth but who were without affiliation to any particular organization. It is impossible to tell on what grounds this observation was made and exactly how far such a change had progressed. It is significant that, in 1921, the Kiangsu chambers of commerce were successful in dominating the provincial assembly and initiating a campaign for provincial autonomy.[23] Also, at the same time, much the same development took place in Shantung.[24]

From this review of the effects of warlord politics on the intellectual and the business communities, it would appear that the intellectuals had a more difficult time adjusting to competitive politics, even though, in their professional domain, they were free to improve themselves. Yet, at the same time, it is important to recognize that this degree of freedom to escape from politics represented a singular departure in the relationship of politics to society in China. Previously the world of officialdom always felt that it had the right and obligation to penetrate all spheres of life and particularly to declare what was or was not officially acceptable in the realm of thought and political philosophy. After the relative openness of the competitive politics of the warlord period, China again returned to a more monolithic system, which brought a different kind of hardship on the intellectuals.

Similarly, some elements of the business community found that they could operate with a respectable degree of political freedom in spite of the warlord system. Other elements showed signs of adapting to the logic of competitive politics and began to organize themselves into embryonic pressure groups. In spite of the violence and the extremely costly character of the competitive politics of the warlord system, which were particularly threatening to the relatively vulnerable businessman, they were beginning to operate as a modern interest group. The very competitiveness gave them some advantages, which they were soon to lose when confronted with the more monolithic political power of the Nationalists and even more the Communists.

10. CONCLUDING REMARKS

In this study of a confused and relatively neglected period of Chinese history, I have sought to do three things. First, I have endeavored to clarify the relations among the warlords and show that they were essentially rational men dealing with very complex problems of political survival and adjustment. Second, I have tried to suggest that, by focusing on the problems of power in Chinese society, and analyzing situations according to the "logic of power," it is possible to obtain important insights into both individual political behavior and the behavior of the entire Chinese political system. Third, I have sought to demonstrate that the modernization of China can be usefully viewed as a profound tension between tendencies toward the restoration in modern guise of an essentially monolithic structure and tendencies toward more open and competitive politics, of which the warlords were a principal but not always happy example.

I have not had much to say about the warlords as individuals. Instead, I have accepted them as a diverse group of men who blended traditional Chinese views and modern ideas in about the same proportion as would be expected of a political class that still had roots in a society that was only beginning to modernize. In dwelling mainly on their organizational and power concerns, I have tried to identify the real problems that they saw as governing their behavior and point out that their limitations as modernizers of China were linked to the basic facts of political life in a society in which the traditional forms of power had crumbled. My analysis suggests that little improvement or, for that matter, even significant change would have occurred if the warlords, either individually or collectively, had had different views on questions of public morality and had adopted new ideologies. Their behavior was controlled too much by the nature and distribution of power in the Chinese society of that era to have been greatly influenced by values and objectives unrelated to the requirements of political survival.

The scarcity of power in the Chinese political system after the fall of the Imperial structure forced those who were in any position to be politically influential to adopt attitudes very similar to those common to people living near a poverty level. In their dealings with each other, the warlords were tight-fisted, instinctively suspicious, quick to suspect that their interests might be threatened, and unwilling to take any avoidable risks. The reality of the scarcity of power made them hard-headed, devoted to the short run, and impervious to idealistic abstractions.

These tendencies to emphasize the short run and to suspect compromise as more likely to threaten one's own interests than others' as we have seen, arise not only from the scarcity of power but also from the way it was competitively distributed. The complex balance of power among the warlords compelled them to be highly pragmatic about power, but it did not produce the easily adjustable system that theories of the balance of power suggest as being normal. Instead, the warlords felt the need to stress always extremely short-run calculations so that immediate and often petty advantages outweighed long-run opportunities for greater benefits.

In this respect, the warlords' behavior may be a significant guide to Chinese behavior when confronted with an open, competitive power situation. Clearly, the phenomenon of competition with respect to power was seen by the Chinese as being unhealthy, absurd, and without any redeeming merits as compared with their traditions of a monolithic and hierarchical system of power. The warlords demonstrated that Chinese have no difficulty in responding pragmatically to the realities of competitive power, but their behavior also suggests that Chinese "pragmatism" in such power situations is likely to be hypersensitive to short-run considerations and prone to a sense of great vulnerability.

Thus, although the warlords represented a high point in the development of a pluralistic and diversified power system in modern China, their anxieties about the "unnatural" and uncomfortable characteristics of open, competitive politics emphasizes the pull toward more monolithic and hierarchical arrangements among Chinese. My analysis of the *tuchün* system suggests that it is useful to put as a central question in the study of Chinese political development the extent to which forces have tended to promote either a more monolithic structure of politics or greater group competition for power. Unquestionably, the apparent futility and impotence of much warlord activity caused the vast majority of politically conscious Chinese to reject the concept that a society might maximize freedom and opportunity by maintaining a division of powers and ceaseless competition among groups. Unquestionably, their experience paved the way for the Chinese to welcome the restoration of a more monolithic system. On the other hand, the analysis has indicated that there is considerably less certainty as to whether all elements of the society actually fared badly with the emergence of a form of competitive politics.

By stressing the structure of power, whether it tends to be competitive or monolithic, I have shifted the customary focus in the study of modern China away from issues of ideology and the value conflicts that accompanied "the Western impact" and toward the realities of power and the considerations that have governed the organizational basis of those most effective in politics. Those who came after the warlords certainly had more potent ideologies, but, probably even more important, they had enough strength to bring China back to a more unified and monolithic structure of politics. And possibly the realities that followed from these more monopolistic power arrangements have been more important than the particular ideologies of the Nationalists and the Communists in preventing China from becoming more democratic politically.

The cost to China of the inability of the warlords to produce a more satisfactory system of competitive politics involved more than just producing a craving for one-party rule and general disillusionment with pluralistic politics. The warlords established the fact that in modern China political power cannot be divorced from military power. The power of the warlords rested upon their armies, and they could only be destroyed by those who had stronger armies. And, so far, no one has been able to discover the secret of how to remove armies from the center of the Chinese political scene.

The warlords thus contributed to the continuing emphasis upon the role of violence in modern Chinese politics. They showed that the mere expectation that violence would be decisive in influencing events was enough to keep many elements out of Chinese politics. This tendency encouraged a passive attitude on the part of citizens and a general inclination to follow docilely the dictates of the "logic of violence"—that is, to accept the requirements of expediency and support whomever had the military preponderance of force.

The analysis of *tuchün* politics thus serves as a key to understanding many of the fundamental features of modern Chinese politics. Within the maze of *tuchün* politics can be found all the domestic issues and conflicts in modern Chinese society. These issues, when they became a part of the political struggle, were never clear cut, and the development of modern Chinese society did not follow a definite pattern toward any established goal. Many of the actions designed to bring about a new and more Westernized society produced in their wake a strengthening of the old qualities of Chinese society, whereas many avowed attempts to reassert the traditions of the old society tended to weaken the monolithic quality of Chinese culture. The struggle in Chinese society over social values has not been able to proceed without regard for the implications of power. Behind all issues has lain the question of power, and, in Chinese society, the distribution of power has not been conducive to the development of positive political programs.

On balance, the warlords probably contributed more to the modernization of China than critics of their day recognized. Compared with military rule in some of the new states, that of the *tuchüns* permitted greater freedom for future-oriented groups to improve themselves. On the other hand, the warlords' failure to provide the Chinese with a more tolerable and respectable system of rule also set back whatever chances there may have been for China to develop a more open, competitive, and democratic system of government.

NOTES

Chapter 1

1. Discussions of the attitudes and behavioral patterns of the Chinese peasant are to be found in such anthropological studies as Martin C. Yang, *A Chinese Village* (New York: Columbia University Press, 1945); Lin Yüeh-Nwa, *The Golden Wing* (New York: Oxford University Press, 1948); Olga Lang, *Chinese Society and Family* (New Haven, Conn.: Yale University Press, 1946); and, particularly, Francis L. K. Hsü, *Under the Ancestors' Shadow* (New York: Columbia University Press, 1948). Hsü, in ch. X, attempts to describe a basic personality configuration based on a modified form of the Linton-Kardiner hypothesis. A traditional study is Arthur H. Smith, *Village Life in China* (New York: Revell, 1899).
2. See Max Weber, *The Theory of Social and Economic Organization*, tr., A. M. Henderson and Talcott Parsons (New York: Oxford University Press, 1947), pp. 333–36.
3. See Ch'ao-ting Chi, *Key Economic Areas in Chinese History as Revealed in the Development of Public Works for Water Control* (New York: P. Smith, 1936).
4. For the most complete general study of a secret society (the Triad Society), see J. S. M. Ward and W. G. Sterling, *The Hung Society, or the Society of Heaven and Earth* (London: Baskerville Press Ltd., 1925), 2 vols.; see also T'ai-ch'u Liao, "The Ko Lao Hui in Szechuan," *Pacific Affairs* XX, no. 2 (June, 1947), 161–73.
5. For a study of the Chinese civil service system, see Pao Chao Hsieh, *The Government of China, 1644–1911* (Baltimore: Johns Hopkins Press, 1925), ch. 6; and Etienne Zi, *Pratique des examens littéraires en Chine* (*The Literary Examination Practice in China*) (Variétés Sinologiques) (Shanghai: Mission Catholique, 1894), no. 5, especially pp. 34–39.

Chapter 2

1. For material on the programs and policies of Yüan Shih-k'ai in developing the Peiyang Army, see Wen Kung-chih, *Tsui-chin' San-shih-nien Chung-kuo Chünshih Shih* (*History of Chinese Military Affairs in the Last Thirty Years*) (Shanghai, 1930), 2 vols., vol. 1, book I, pp. 39–60 and vol. 1, book II, pp. 1–14; Shen Chien, "Hsin-hai Ko-ming Ch'ien-hsi Wo-kuo Chih Lu-chun Chi Ch'i Chun-fei" ("The Chinese Army and Its Finances on the Eve of the 1911 Revolution") *She-hui K'o-hsüeh* (*The Social Sciences*) III, no. 2 (Jan., 1937); Raphael Verbrugge, *Yuan Che-k'ai, sa vie, son temps* (Paris, 1904). For the report of a Western observer, see William de la Tour (Lord Charles Beresford), *The Break-up of China* (New York and London: Harper, 1899).
2. For discussions of the Chinese armies developed during the Taiping Rebellion, see Lo Erh-kang, *Hsiang-chün Hsin-chih* (*New Gazetteer of the Hunan Army*) (Shanghai, 1937); W. L. Bales, *Tso Tsung-t'ang, Soldier and Statesman of Old*

China (Shanghai: Kelly and Walsh, 1937); W. J. Hail, *Tseng Kuo-fan and the Taiping Rebellion* (New Haven, Conn.: Yale University Press, 1927); and Arthur W. Hummel, ed., *Eminent Chinese of the Ch'ing Period* (Washington, D.C.: U.S. Government Printing Office, 1943).

3. Wang Shih-chen took little part in the later politicomilitary developments and finally retired from public life in 1918.

4. The split within the Peiyang Army was accelerated by the decision of the Throne to decentralize the army because of financial considerations. By moving parts of the army out of Chihli Province, the Throne could obtain the financial support of the other provinces. Wen Kung-chih, *op. cit.*, vol. I, book 2, pp. 3–4.

5. For discussions of the last efforts of the Manchus to retain authority and of Yüan's position, see John Gilbert Reid, *The Manchu Abdication and the Powers, 1908–1912* (Berkeley: University of California Press, 1935), chs. XII and XIII; and J. O. P. Bland, *Recent Events and the Present Policies of China* (London: William Heinemann, 1912).

6. Wen Kung-chih, *op. cit.*, vol. I, book 1, p. 8.

7. For accounts of Yüan's maneuvering, see Harley F. MacNair, *China in Revolution* (Chicago: University of Chicago Press, 1931), pp. 34–35; and Stanley K. Hornbeck, *Contemporary Politics in the Far East* (New York: Appleton, 1916), chs. V and VI.

8. In 1911, Li Yüan-hung was a colonel in the Imperial forces at Hankow and had, somewhat against his will, been forced to support the revolutionary cause. He represented the strongest military commander whom the group under the leadership of Sun Yat-sen felt they could control. Thus he became an ideal compromise for the Vice-Presidency when it was decided that Yüan Shih-k'ai should be President. See MacNair, *op. cit.*, pp. 37–38.

9. For discussion of the issue of China's entry into World War I, see Thomas LaFargue, *China and the World War* (Stanford, Calif.: Stanford University Press, 1937); W. R. Wheeler, *China and the World War* (New York: Macmillan, 1919); and Putnam Weale (B. Lenox Simpson), *The Fight for the Republic of China* (New York: Dodd, Mead, 1917), chs. XIV–XVI.

10. MacNair, *op. cit.*, p. 48.

11. The *coup d'état* and the dissolution of Parliament led directly to the establishment of the Canton government. The Kuomintang members of Parliament moved to Canton and, there, depending on the strength of the southern *tuchüns*, formed the southern regime, of which Sun Yat-sen, in 1921, was elected President. From this time on, one of the main issues in the politics of the northern warlords was the problem of relations with the South. See Chapters 4 and 5 of this volume.

12. Wen Kung-chih, *op. cit.*, vol. I, book 2, pp. 8–9.

13. For discussion of the activities of the Chinese Parliament during this period, see Harold M. Vinacke, *Modern Constitutional Development in China* (Princeton, N.J., Princeton University Press, 1922), especially pp. 141–47; and Paul M. A. Linebarger, *Government in Republican China* (New York: McGraw-Hill, 1938), pp. 155–60.

14. For the early history of the Chihli faction, see Wen Kung-chih, *op cit.*, vol. I, book 2, pp. 11–29; and *The China Year Book 1924–1925*, ed., H. G. W. Woodhead (Tientsin: Tientsin Press, 1925), pp. 1179–81.

15. For an account of Chinese attitudes toward Anfu policies, see *North China Herald*, May 10, 1919, pp. 348–49.

16. For an interesting, if overly optimistic, interpretation of the potential role of students in the May Fourth Movement by one of its inspirational leaders, who happened to be in Peking at the time, see John Dewey, "The Student Revolt in China," *New Republic* XX (Aug. 6, 1919).

17. Wen Kung-chih, *op. cit.*, vol. I, book 2, p. 11.

18. *North China Herald*, May 29, 1920, p. 506.

19. For discussion of Japan's economy at this time, see Chitoshi Yanaga, *Japan Since Perry* (New York: McGraw-Hill, 1949), pp. 379–97.

20. *New York Times*, Jan. 30, 1920, p. 19.

21. Wen Kung-chih, *op. cit.*, vol. I, book 1, p. 11.
22. Feng Yü-hsiang, *Feng Yü-hsiang Jih-chi* (*The Diary of Feng Yü-hsiang*) (Peiping, 1930), 2 vols., vol. I, book 1, p. 7. This work will hereafter be cited as Feng's *Diary*.
23. Feng Kuo-chang, after his failure to be re-elected to the Presidency, retired to Central China in ill health and died on January 2, 1920. (*New York Times*, Jan. 3, 1920, p. 11.)
24. For the history of the early period of Chang Tso-lin's career, see Wen Kung-chih, *op cit.*, vol. I, book 2, pp. 49–100.
25. *North China Herald*, June 18, 1920, p. 184.
26. H. G. W. Woodhead, *Occidental Interpretations of the Far Eastern Problem* (Harris Foundation Lecture, 1925) (Chicago: University of Chicago Press, 1926), p. 33. Liang Shih-i had been a supporter of Chang Hsün's and was generally regarded as loyal to the Manchu Imperial Family. As a result of this, the Chihli faction was able to exploit this sentiment by identifying the policies of Chang Tso-lin as intended to achieve a Manchu restoration. See Chapters 4 and 5 of this volume.
27. Wen Kung-chih, *op. cit.*, vol. II, book 3, p. 118.
28. For the details of the first Chihli-Fengtien war, see Wen Kung-chih, *op. cit.*, vol. II, book 3, pp. 115–32.
29. Feng Yü-hsiang understood Wu's objectives in moving him to Peking, but Feng also felt that Wu was interested in removing him from Honan, where he might, if allowed to remain there, have threatened Wu's supreme control over that area, which was his central base of power (Feng's *Diary*, book 4, p. 30.)
30. MacNair, *op. cit.*, pp. 52–53.
31. See Chapter 4 of this volume.
32. The Parliament that was reconvened was the so-called Old Parliament, which had been first formed in 1912 under Yüan Shih-k'ai. Because this body included representatives of the Kuomintang, it was hoped that, by calling it back into session, it would be possible to bring the Canton regime into cooperation with the Peking government. Vinacke, *op. cit.*, pp. 156–57.
33. For details on the financial problems of the Peking government and how they affected the actions of the *tuchüns*, see Chapters 8 and 9 of this volume.
34. President Li was able temporarily to strengthen his position as a result of developments in the field of foreign affairs. On March 10, 1923, a decision was made by President Li to send a note to Tokyo demanding the cancellation of the remaining terms of the Treaty of 1915 (Twenty-one Demands). The rejection of the note by the Japanese Government was followed by a major boycott of Japanese goods entering China. Although the boycott was a spontaneous and popular movement without official inspiration or organization, the President sought to identify himself with the public sentiment and claim credit for the movement. For the organization and effectiveness of Chinese boycotts, see Charles F. Remer, *A Study of Chinese Boycotts* (Baltimore: Johns Hopkins Press, 1933).
35. Feng's *Diary*, book 5, pp. 57–59.
36. *Ibid.*, pp. 56, 64.
37. Woodhead, *op. cit.*, p. 37.
38. *North China Herald*, Aug. 11, 1923, p. 371.
39. *Ibid.*, Oct. 27, 1923, p. 226.
40. For an interview with Ts'ao K'un, see *North China Herald*, Aug. 4, 1923, p. 300.
41. Although no accurate records are available, it was generally believed that Ts'ao K'un spent $15,000,000 (silver) to "win" the election. (MacNair, *op. cit.*, p. 54.)
42. See Chapter 6 of this volume.
43. *North China Herald*, Dec. 29, 1923, p. 873.
44. Wen Kung-chih, *op. cit.*, vol. II, book 3, p. 181.
45. For discussion of the importance of Shanghai and Chekiang, see Chapter 6 of this volume.

46. Feng's *Diary*, book 6, p. 96.
47. *Ibid.*, pp. 100–102.
48. For the organization of Lu Yung-hsiang's armies and the nature of the revolt, see Chapter 5 of this volume.
49. On the campaigns and fighting in the Chekiang-Kiangsu war, see *North China Herald*, Aug. 30 and Sept. 6, 1924; on the devastation caused by the fighting and troop movements, see *Chiang-su Ping-tsai Tiao-ch'a Chi-shih (Factual Record of a Survey of the War Devastation in Kiangsu)*, ed., Fu Huan-kuang (Shanghai, 1924).
50. Feng's *Diary*, book 6, pp. 100–102; MacNair, *op. cit.*, p. 56.
51. For an analysis of the strategic and political problems peculiar to those *tuchüns* who, like Feng Yü-hsiang, had no secure geographic base, see Chapter 3 of this volume.
52. Feng's *Diary*, book 6, p. 111.
53. For the details of the campaigns of the second Chihli-Fengtien war, see Wen Kung-chih, *op. cit.*, vol. II, book 3, pp. 180–205; and *North China Herald*, Aug. 30 and Sept. 6, 1924.
54. Feng himself, in his *Diary*, mentioned all of these considerations but primarily defended his actions in terms of a strong moral denunciation of Wu P'ei-fu for instigating a costly war that could only weaken China. (Feng's *Diary*, book 6, pp. 113–15.) For an account of the personal break between these two men, which had been developing since 1920, see Chapter 3 of this volume.
55. Wen Kung-chih, *op. cit.*, vol. II, book 3, p. 187.
56. The *North China Herald* of November 1, 1924, gives the report of a personal interview with Wu P'ei-fu at the Shanhaikuan front.
57. The terms of the abdication of the Manchu dynasty included the stipulation (Article 2) that the Throne was to receive an annuity of $4,000,000. The Articles of Favorable Treatment are published in Putnam Weale (B. L. Simpson), *The Fight for the Republic of China* (New York, 1912), pp. 399–400.
58. For the formation and organization of the Kuominchün, see Chapter 3 of this volume.
59. Since 1917, Sun Yat-sen had been seeking the support of various northern warlords who were temporarily out of power but who had prospects of regaining control of the Peking government. Thus, he first had contacts with the defeated Anfuites after 1920, and later he negotiated with Chang Tso-lin. The appeals of Feng, Chang, and Tuan were sufficient to interest Sun in making the trip to the North.
60. Feng also had made preliminary negotiations with Tuan Ch'i-jui before he carried out his *coup d'état*. (Feng's *Diary*, book 6, p. 115.)
61. For details on the results of the Tientsin Conference, see *The China Year Book 1925–26*, *op. cit.*, p. 847.
62. *North China Herald*, Nov. 1, 1924, p. 175.
63. See Chapter 3 of this volume.
64. For a report, based on Russian sources, of this conference, see Louis Fischer, *The Soviets in World Affairs* (London: Jonathan Cape, 1930), 2 vols., vol. II, pp. 648–50. Feng himself minimized the importance of the Borodin meeting. (Feng's *Diary*, book 7, p. 25.)
65. See Dorothy Borg, *American Policy and the Chinese Revolution, 1925–1928* (New York: Macmillan, 1947), ch. 2.
66. *The China Year Book, 1926–27*, p. 1023.
67. For a discussion of the Kuo Sung-ling revolt, see Chapter 4 of this volume.
68. The popular belief at the time was that Japan was unofficially supporting Kuo Sung-ling. See *The China Year Book, 1926–27*, *op. cit.*, p. 1028. However, there is little evidence to support this belief. See Chapter 3 of this volume.
69. The Japanese statement is to be found in *The China Year Book, 1926–27*, p. 1027.
70. *Ibid.*, p. 1029.
71. Feng's *Diary*, book 7, p. 54.
72. For Feng's relations with Russia, see Chapter 3 of this volume.

73. *The China Year Book, 1926–27*, p. 1032.
74. Text of note in *The China Year Book, 1926–27*, p. 1032.
75. *New York Times*, March 19, 1926, p. 4.
76. *Feng's Diary*, book 7, p. 73.
77. *New York Times*, March 20, 1926, p. 6.
78. *Ibid.*, April 16, 1926, p. 4.

CHAPTER 3

1. Wolfram Eberhard, *A History of China* (Berkeley: University of California Press, 1950), pp. 102–05. However, it was at the end of the T'ang that the problem became especially serious, as the autonomous position of the military leaders was institutionalized by the granting of official posts to them without establishing any formal controls over their actions. The leading military commanders were given the title of Chao-t'ao Shih. (Robert des Rotours, *Traité des Fonctionnaires et traité de l'armée, traduits de la nouvelle histoire des T'ang* [Leyde: E. J. Brill, 1948], p. 650ff.) The autonomy of these "Pacifiers of Rebels" was ensured by the system of the Hsing-ying, or traveling headquarters, which had their own Chüeh-tu Shih or administrative officers (des Rotours, *op. cit.*, p. 716) and their own methods of collecting taxes. (For historical examples of these practices, see *The Cheng Shih*, K'ai-ming edition, pp. 3505.c and 4199.b.)
2. See Chapter 7 of this volume.
3. *Lu-chun Hsing-cheng Chi-yao* (*An Account of Important Aspects of Army Administration*), ed., published, Lu-chun Pu (Ministry of War) (Peking, 1916), 4 vols., vol. 1, ch. 2, pp. 1–2.
4. *Ibid.*, vol. 1, ch. 3, p. 2.
5. Chiang T'ing-fu, *Chung-kuo Chin Tai-shih* (*History of Modern China*) (Changsha, 1938), pp. 47–48.
6. U.S., Department of State 893.01A/56. The attention reserved for purely military affairs and training further reflects the fact that the key to the *tuchün*'s success in the political arena was the effectiveness of the troops under his command.
7. *Far Eastern Times* (Peking), Sept. 15, 1923, p. 2, quoting charges listed in the Tientsin *Ta Kung Pao* of unspecified date.
8. The ability to command the loyalties of military forces was still important for the members of this third group because seniority and prestige were not sufficient, as can be seen from the fact that the College of Marshals was never important in the relations of the *tuchüns* and was therefore insignificant in Chinese politics. The College of Marshals was established in 1912 and consisted of seventy of the highest ranking military officers in the country. (*Lu-chün Hsing-cheng Chi-yao, op. cit.*, vol. I, ch. 3, p. 5.) The original intention was that the college should serve as a body of elder statesmen in advising the government, much as the *genro* and *jushin* functioned in Japan. However, it was never more than a roll of honor and at no time held any effective power as a group. (U.S., Department of State 893.00/49.)
9. For a factual account of these parties and associations that outlines the policies and leadership of each group, see Hsieh Pin, *Min Kuo Cheng-tang Shih* (*History of Political Parties Under the Republic*) (Shanghai, 1926), especially pp. 11–37; and Ch'ien Tuan-sheng, *The Government and Politics of China* (Cambridge, Mass.: Harvard University Press, 1950), pp. 346–50.
10. See Liu Ch'i-hung, *Political Parties in China* (Peking: Henri Vetch, 1930).
11. For a discussion of the ideology and propaganda efforts of the *tuchüns*, see Chapter 6 of this volume.
12. Captain Anatol M. Kotenev, *The Chinese Soldier* (Shanghai: Kelly and Walsh, 1937), p. 99.
13. W. S. A. Potts, "Demilitarizing Unmilitary China," *Millard's Review* XV, no. 3 (Dec. 18, 1920), p. 46.
14. Feng Yü-hsiang, *Feng Yü-hsiang Jih-chi* (Feng's Diary) (Peiping, 1930), book 7, p. 79; book 2, pp. 8, 10.
15. *North China Herald*, Oct. 16, 1924, p. 178.

16. For a discussion of efforts to subvert the loyalties of subordinate commanders, see Chapter 5 of this volume.

17. Throughout this study, emphasis will be given to the problems that arose out of the necessities and efforts to achieve a more impersonal form of political relationship, given the highly personal form of political and social relations so characteristic of Chinese life. However, it should be noted that these problems are not characteristic solely of Chinese life, and, as more extensive studies have been made of Western institutions, there has been a greater appreciation of the problems of cliques and personal relations in what had been idealized as highly impersonal organizations and relationships. Thus, although the West, with its industrial society, has been characterized as having carried the institutionalization of universalism and impersonal relations further than any other society, it is still true that, even in such societies, there has persisted a high incidence of particularism, albeit in a far more subtle form than found in China. However, as Marion J. Levy (*The Family Revolution in Modern China* [Cambridge, Mass.: Harvard University Press, 1949], pp. 222–23) has pointed out, in the West there are many aspects of life in which universalism has been institutionalized, such as in industry, business, government service, education, and the like, whereas, in China, there was only the bureaucracy, and even the bureaucracy continued to degenerate toward accepting personal and clique considerations. Thus the difference in degree between China and the West was so great as to make the problem really one of a difference in kind. The presence of personal politics in the West, in spite of the stress placed upon universalism, only serves to emphasize the magnitude of the problem as it existed in China.

18. The literature on the Chinese family and its unique and pervasive demands on the individual is legion. The most penetrating works include Marion J. Levy, *op. cit.*; Olga Lang, *The Chinese Family and Society* (New Haven, Conn.: Yale University Press, 1945); F. L. K. Hsü, *Under the Ancestor's Shadow* (New York: Columbia University Press, 1948); Ida Pruitt, *A Daughter of Han* (New Haven, Conn.: Yale University Press, 1945); H. Wilkinson, *The Family in Classical China* (Shanghai: Kelly and Walsh, 1926); Lin Yueh-hwa, *The Golden Wing* (New York: Oxford University Press, 1948).

19. Wen Kung-chih, *Tsui-chin San-shih-nien Chung-kuo Chun-shih Shih* (*History of Chinese Military Affairs in the Last Thirty Years*) (Shanghai, 1930), 2 vols., vol. I, book 2, p. 63.

20. *Ibid.*, p. 88, and U.S., Department of State 893.00/3612.

21. Lawrence Impey, *The Chinese Army as a Military Force* (Tientsin: Tientsin Press, 1926), p. 12.

22. Li Chien-nung, *Tsui-chin San-shih Nien Chung-kuo Cheng-chih Shih* (*Political History of China in the Last Thirty Years*) (Shanghai, 1930), pp. 580–81.

23. Often the commanders would refer to each other in the terms applicable to such familial relationships. In particular, they would call their superiors "elder brother" and themselves "younger brother." See the circular telegram quoted in Sun Yao-pien, *Chung-hua Min-kuo Shih-liao* (*Historical Data on the Chinese Republic*) (Shanghai, 1930), 3 vols., especially vol. III, pp. 161, 169, and 176ff.

24. *North China Herald*, Dec. 15, 1923, p. 737.

25. U.S., Department of State 893.00/4522.

26. *Tung-fang Tso-chih* (*Eastern Miscellany*) 20, no. 10 (May 25, 1925), p. 5.

27. *Feng's Diary*, book 5, p. 142.

28. *Ibid.*, p. 126.

29. U.S., Department of State 893.00/6266.

30. *New York Times*, March 2, 1922, p. 8.

31. U.S., Department of State 893.00/5337.

32. *North China Herald*, Nov. 1, 1924, p. 178.

33. It is significant that Olga Lang (*op. cit.*, pp. 183–95), in investigating the incidence of nepotism in business establishments in China, found that managers felt strongly that relatives were highly inefficient, more demanding than other employees, and could not be called upon to work as hard as the latter, but that

they did have the virtues of being more trustworthy and loyal to the establishment. The policies of the *tuchüns* appear to confirm this conclusion.

34. U.S., Department of State 893.00/5018 (July 7, 1922).
35. *North China Daily News* (Shanghai), April 27, 1923.
36. It is significant that in traditional China there was almost no formal recognition of the legitimacy of sectional or provincial sentiments. The Ch'ing prohibition against the official's serving in his own province typified the Chinese feelings about the impropriety of such sentiments, and the need to repress them rather than to build political life upon them as happened in Europe, America, Japan, and nearly all societies that have developed along democratic lines.
37. U.S., Department of State 893.00/6358 (Dec. 15, 1923).
38. F. C. H. Dryer, "Yen Hsi-shan: A Progressive Governor," *Chinese Recorder*, vol. 51 (1920), p. 461.
39. Wu Liao-tzu (pseudonym), *Hsien-tai Chih Chang Tso-lin* (*The Present-Day Chang Tso-lin*) (Shanghai, 1924), p. 30. The author of this volume used the pseudonym "The Dejected One." By and large, he gives a fairly objective account of Chang Tso-lin's policies, but he did hold a bias favorable to Chang and regretted that Chang had not been able to achieve greater successes in bringing unity to China.
40. The large migrations of peasants from overpopulated Shantung to Manchuria, which commenced with the fall of the Ch'ing government, provided a source of manpower for the Fengtien armies, as many of the Shantungese failed to find in Manchuria the hoped-for opportunities to procure new farm land. Also the land speculators in Manchuria were able to defraud sufficient numbers to force them into accepting the military service. Walter H. Mallory, *China: Land of Famine* (New York: American Geographical Society, 1926), p. 72; and Franklin L. Ho, "Population Movement to Manchuria," *Chinese Political and Social Science Review* XIV, no. 3 (Oct., 1931). That the Shantung peasants were aware of the dangers of being conscripted into the Fengtien armies is attested to by the fact that, when it was apparent that Fengtien was about to launch a military campaign, there was a sharp decline in the movement of peasants from Shantung to Manchuria. (U.S., Department of State 893.00/6372.)
41. Li Chien-nung, *op. cit.*, p. 601.
42. T'ao Chü-yin, *Wu P'ei-fu Chiang-chun Chuan* (*Biography of General Wu P'ei-fu*) (Shanghai, 1941), p. 29.
43. Of Feng's ten leading subordinates, four were natives of Chihli; Shensi and Honan were each represented by two officers; and the others were from Fengtien and Anhwei. (Pai Ying-hsing and Chin Yu-k'un, *Kuo-min-chun Shih-kao* [*Draft History of the Kuominchün*] [Peking, 1930], pp. 99–100, 157, 173.) Feng himself states that he sought to follow such a policy in order to ensure uncompromising loyalty to himself. (Feng's *Diary*, book 3, p. 12.)
44. Feng's *Diary*, book 3, p. 26.
45. *Ibid.*, pp. 13, 19, 22.
46. *North China Herald*, Oct. 14, 1922, p. 164.
47. *Ibid.*, Sept. 6, 1924, p. 363.
48. *Ibid.*, Sept. 20, 1924, p. 452.
49. U.S., Department of State 893.00/7108. A further discussion of the difficulties the *tuchüns* confronted in attempting to direct troops who were natives of different provinces is offered in Chapter 5 of this volume.
50. Lo Erh-kang, *Hsiang-chun Hsin-chih* (*New Gazetteer of the Hunan Army*) (Shanghai, 1938), p. 15.
51. U.S., Department of State 893.00/5482.
52. Wen Kung-chih, *op cit.*, vol. I, book 2, pp. 49–50.
53. *Ibid.*, p. 52.
54. U.S., Department of State 893.00/3748; 893.00/6108; 893.00/6586.
55. *North China Daily News*, Sept. 11, 1925, pp. 4–5.
56. U.S., Department of State 893.00/6108.
57. Wen Kung-chih, *op. cit.*, vol. I, book 2, pp. 62–63. For further discussion of the Kuo revolt, see Chapter 4 of this volume.

58. Chang also faced further difficulties of a similar nature when he commenced to incorporate large numbers of White Russian officers and men into his armies. This was an additional factor in increasing tensions, because the Russians were active in the formulation of plans for the campaigns of 1924. (U.S., Department of State 893.00/5904.)

59. *North China Herald*, Nov. 1, 1924, p. 178.

60. T'ao Chü-yin, *op. cit.*, p. 109.

61. *North China Herald*, Nov. 8, 1924, p. 214, gives the text of circular telegrams issued by Wu's supporters.

62. *Tung-fang Tsa-chih* XXI, no. 23 (Dec. 10, 1924), p. 3. The local leaders appeared to have been put off-balance by Wu's unexpected announcement. They hesitated to deny any knowledge of the plans until they were certain of Wu's potentials and the attitudes of the other Yangtze leaders. (Li Chien-nung, *op. cit.*, p. 591.)

63. T'ao Chü-yin, *op. cit.*, pp. 125–26.

64. *Ibid.*, p. 130. The Fengtien commander, Chang Tsung-ch'ang, at this point did issue a circular telegram stating that "I, Chang Tsung-ch'ang, am a Shantung man, and you, Marshal Wu, are also a Shantung man. Shantung men do not fight Shantung men. I want to place myself under your command, and change my Fengtien Army into a Shantung Army. I welcome your return to Shantung. . . ." (*Ibid.*, p. 133, author's trans.) The telegram was degrading to Wu P'ei-fu because it suggested that he was so weak that his former enemies were willing to accept him as a subordinate without fear that he would become a disruptive element in their organization.

65. U.S., Department of State 893.00/5988.

66. *Central China Post* (Hankow), Dec. 5, 1924. Although Hsiao's words may sound hollow, it should be remembered that Wu had lost his military power at this time, and thus the deference shown him was to some degree sincere.

67. U.S., Department of State 893.00/6765.

68. U.S., Department of State 893.00/6141.

69. U.S., Department of State 893.00/6826. Even a large group of strictly political officials joined the bandwagon, including Wellington Koo.

70. Feng's *Diary*, book 2, pp. 2, 3, 10; book 4, p. 43; book 5, p. 138. Feng also received tutelage in the works of the classical military writers such as Sun Wu and Yang Fang. See book 4, p. 40. Yang Fang and Yang Yü-chun were both distinguished writers of military treatises. (Hummel, *op. cit.*, vol. II, pp. 884–85.)

71. Wu Liao-tzu, *op. cit.*, p. 24.

72. U.S., Department of State 893.00/4010 (Aug. 23, 1922).

73. U.S., Department of State 893.00/5378. Chang Tso-lin employed a scholar, Chang Hsüan-hsiang, to maintain relations with the Anfu group before 1920. (*Ibid.*, 893.00/3748.)

74. For a frank discussion of the dilemma of the Western-trained man, see L. K. Tao, "Unemployment Among Intellectual Workers in China," *Chinese Social and Political Science Review*, 13 (1929), pp. 251–356; Y. S. Tsao, "A Challenge to Western Learning," *News Bulletin*, Institute of Pacific Relations, Dec., 1927; and Chapter 8 of this volume.

75. This fact is well illustrated in *Chung-hua Min-kuo Ming-jen Chuan* (*Biographies of Famous Men of the Republic of China*) (Peking, 1932), pp. 13, 22, 43, 45, 56, *passim*. It is striking to observe, of the careers of Western-trained men in this work, how often they followed a similar path to prominence, in that they established contacts by initially serving in the administration of some *tuchün*, usually the leader of their native province. The *North China Herald* (March 8, 1924, p. 358) reported that young men were flocking to Wu P'ei-fu's headquarters and that life in Loyang was much like the old court life in Peking.

76. The *North China Herald* (Sept. 1, 1923) carried a detailed account of Wu's methods in making these appointments.

77. Dr. C. T. Wang was the first Director General for the Rehabilitation of Shantung Rights and initiated the policy of utilizing returned students in the Kiaochow administration. However, on October 20, 1922, Wu P'ei-fu assumed the

responsibility of appointing the administrator. (U.S., Department of State 893.00/4868.)

78. Pai and Chin, *op. cit.*, pp. 57–60. The question of skills did not serve as an absolute standard for Feng. It is interesting to observe that Feng refused to employ a returned student from Germany who was trained in military science, because he was "too august and probably only wanted a sinecure." (Feng's *Diary*, book 2, p. 5.) However, he happily employed two students trained in France and Germany when they had been discreet enough to present Feng with a scroll bearing the legend "Pillar of the State, Star of the Army." (Feng's *Diary*, book 2, p. 7.)

79. U.S., Department of State 893.00/5082; 893.00/6054; 893.00/5391.

80. U.S., Department of State 893.00/6098; 893.01A/56; 893.00/5949.

CHAPTER 4

1. Odoric Ying-kwang Wou has, however, overcome these obstacles to produce a detailed biography of Wu in his "Militarism in Modern China as Exemplified in the Career of Wu P'ei-fu, 1916–1928" (Ph.D. diss., Columbia University Department of Political Science, 1970).

2. James E. Sheridan, *Chinese Warlord: The Career of Feng Yu-hsiang* (Stanford, Calif.: Stanford University Press, 1966).

3. Feng Yü-hsiang, *Feng Yü-hsiang Jih-chi* (Feng's *Diary*) (Peiping, 1930), book 1, p. 2.

4. *Ibid.* One of the reasons that the province of Anhwei produced so many men of importance during the early years of the Republic was that Li Hung-chang had built up a large following from his home province, and these men continued to follow the practice of giving preference to coprovincials. Lu Kuang-yu, *Min-kuo Shih-yao* (*A Historical Summary of the Republic*) (Peking, 1927), p. 44.

5. Feng's *Diary*, book 1, p. 3.

6. *Ibid.*, book 2, p. 6.

7. *Ibid.*, book 1, p. 4.

8. At the time of the Revolution, Feng supported the demands of the Fengtien viceroy, Chang Shao-tseng, for nineteen specific reforms. He also identified himself with the move of Wang Shin-min and Shih Tsung-yün in attempting to take over the Fengtien government, but, when the revolt of his superiors failed and they were executed by the troops loyal to the Manchus, Feng escaped with a brief period in prison before the province declared its loyalty to Yüan Shih-k'ai. For details of Feng's activities during this period, see Pai Ying-hsing and Chin Yu-k'un, *Kuo-min-chün Shih-kao* (*Draft History of the Kuominchün*) (Peking, 1930), pp. 6–7.

9. Feng attempted to expand his power in Szechwan by having his subordinate, Chang Chih-chiang, negotiate an agreement with Ts'ai Sung-p'o, the Yünnan leader, while, at the same time, he brought pressure on the Szechwan civil governor, Cheng Yu, to declare the independence of the province. (Feng's *Diary*, book 1, p. 4; Pai and Chin, *op. cit.*, p. 45.)

10. Feng's *Diary*, book 1, p. 7. This action on the part of Ts'ao appears to have made a great impression upon Feng, and later, when he revolted against the Chihli faction, he was always careful to announce that he still held Ts'ao K'un in the greatest esteem.

11. U.S., Department of State 893.00/4011 (June 29, 1920).

12. Pai and Chin, *op. cit.*, pp. 48–49.

13. Feng's *Diary*, book 3, pp. 23–24.

14. *Ibid.*, p. 27. For the details of Hu Ching-i's military career and his acceptance of Feng's leadership, see Pai and Chin, *op. cit.*, pp. 49–52.

15. Feng's *Diary*, book 3, p. 31.

16. *Ibid.*, p. 37.

17. *Ibid.*, book 1, p. 9, and Pai and Chin, *op. cit.*, pp. 54–55.

18. Thus, for example, Han Fu-chü was transferred from the post of Feng's *aide de camp* to the office of regimental commander in the Twelfth Division (Feng's *Diary*, book 4, p. 11), Liu Yu-feng and Lu Chung-lin were raised to brigade

commanders from the rank of battalion commander (*ibid.*, book 1, p. 9), and Chang Chih-chung was placed in command of a regiment of the Eleventh (*ibid.*, book 4, p. 22).

19. Han Fu-chü was certainly very close to Feng when it came to political policy decisions. However, it appears that, when Feng gave personal gifts to his subordinates, those received by Chang Chih-chiang were the most valuable. (*Ibid.*, p. 151.)

20. Feng was able to maintain the semblance of a teacher-student relationship with his subordinate commanders even after they held commands that were geographically isolated from his headquarters by organizing the regimen and daily schedules of training and education for all the troops under his authority. To ensure compliance with the routine, he communicated each day by either telephone or telegraph with his subordinates. (Pai and Chin, *op. cit.*, pp. 56–60.) Feng's practice of refusing to delegate authority was observable to foreigners. (Arthur Holcombe, *The Chinese Revolution* [Cambridge, Mass.: Harvard University Press, 1930], p. 23.)

21. Pai and Chin, *op. cit.*, pp. 112–13. Feng's contribution to the first Chihli-Fengtien war and the subsequent assistance he rendered to Wu P'ei-fu in ousting Chao Ti from Honan (see Chapter 4 of this volume) did not result in any radical changes or create any problems within Feng's organization. Also Feng's *coup d'état* of 1923 (see ch. 6 of this volume) primarily influenced his relations with other *tuchüns* and did not lead to any unique internal problems.

22. Feng's *Diary*, book 6, p. 103. For other details of the reasons for Feng's actions at this time in terms of his relations with Wu P'ei-fu and the Chihli alliance, see Chapter 5 of this volume.

23. For Feng, this was a particularly radical change because he, more than most of the *tuchüns*, insisted upon making all policy, as well as administrative, decisions and had given his subordinates little independence or responsibility. In this respect, Feng was the direct opposite of Tuan Ch'i-jui, who permitted his subordinates a great deal of freedom. (U.S., Department of State 893.00/4652.)

24. Ch'en Kung-fu, *Chung-kuo Tsui-chin San-shih-nien Shih* (*History of China in the Last Thirty Years*) (Shanghai, 1928), p. 237.

25. Feng's *Diary*, book 6, p. 104.

26. *Ibid.*, pp. 101, 107.

27. The Second Kuominchün consisted of three divisions. Hu Ching-i served concurrently as commander of the First Division, which included in its table of organization six brigades and one artillery regiment. The Second Division included five infantry regiments. (Pai and Chin, *op. cit.*, pp. 134–36.) The Third Kuominchün consisted of four divisions. Its First Division included one artillery regiment and two brigades of two infantry regiments each. The Second Division contained seven mixed brigades but with only ten regiments in all. The Third and Fourth Divisions had only two regiments each. (*Ibid.*, pp. 138–40.) It is impossible to determine the exact manpower that all this represented. Wen Kung-chih gives as the figures for the maximum size that each of the Kuominchün armies ever achieved the following: the First Kuominchün, a little less than 900,000; the Second Kuominchün, about 250,000; the Third Kuominchün at one time achieved a total of 50,000 men. (Wen Kung-chih, *op cit.*, vol. I, book 2, pp. 32 and 42–43.) However, these figures appear excessively high, and it is doubtful if the Kuominchün's normal complement was half these numbers. H. G. W. Woodhead estimated that the Kuominchün totaled 250,000 men in 1925. (*Occidental Interpretations of the Far Eastern Problem*, Harris Foundation Lecture, 1925 [Chicago: University of Chicago Press, 1926], p. 76.)

28. Wen Kung-chih, *op. cit.*, vol. I, book 2, p. 30. This increase was made possible by the incorporation of elements of the defeated troops of Wu P'ei-fu.

29. Sun Yüeh also reorganized the troops that had been under the command of Ts'ao K'un and the Presidential bodyguard. (Feng's *Diary*, book 6, p. 123.) Of the forty-one men who held the rank of regimental commander or above in the Third Kuominchün, twenty-one were natives of Hopei, as was Sun Yüeh. The rest, however, included five Hunanese, four Shantungese, three men from Fu-

kien, two each from Anhwei, Manchuria, and Shansi, while, of Kiangsu and Yünnan, each was represented by one officer. (Pai and Chin, *op. cit.*, pp. 138–40.)

30. No effort was made to alter the internal structure of Hu's organization when it became the Second Kuominchün. It was in essence the same army of Shensi troops that Hu had previously been commanding. Of the twenty-four officers who held regimental command and higher rank, all except five were natives of Shensi. (*Ibid.*, pp. 134–36.)

31. Feng's *Diary*, book 6, p. 124.

32. *Ibid.*, book 7, pp. 6, 9.

33. Pai and Chin, *op. cit.*, p. 121.

34. Feng's *Diary*, book 6, p. 138.

35. Wen Kung-chih, *op. cit.*, vol. I, book 2, p. 30. The Fourth Kuominchün was established in Anhwei under the Li Ch'un-yeh but was soon defeated and never was an important factor in the total organization of the Kuominchün.

36. The creation of the Fifth and Sixth Kuominchün did not affect the military power of the first Kuominchün, because the Fifth and Sixth continued to function militarily as component parts of the First, and, when Feng left for Moscow, they again became officially a part of the First. (Pai and Chin, *op. cit.*, p. 140.)

37. Feng's *Diary*, book 6, p. 128.

38. U.S., Department of State 893.00/5990, 893.00/6058.

39. Feng's *Diary*, book 7, p. 5. Feng made it clear to Hu that he would have a better chance to gain control of the Honan area if he showed a greater willingness to attend to the problems of provincial finance and civil rule. He also indicated that Hu would have to desist from entertaining representatives from Central and South China who were pressing Hu to enter the Yangtze area. Feng felt that, if Hu attempted any such extended campaign, it would unify all forces against the Kuominchün and threaten the possibilities of its obtaining control of North China. (*Ibid.*, book 6, p. 142.)

40. Lu Kuang-yu, *op. cit.*, p. 127.

41. *Ibid.*, pp. 127–28. The technique of a leader's temporary retirement in the midst of a political controversy with his subordinates was a phenomenon common in Chinese politics. Chiang Kai-shek employed it four times and threatened to do so on numerous other occasions. This technique is indicative of the highly personal form of politics that persisted in modern China, as such moves were calculated to demonstrate the indispensability of the leader's personal role in existing political relations. Thus, as long as these relations were ordered, to a large degree, in terms of personal relations, the withdrawal and reappearance of specific personalities had a profound effect on all the other relations in the political arena.

42. Pai and Chin, *op. cit.*, p. 239.

43. *Ibid.*, p. 242.

44. U.S., Department of State 893.00/5939 (Feb. 3, 1925).

45. Pai and Chin, *op. cit.*, p. 242. The clashes did not develop into a major conflict at this time, because neither Feng nor Chang was prepared. Just as Feng had found it necessary to permit some of his subordinates to expand their power, so was Chang Tso-lin faced with the problems of giving some of his subordinates greater freedom. (U.S., Department of State 893.00/5843.) Thus, both of the leaders were in the position of desiring to proceed more cautiously and to strengthen the bonds of loyalty within their organizations, but they were forced to sanction moves of their subordinates. Feng, himself, sought to identify the tension at the time as only the result of a personal clash between Hu and Sun, on the one hand, and Li Ching-lin, on the other, and, thus, one which did not involve the entire Kuominchün (Feng's *Diary*, book 7, pp. 10, 32). The very fact that he could claim that it was possible for subordinates to conduct personal campaigns was indicative of the weakening of the control he had over the entire organization.

46. U.S., Department of State 893.00/5962 (Feb. 17, 1925).

47. It is impossible to determine exactly who was involved in making this decision. Feng hints that it was his suggestion. (Feng's *Diary*, book 7, pp. 5–6.) However, there was no official order for the action from the office of the commander in chief of the Kuominchün. (Pai and Chin, *op. cit.*, p. 192.) But it is clear that, regardless of the initiator of the move, there was no opposition from the First Kuominchün, and thus it can be assumed that Sun Yüeh had the tacit approval of Feng.

48. On February 9, 1925, Feng had issued a circular telegram stating that the Kuominchün was responsible for Shensi. (Text in Sun Yao-pien, *op. cit.*, vol. 3, pp. 78–79.) Feng was, at the time, seeking to check Hu's ambitions in Honan (Feng's *Diary*, book 7, p. 7), and thus the implication of the circular telegram was that, if Hu cooperated with the Kuominchün, he would be rewarded in Shensi and not in Honan.

49. Although there were rumors that there might have been foul play in connection with the unexpected and opportune death of the commander of the Second Kuominchün, there is no evidence to prove that the ailing Hu had not finally succumbed to a weak heart aggravated by his obesity and love of drink. At any rate, the political speculators soon lost interest in the case after the May 30 incident, and other leaders of the Kuominchün were never openly charged with having eliminated their former colleague.

50. Feng's *Diary*, book 7, p. 40. The Fengtien leaders did attempt to create confusion at the time by publicly announcing that they felt that Sun Yüeh should incorporate into his armies the former troops of Hu, and that they would be willing to support Sun if he desired to do so. (*Tung-fang Tsa-chih* 22, no. 9 [May 10, 1925], p. 3.) The appointment did not create the degree of internal dissension that might have been expected, probably because the other possible candidates realized that it would be no easy task to retain the loyalties of the Shensi troops if they were not natives of the province.

51. For a discussion of the balance that existed among the leading *tuchüns* at this time, see Chapter 6 of this volume.

52. U.S., Department of State 893.00/6765. To a certain extent, the conservative attitude of the military commanders reflected their unwillingness to risk losing their new posts in Jehol and Suiyüan, for they were willing for the Second and Third Kuominchün to fight.

53. Text of Feng's telegram in Sun Yao-pien, *op. cit.*, vol. III, pp. 169–70.

54. The details of the general balance of power in North China during autumn, 1925, are given in Chapter 6 of this volume. It is sufficient at this time to note that the lack of unity in the Kuominchün had prevented Feng from initiating any independent policies. Rather, he was forced to seek the best possible bargains with each of the other leading *tuchüns*, with the hope that these bargains would be attractive enough to satisfy all of his subordinates, thereby restoring unity to his organization. Thus, Feng sought in addition to the agreements with Sun Ch'uan-fang and Kuo Sung-ling, to establish an alliance with Yen Hsi-shan. (Feng's *Diary*, book 7, pp. 110, 125.) Feng hoped that, by entering into such an agreement, he would be able to entice the Shansi leader out of his policy of isolation and thus alter the general balance of power in North China in such a manner that it would result in clearly giving all elements in the Kuominchün the opportunity to satisfy their expectations of greater personal power. At the same time that Feng was making these agreements directed against the rising power of Fengtien, it was also necessary for him to meet the immediate threat of the Mukden forces. To this end, on November 13, 1925, he signed an agreement with Chang Hsüeh-liang, which was intended to define clearly the spheres of influence of the Kuominchün and the Fengtien forces south of the Wall. (For the terms of the agreement, see *The China Year Book, 1926–1927*, ed., H. G. W. Woodhead [Tientsin, 1927], p. 1025.) This agreement was violated almost as soon as it was made, but it did have the temporary effects of (1) reducing the pressure of Fengtien on the Second and Third Kuominchün in Honan and Shantung and (2) giving Sun Ch'uan-fang the opportunity to consolidate his positions on the southern border of Shantung.

55. Pai and Chin, *op. cit.*, p. 254.
56. U.S., Department of State 893.00/6886 (Dec. 29, 1925).
57. Feng's *Diary*, book 7, p. 145.
58. U.S., Department of State 893.00/6922 (Jan. 17, 1926).
59. For details of the fighting that led up to the Taku incident and of the correspondence between the diplomatic corps and the Chinese Ministry of Foreign Affairs, see *The China Year Book, 1926–27, op. cit.*, pp. 1029–30.
60. U.S., Department of State 893.00/6993 (Jan. 25, 1926).
61. Feng did order Lu Chung-lin to disband Tuan Ch'i-jui's bodyguards and to maintain law and order in the capital, but he refused to permit any element of the First Kuominchün to assume the responsibility for the government. (U.S., Department of State 893.00/7289.) At the same time, Feng initiated a policy of exploiting the resources of the Northwest in order to strengthen the structure of the Kuominchün and to ensure continued finances. To this end, Feng organized the Executive Society of the Mongolian Party of the Chinese Republic. (U.S., Department of State 893.00/7085.) By establishing headquarters for the Mongolian leaders at Kalgan, Feng hoped to be able to incorporate this ethnic group into the Kuominchün. This policy was intended so to strengthen the organization that it would be capable of countering any influence of Chang Tso-lin's in the the areas of Inner Mongolia and possibly even helping to obtain the support of the Mongolians in a conquest of Western Manchuria. (Feng's statement to the American consul at Kalgan, see U.S., Department of State 893.00/7088.)
62. Feng gave as his reasons for retiring at this time the conventional argument that he had failed to bring peace to the people. (Feng's *Diary*, book 8, pp. 1–2.) However, he also charged Chang Tso-lin and the Fengtien leadership with seeking to foment conflicts among his subordinates and weakening the relationships within the Kuominchün. (Pai and Chin, *op. cit.*, pp. 258–59.)
63. U.S., Department of State 893.00/6920. It would appear from Feng's record of his activities during this period of retirement that, by announcing he had stepped out of the political and military arena, he had, in fact, increased his opportunities to negotiate with all groups in North China. He records daily visits from leaders or representatives of important military and political figures, who sought him out in his retreat in the Western Hills. (Feng's *Diary*, book 8, pp. 3–5.)
64. U.S., Department of State 893.00/7193 (March 12, 1926).
65. Only Lu Chung-lin remained unconvinced, and he actually attempted to negotiate agreements with Wu P'ei-fu and Tuan Ch'i-jui. Tuan's proposition was the most appealing; he proposed that Lu join in attempting to restore the Anfu Club, and he pointed out that, in such an arrangement, Lu would be certain of having a great deal of influence because he would be the only member with any military power. (U.S., Department of State 893.00/7274.)
66. In this move, the First Kuominchün did lose one division, the Ninth, which consisted of men and officers who had formerly been in the Fengtien armies but who had been incorporated into the Kuominchün after the defeats of Chang in December, 1925. (U.S., Department of State 893.00/7334.) This was an example of the dangers of depending upon defeated forces for augmenting one's power, because they were willing to be loyal only as long as there were hopes for immediate victories. When the expectations of rewards were delayed, they were the first to feel that they had no binding ties with the organization.
67. *North China Herald*, May 8, 1925, p. 243.
68. *Ibid.*, book 1, p. 11.
69. See Chapter 6 of this volume.
70. The First Division of the First Kuominchün soon ran into difficulties in the area and, in heavy fighting, sustained up to 50 per cent casualties. It had to call upon the assistance of Sun Chih-yüan's forces in Suiyüan. (U.S., Department of State 893.00/7546.)
71. These operations also proved costly and resulted in the negotiation of an agreement with Yen Hsi-shan by which the Kuominchün pledged itself to recognize the authority of Yen in the Northwest but, in return, was granted the right to

move troops through the area and maintain communications along the Peking-Suiyüan Railroad. This was the beginning of the policy of cooperation between Feng and Yen, which was to last into the Nationalist period.

72. Feng's *Diary*, book 8, pp. 19, 28, 30, 40, *passim*.
73. *Ibid.*, p. 32. Both the Second and the Third Kuominchün were endangered by the victories of Fengtien and the new armies of Wu P'ei-fu. The Second was forced to withdraw from western Honan in October, 1926, when the Fengtien armies succeeded in dislodging the First Kuominchün from Nankow and were prepared to commence a new drive into Central China by way of the Peking-Hankow Railroad. (U.S., Department of State 893.00/7936.)
74. Feng's *Diary*, book 8, p. 67.
75. U.S., Department of State 893.00/7994.
76. U.S., Department of State 893.24/28.
77. *Public Documents Supplement*, *op. cit.*, document 12, p. 210.
78. *Ibid.*, p. 218.
79. Pai and Chin, *op. cit.*, p. 474.
80. Feng's *Diary*, book 8, p. 85.
81. Feng's policies of strengthening the Kuominchün at this time also included his first efforts at working with the secret societies in the· Northwest. To this end, Feng incorporated the Ke Lao Hui (Elder Brother Society) into the Kuominchün, and he himself became a Ta Ke in the Society. (U.S., Department of State 893.00/7994.)
82. For the role that Feng did play in this settlement, see Chapters 5 and 8 of this volume. On October 27, 1926, the Kuomintang promised to pay Feng $100,000 per month for the support of his troops. (Feng's *Diary*, book 8, p. 79.)
83. On May 24, 1929, Han Fu-chü and Shih Yu-san, without warning, declared their allegiance to Chiang Kai-shek. This was the only case of outright betrayal in the entire history of the Kuominchün. Although there were many incidents in which subordinates refused to comply with Feng's orders, this was the only occasion on which a trusted leader actually went so far as to denounce Feng and shift his allegiance.

Chapter 5

1. Lu Kuang-yu, *Min-kuo Shih-yao* (A Historical Summary of the Republic) (Peking, 1920), pp. 44–45.
2. For details on these developments in the Anfu and Chihli factions, see Li Chien-nung, *Tsui-chin San-shih-nien Chung-kuo Cheng-chih Shih* (Political History of China in the Last Thirty Years) (Shanghai, 1930), pp. 404–11, 451–55.
3. *Tung-fang Tsa-chih* 21, no. 23 (Dec. 10, 1924), pp. 2–3.
4. An extremely interesting work, which illustrates the use of "personal cues" by the *tuchüns*, is Ts'ai Tung-fang, *Min-kuo T'ung-shu Yen-I* (A Popularized Discussion of the Republic) (Shanghai, 1930). This work is a "romantic history" of the early years of the Republic written in the tradition of such romantic histories of other periods of Chinese history as the *San-kuo Chih Yen-I* (Romance of the Three Kingdoms). The author, who was an active observer of, and at times a participant in, the events, employs facts where available, but he also incorporates all the rumors, tea-shop talk, and the reports of personal acquaintances who were intimate with the developments. The defect of such a work is that it makes no effort to distinguish or document the sources employed. However, possibly better than any other study, it shows the atmosphere within which the *tuchüns* conducted their politics. The author reflects the attitudes of that group of Chinese intellectuals who were disgusted with the general drift of Chinese politics but fascinated with, and entranced by, the political process. The principal weakness of the work, however, is that it shares with other such "intimate histories" the characteristic of oversophistication to the extent of attributing far too much to personal manipulations and personality factors. For a study that concludes that the tradition of "romantic histories" was one of great fidelity to the historical "facts" as described in the *Standard Dynastic Histories*, see

James I. Crump, "Some Problems in the Language of the Shin-bian Wu-day Shyy Pyng-huah," Ph.d. diss., Yale University, 1949, p. 15.

5. For a discussion of changes in the symbols employed in *tuchün* politics, see Chapter 7 of this volume.
6. Li Chien-nung, *op. cit.*, pp. 517–18.
7. *Tung-fang Tsa-chih* 20, no. 13 (July 10, 1923), pp. 3–4.
8. Ch'en Kung-fu, *Chung-kuo Tsui-chin San-shih-nien Shih* (*A History of China in the Last Thirty Years*) (Shanghai, 1928), p. 225.
9. Feng Yü-hsiang, *Feng Yü-hsiang Jih-chi* (Feng's *Diary*) (Peiping, 1930), book 5, p. 68.
10. Li Chien-nung, *op. cit.*, p. 477. Evaluations of Chang's contributions to the defeat of Anfu differ. Actually, the troops of Tuan Ch'i-jui and Hsü Shu-cheng had been routed before Chang declared his intention to intervene. (U.S., Department of State 893.00/3581.) On the other hand, it was the knowledge of Chang's decision to enter the conflict at this time that forced Tuan and Hsü to realize it was hopeless to attempt to regroup their troops and prolong the struggle. (U.S., Department of State 893.00/3468.) Tuan later reported that Chang had personally promised him that, should there be a conflict between Chihli and Anfu, he would remain neutral. (*North China Daily News*, Nov. 25, 1920, p. 7.)
11. For the appointments that Chang made to the cabinet of 1920, see Chapter 8 of this volume. The Chihli faction was willing to comply with Chang's wishes because of disagreements within their own camp, and Ts'ao K'un saw in Chang a possible check to the meteoric rise of Wu P'ei-fu's influence in the councils of the Chihli military faction (*Peking and Tientsin Times*, Oct. 27, 1920.)
12. Chang's efforts to form a coalition with Sun Yat-sen and the remnants of the Anfu faction were referred to in the press as the "Unholy Alliance." In particular, Chang sought to reach an agreement with the Chao brothers in Honan to revolt against Wu P'ei-fu if Chihli should attempt to initiate a conflict with Fengtien. (U.S., Department of State 893.00/4761.) Chang also welcomed Hsü Shu-cheng ("Little Hsü") to Mukden in 1920 and again in April, 1924. (U.S., Department of State 893.00/6108.)
13. U.S., Department of State 893.00/4261 (April 12, 1921).
14. During the Chihli-Anfu conflict of 1920, the Shanghai community, including foreign groups, had issued a strong statement to the effect that Shanghai should be recognized as neutral territory, which had deterred the Chihli *tuchün* of Kiangsu, Li Shun, from an attack upon Lu Yung-hsiang. (U.S., Department of State 893.00/6102.)
15. Lu issued a circular telegram at the time, stating that others could fight for power, but he sought only a just rule of law. (Text of telegram in Sun Yao-pin, vol. II, book 3, pp. 72–73.)
16. U.S., Department of State 893.00/5337.
17. In particular, Wu challenged the policies of Premier Liang Shih-yüan, who was a Chang appointee. (Ch'en Kung-fu, *op. cit.*, pp. 216–17.) Wu's threatening denunciations of Chang included the charge that the Mukden leader had been responsible for the unpopular Shantung Settlement at the Washington Conference, and Wu issued a circular telegram stating that "Of all the evils, the greatest is the selling out of one's country." (U.S., Department of State 893.00/4185.) Wu's accusations were in tune with public opinion, but it is difficult to determine whether Chang had any influence upon the Chinese delegation at Washington. It might be significant that he informed the American consul at Mukden that he was "extremely concerned that the Washington Conference would give Japan a strong position in Manchuria in lieu of their former 'rights' in Shantung." (U.S., Department of State 893.00/4200.) Also, an unidentified Chinese delegate, in informal conversation, stated that the Chinese delegation was conscious of Chang Tso-lin's fears that, if China struck too hard a bargain over the Shantung question, Japan might seek to obtain compensations in Manchuria. (*New York Times*, Dec. 20, 1921, p. 3.)
18. Wen Kung-chih, *op. cit.*, vol. II, book 3, p. 181.

19. Chang, at this point, initiated his major effort to build up his power. This program included the expansion of the Mukden arsenal and the employment of foreign advisers. (*Tung-fang Tsa-chi* 20, no. 5 [March 10, 1923], p. 6.) Chang also initiated his policy of using White Russians, not only as advisers but as common soldiers too. (Many of the White Russians were driven into the Fengtien Army by economic necessity, but interviews with many of these men indicate that they had been motivated by anti-Bolshevik sentiments and that they identified Feng Yü-hsiang with Communist expansion. [*North China Herald*, September 11, 1926, p. 486].) In addition, Chang began his extensive program of training his officers in Japanese academies and reorganizing his entire army. (*Ibid.*, Aug. 18, 1923, p. 401; Wen Kung-chih, *op. cit.*, vol. I, book 2, pp. 55–57.)

20. U.S., Department of State 893.00/5335.

21. U.S., Department of State 893.00/5337.

22. *Ibid.*

23. U.S., Department of State 893.00/6108.

24. See Chapter 6 of this volume.

25. Tuan at this juncture made a striking bid for control of the politicians in Peking by announcing, on August 6, 1923, that, before the election of the President, there should be a conference of all the political leaders in China to discuss the new Constitution. This was interpreted not only as a move to undermine Chang Tso-lin's position as leader of the anti-Chihli forces but also as a challenge to Ts'ao K'un, who was endeavoring to force the Parliament to complete its work on a new constitution before his election to the Presidency. (*Tung-fang Tsa-chih* 20, no. 16 [Aug. 25, 1923], pp. 3–4.) The Chihli alliance immediately acted to counter the threat of Tuan Ch'i-jui's return to the political scene. Ts'ao K'un proposed that, because Tuan had served the Republic so well, he should be granted a pension by the Peking government. (U.S., Department of State 893.00/5267.) Wu P'ei-fu seconded the suggestion with the public statement that "Although Tuan Ch'i-jui does not agree with us in his political ideas, we must respect him as a senior member of the Peiyang Army. Therefore, his pension must be fixed and his meritorious services be remembered by the Government." (*Peking and Tientsin Times*, Oct. 15, 1923.) This would have "officially" retired Tuan from politics, and he could hardly return as a threat to the Chihli faction after receiving payments from Ts'ao K'un.

26. *Peking and Tientsin Times*, Oct. 8, 1923. The Tientsin clique was unsuccessful because it could not meet Chang's terms, which included the complete control of Jehol by Fengtien.

27. *Chiang-che Chan-shih* (*History of the Kiangsu-Chekiang War*), compiled, published, the Hung Wen Library (Shanghai, 1924), 4 vols., vol. I, p. 102.

28. U.S., Department of State 893.00/5482.

29. U.S., Department of State 893.00/5490.

30. In particular, Lu turned to the local Chambers of Commerce in Shanghai and the rest of Chekiang for funds to increase his army, and he also asked these groups to assume the initiative in seeking a peace pact with Kiangsu and Ch'i Hsüeh-yüan. This movement resulted in the signing of a treaty by Lu and Ch'i on August 20, 1923. (For text of treaty, see *Chiang-che Chan-shih, op. cit.*, vol. I, pp. 7–8.) The treaty, clearly a nonaggression pact, even included a pledge that each would maintain peace and stability within his own province and not interfere in the internal affairs of the other's. (Article II.)

The existence of such a formal treaty to regularize the relations between two opposing *tuchüns* was unique. It was heralded as a definite step in the direction of peace, especially because the treaty recognized the contribution that public groups had made to its formation. At the time the treaty was concluded, it was considered successful in reducing the tension between the two provinces, because neither Lu nor Ch'i was in a position to initiate aggressive acts. However, after Ch'i Hsüeh-yüan obtained substantial backing from the other Chihli leaders and appeared to have the potential power of Wu P'ei-fu in reserve, the balance was radically altered; the treaty now became an element in the complex of relations that served to increase, rather than diminish, tensions. The two leaders were engaged in one of the most intense "wars of circular telegrams" of the period, which further added to the tensions that culminated in military conflict. (For the texts of the telegrams, see *Chiang-che Chan-shih*, vol. I, pp. 14–31; *North China Herald*, Aug. 23 and 30, 1924.)

31. Tuan Ch'i-jui agreed to come to Chekiang and give full support to Lu on the condition that Lu raise six more divisions. However, Lu's efforts to obtain the troops proved unsuccessful and the plan failed to materialize. (U.S., Department of State 893.00/5362.)

32. In order to keep the Chihli alliance off balance at this time, Chang pleaded with Tuan Ch'i-jui to emerge from his retirement. He was finally successful in persuading Tuan to issue a circular telegram denouncing the Chihli alliance and the Peking government. (*North China Herald*, Sept. 20, 1924, pp. 450, 452.)

33. Texts of Chang's statements are to be found in *Feng-chih Chan-shih*, pp. 5–6. On October 1, 1923, Chang Tso-lin gave a dinner for the European and American residents of Mukden and announced rather pointedly that "In case of further conflicts, the Yangtze River Valley which up until now has been immune to conflict might be the center of great chaos" and that it was the responsibility of the leaders in this area to prepare to preserve law and order. (U.S., Department of State 893.00/5248.)

34. Wen Kung-chih, *op. cit.*, vol. II, book 1, p. 181. In addition, in July, 1924, Lu attempted to strengthen his armies by receiving into Chekiang the remnants of the Chang Chih-ping and Yang Hua-chao armies, which had been driven out of Fukien by Sun Ch'uan-fang, acting under the orders of Wu P'ei-fu. These troops were considered to be loyal to the Anfu leaders, and that they were Shantungese was interpreted to mean that Lu Yung-hsiang, himself a native of this province, could fully rely upon them to defend Chekiang from Ch'i Hsüeh-yüan. (U.S., Department of State 893.00/5635.) However, Lu needed funds from Chang Tso-lin to equip these troops before they would be an effective addition to his power, and Chang hesitated to give such direct assistance to troops whose first loyalty was to Anfu and Tuan Ch'i-jui. (U.S., Department of State 893.00/5672.)

35. Wu P'ei-fu fully appreciated Lu's nuisance value and was unwilling to make any move against Fengtien until he was confident that Ch'i Hsüeh-yüan would be able to neutralize Lu in Chekiang. (T'ao Chü-yin, *op. cit.*, p. 104.)

36. *Feng-chih Chan-shih*, *op. cit.*, p. 69.

37. *Tung-fang Tsa-chih*, 20, no. 21 (Nov. 10, 1924), pp. 4–5.

38. U.S., Department of State 893.00/6585 (Dec. 8, 1924).

39. U.S., Department of State 893.00/5928.

40. Wu Liao-tzu, *op. cit.*, p. 72.

41. Wen Kung-chih, *op. cit.*, vol. I, book 2, p. 88.

42. On September 10, 1925, Chang announced the appointment of his chief of staff, Yang Yu-ting, *tuchün* of Kiangsu and thus ended all pretense of cooperating with Anfu in the Yangtze area. (U.S., Department of State 893.00/6646.)

43. A great deal has been made of the charges that both Mukden and the Anfuites, including Lu Yung-hsiang, were bound by a common factor of being amenable to Japanese influence and thus did have a common basis for their actions. However, it has been impossible to uncover any evidence that these leaders found, in their readiness to turn to Japan, any common ideological ground. It would appear to be far more correct to assume that their Japanese orientation was primarily dictated by expediency and that these groups as "out-groups" did find Japan desirous of supporting such elements in the hope that, if they should be successful, they would be obligated to Japan.

In this respect, it is significant that Sun Yat-sen during this period showed a readiness to join the various *tuchüns* who were out of power in the capital and that, as a consequence, he showed a strong pro-Japanese bias. Immediately after the defeat of the Anfu faction in 1920, Sun championed the cause of Tuan Ch'i-jui and the Anfuites in spite of the strong criticism that they had sold out China to Japan. (Sun justified this policy by saying that Tuan was the only northern *tuchün* whom he could trust and that he was "the only militarist in Peking who is not a liar" [*North China Herald*, Nov. 27, 1920].) In fact, throughout the period that Tuan was out of power, Sun sought to establish close relations with the old Peiyang leader, and it was the expectation that Tuan would return to power that brought Sun to Peking in 1925 just before his death. Sun, however, also sought ties with Chang Tso-lin, in spite of all the charges that he was pro-Japanese and a monarchist. (In the 1922 Fengtien-Chihli war, Sun had promised to attack Wu P'ei-fu through Kiangsi in support of Chang's move south of the Wall, but the revolt at Canton after the Southern armies had left the city caused Sun to recall his troops and finally to flee the city. (U.S., Department of State 893.00/5252.) There is little doubt that Sun saw the need for supporting the out-groups in any alliance that might be formed out of expediency and that he provided grounds for charges that he was playing into the hands of Japan or even becoming pro-Japanese himself. In fact, as indicated in the following interview, given while he was a political refugee in the French Concession in Shanghai in December, 1922, Sun was more than willing to obtain any assistance that he might get from Tokyo. "In joining in the World War on the side of the Allied Powers, Japan failed to utilize a golden opportunity of making Asia exclusive for the Asiatics. Such an Asia would have opposed the Whites, especially the Anglo-Saxons. At the beginning of the World War, I wrote Mr. Inukai, President of the Kokuminto (Nationalist Party), urging Japan to assist the Teutonic Powers, thereby impairing the strength of the Anglo-Saxons and balancing the power of the world. The result of such a situation would have been the promotion of the position of Japan to the real leadership of the Asiatics." (*The Weekly Review of the Far East* XXIII, no. 2 [Dec. 16, 1922], p. 88.)

44. That not all of the *tuchüns* acted outside of the law led to some interesting, if somewhat naïve, proposals by the more legalistically inclined Chinese intellectuals. The argument was that, because the Chinese legal structure was so loosely defined, it was possible for those *tuchüns* who still claimed legitimacy to conduct policies that degraded the spirit of the law, and therefore they were little better than those who openly flaunted the laws of the land. This led to the proposal that, if the legal system was revised and made more precise and rigid, many of the *tuchüns* would still attempt to satisfy its requirements, but, in order to do this, they would have to make the law supreme. This would have the effect of forcing these *tuchüns* to comply with a meaningful system of law and would make it possible for the public clearly to classify the *tuchüns* in terms of their ideological differences in accordance with the respect they showed for the principles of legal rule. See Wang Shih-mu, "Chun-jen te jen-sheng tzu-yu yen-lun Tzu-yu yu Cheng-chih Hsuan" ("The Personal Freedom and the Freedom of Speech of the Military and the Power of Governmental Administration"), *Tung-fang Tsa-chih* 22, no. 3 (Feb. 10, 1925), pp. 13–20.

45. For a more extensive discussion of the problems of patronage and the division of offices among lesser followers, see Chapter 8 of this volume. The question here is not how to obtain posts for deserving associates but, rather, what were to be the formal positions of the leaders of a victorious coalition.

46. Examples of such newly created posts designed to represent the power positions of the *tuchüns* were those of defense commissioner of the Northeast and defense commissioner of the Northwest, set up in 1924 and held by Chang Tso-lin and Feng Yü-hsiang, respectively. (Li Chien-nung, *op. cit.*, pp. 591–92.) At the time of the Tientsin Conference, it was agreed that Tuan Ch'i-jui would become the provisional chief executive, but it was impossible, without creating the two new positions, to arrive at a settlement that would give both Chang and Feng full formal recognition of their dominant roles in the new regime.

47. For the optimistic comments that appeared in both the Chinese and foreign press, see *North China Herald*, July 15, 1920, pp. 165–66.

48. For a discussion of the problems that arose in attempting to form a cabinet at this time, see Chapter 8 of this volume.

49. *Peking and Tientsin Times*, Oct. 27, 1920.

50. U.S., Department of State 893.20/43.
51. *North China Herald*, Aug. 7, 1920.
52. T'ao Chu-yin, *op. cit.*, pp. 41 and 48.
53. As early as April, 1921, Li Shun had informed the American Consul at Nanking that he was planning, with Ts'ao K'un and Wu P'ei-fu, to eliminate the Anfuites. (U.S., Department of State 893.00/3894.)
54. U.S., Department of State 893.00/3572 (June 25, 1920).
55. Wu stated that he felt that Li Shun had designs on Hupei and Hunan and that he was interested only in the war against Anfu as a means of drawing Wu's armies away from this region. (Ch'en Kung-fu, *op. cit.*, p. 206.)
56. U.S., Department of State 893.00/3611.
57. U.S., Department of State 893.00/3609.
58. U.S., Department of State 893.00/3612 (June 17, 1920).
59. U.S., Department of State 893.00/3707 (July 3, 1920).
60. *Peking and Tientsin Times*, Dec. 6, 1920.
61. U.S., Department of State 893.00/3894. Ni Ssu-ch'un, by retiring as he did, was able to obtain the support of Li Shun, who was willing to have Ni restored to his old post as long as Li was able to sponsor the move.
62. Chang Tso-lin's decision to support the candidacy of Chang Hsün gave rise to numerous rumors that the Mukden leader was plotting the restoration of the Monarchy, and these reports were exploited later by the other *tuchüns* to discredit Chang Tso-lin. See Chapter 6 of this volume.
63. *Peking and Tientsin Times*, Sept. 23, 1930.
64. U.S., Department of State 893.00/3612. Chang Wen-sen at one time had served under Chang Hsün but had recently been the defense commissioner at Hsuchow and showed his willingness to support Ts'ao K'un.
65. U.S., Department of State 893.00/3478 (July 18, 1920).
66. U.S., Department of State 893.00/3490 (Aug. 7, 1920).
67. Wen Kung-chih, *op. cit.*, vol. I, book 2, p. 166.
68. U.S., Department of State 893.00/5397.
69. T'ao Chu-yin, *op. cit.*, p. 94.
70. U.S., Department of State 893.00/4868.
71. *Peking and Tientsin Times*, Nov. 16, 1920.
72. U.S., Department of State 893.00/6206. Chao Ti had been appointed *tuchün* of Honan in 1916, immediately before the death of Yüan Shih-k'ai and, by 1918, had been able to strengthen his position in the province by becoming also the civil governor. All during the period that the Anfu faction held sway in Peking, Chao Ti remained in control of local affairs, because the Anfuites feared that trying to remove him would cause the Yangtze commanders and the other members of the Chihli faction to interpret the act as an attempt to expand the area of direct Anfu control farther south. When Wu P'ei-fu assumed hegemony over Central China in 1919 and 1920, Chao Ti indicated to Wu that he would be willing to support the efforts of the Chihli alliance if he should be permitted in return to continue to dominate the local affairs in the province. (*Ibid.*)
73. Li Chien-nung, *op. cit.*, p. 485.
74. T'ao Chu-yin, *op. cit.*, p. 56.
75. Wen Kung-chih, *op. cit.*, vol. I, book 2, p. 29.
76. Feng's *Diary*, book 3, p. 55. Feng, however, immediately after he was given the post, made a trip to Paoting to demonstrate his "abiding loyalty" to Ts'ao K'un. (*Ibid.*, book 3, p. 120.)
77. T'so Chü-yin, *op. cit.*, pp. 75–76.
78. Wen Kung-chih, *op. cit.*, vol. I, book 2, p. 166.
79. U.S., Department of State 893.00/5252.
80. T'ao Chü-yin, *op. cit.*, p. 93.
81. One of the first acts of Ts'ao K'un after taking his oath of office was to appoint Wu P'ei-fu to the post of inspector-general of Chihli, Honan, and Shantung. Because Ts'ao had previously held this office, the appointment was considered an indication that Ts'ao still regarded Wu as second in command of the Chihli alliance. In addition, Ts'ao appointed Chiao Yao-nan, the former *tuchün* of

Hupei, to the office of inspector general of Hupei and Honan, and Ch'i Hsüeh-yüan was formerly assigned the post of inspector general of Kiangsu, Kiangsi, and Anhwei. Because these men were both recognized as supporters of Wu P'ei-fu's, the appointments constituted an effort on the part of Ts'ao to conciliate Wu.

CHAPTER 6

1. In general, the occurrence of periodic *coups d'état* in a body politic signified a high degree of political instability. However, it is necessary to distinguish between a situation in which the capture of a relatively few governmental organs guarantees effective political power and the situation in China during the 1920's. Some of the Chinese commentators on *tuchün* politics expressed the feeling that the very ineffectiveness of *coups d'état* was the ultimate proof of the hopeless condition of Chinese politics. Others appeared to find some comfort in the fact that the military leaders were unable to dominate all of China by such acts. See Chang Chia-sen, *Chung-nei Chan-cheng Liu-chiang* (*Six Lectures on the Civil Wars*) (Shanghai, 1927), especially Lectures V and VI.
2. Fei Pao-yen, *Shan-hou Hui-i Shih* (*History of the Reconstruction Conference* [1925] (Shanghai, 1927), pp. 42–43.
3. No exact records of the revenue that Feng received exist. It was reported that he was to be given $200,000 a month from the Honan provincial treasury, which was to be paid through Wu P'ei-fu's headquarters, and, in addition, he was to receive $120,000 a month from the Peking government. (*North China Herald*, July 21, 1923, p. 186.) He received $160,000 from Honan. (*Ibid.*, Aug. 18, 1923, p. 455.) Regardless of the exact sums Feng might have received, he found himself in a disadvantageous position because he was without direct control over his source of revenue and had to depend upon the attitudes of the more powerful members of the Chihli coalition. (Feng Yü-hsiang, *Feng Yü-hsiang Jih-chi* [Feng's *Diary*] [Peiping, 1930], book 4, p. 137.)
4. Feng's *Diary*, book 4, pp. 137, 149; book 5, pp. 1, 11, 33.
5. *Ibid.*, book 4, p. 145; book 5, pp. 15, 33, 43.
6. *Ibid.*, book 4, pp. 149, 152; book 5, pp. 6, 71.
7. *Ibid.*, book 5, pp. 35–38.
8. *Ibid.*, p. 36.
9. On June 7, Feng issued a circular telegram claiming that the President's office had interfered with the functions of the cabinet. Because the cabinet was at the time under the control of the Chihli leaders, the statement appeared to be in defense of the alliance. However, Feng also charged that the President had not been accounting for the disposition of the revenues of the Peking Octroi. (*North China Herald*, June 9, 1923.) Immediately after the coup, Feng appointed his close adviser Hsüeh Tu-pi as the new director of the Octroi. A month later, Hsüeh, in a press interview, was quoted as claiming that, since he had become director, the monthly receipts of the Octroi had been $220,000, of which $100,000 had been used for the support of Feng's troops and the remainder delivered to the ministry of finance. Hsüeh pointed out with pride that this was an increase over the $100,000 a month that had previously been turned over to the government. (*Peking and Tientsin Times*, July 13, 1923.)
10. *Ibid.*, June 15, 16, 1923.
11. In particular, it meant that, with the weakening of Wu's power potential, the Tientsin clique now presumed that it had sufficient "alignment potential" to assert a greater influence in the alliance. (U.S., Department of State 893.00/5372.) Also the shift raised doubts as to the willingness of Ch'i Hsüeh-yüan and the Yangtze members of the alliance to continue to look upon Wu P'ei-fu as the control power around whom they should adjust their relations. (*Tung-fang Tsa-chih* 20, no. 13 [July 10, 1923], p. 4.) Possibly most important of all, the coup so altered relations within the Chihli faction that Ts'ao K'un was no longer dependent upon Wu P'ei-fu's military power, and he was thus free to seek formal office in the Peking government despite the opposition of Wu.
12. At the time of the 1923 coup, the minister of finance, Chang Ying-hua, a sup-

porter of Chang Tso-lin's, had just initiated a policy of unrestricted issuance of paper currency to assist the Fengtien financial position. The coup not only resulted in eliminating Chang's influence at the capital; it also left Feng in control of the newly created currency. (*Tung-fang Tsa-chih* 20, no. 10 [May 25, 1923], pp. 8–9.) The danger of Chang's opposition to the new government under President Ts'ao K'un and the possibility of a Fengtien-Loyang alliance had been recognized by the leaders of the Tientsin clique, and it had been hoped that it would be possible to obtain the participation of Chang in the government or at least to prevent him from actively opposing it by offering him the post of Vice-President under Ts'ao. (*Peking and Tientsin Times*, Aug. 7, 1923.)

13. Li Chien-nung, *Tsui-chin San-shih Nien Chung-kuo Cheng-chih Shih (Political History of China in the Last Thirty Years)* (Shanghai, 1930), p. 528.
14. Feng's *Diary*, book 6, p. 11.
15. *Ibid.*, p. 46.
16. *Ibid.*, pp. 14, 68.
17. *Ibid.*, pp. 104–5.
18. Although it is clear that Feng's objectives at the time were to alter drastically the balance and split the Chihli alliance, it is impossible to determine all the other factors that were involved in his decision. It appears that he was also interested in developing a power base in the Northwest. As early as February 1, 1924, he had discussed with H. H. Kung the possibility of exploiting the area. (Feng's *Diary*, book 6, p. 25.) On March 28, Feng met with representatives from Outer Mongolia, and, on July 8, he discussed with an unidentified American, representing U.S. financial interests, the project of developing that territory. (*Ibid.*, pp. 44, 75.) In addition, Feng commenced on July 29 to study the Russian language, giving as his reason the necessity for close relations with Russia if he should develop the Northwest. (*Ibid.*, p. 85.) At no point in his *Diary* does Feng explicitly state how his plans for expanding into that area were related to his scheme for a coup and the establishment of the Kuominchün. It is not clear whether he expected to turn to the Northwest only if he failed to obtain control of Peking after the coup (as was the case) or whether he envisaged a situation in which he would hold the area as a base of power, much as Chang held Manchuria, while at the same time controlling the Peking government.
19. *North China Herald*, Nov. 1, 1924, p. 177.
20. *Tung-fang Tsa-chih* 21, no. 21 (Nov. 10), 1924, p. 3.
21. *North China Herald*, Nov. 1, 1924, p. 176.
22. Marshal Ch'i's attitude toward the northern coup was not to be ascertained. His confidential adviser indicated that it would be impossible for Marshal Ch'i to determine upon a course until he knew exactly what the situation was. (*North China Herald*, Nov. 1, 1924.)
23. *North China Herald*, Nov. 1, 1924, p. 175.
24. Wen Kung-chih, *Tsui-chin San-shih-nien Chung-kuo Chün-shih Shih (History of Chinese Military Affairs in the Last Thirty Years)* (Shanghai, 1930), vol. I, book 2, p. 30.
25. The *Tung-fang Tsa-chih* (21, no. 20 [Oct. 25, 1924], p. 2) gives a vivid description of the uncertainty that prevailed in the capital. The confusion spread to Shanghai, where it was reported that "Shanghai has become full of representatives of every leader in China who are here bargaining for support." (*North China Herald*, Nov. 8, 1924, p. 218.)
26. U.S., Department of State 893.00/5847.
27. When it was announced that Tuan Ch'i-jui would join with Feng and Chang in forming the new government, there were further reports that the Japanese Government was behind the move. (*Peking and Tientsin Times*, Nov. 22, 1924, p. 1.) The American Embassy obtained from "three separate and reliable sources," in effect, the following report on how Japan was alleged to have instigated the coup: Ever since the Fengtien-Chihli war of 1922, the Japanese had believed that another conflict was inevitable and had maintained their contact with the old Anfu leaders while continuing to strengthen Chang's military power. The problem of how to bring Feng into the plan was solved through a rather

devious course. The Japanese persuaded Hsü Tao-lin, head of the government printing office, to act ostensibly on behalf of Tuan Ch'i-jui in soliciting the aid of Huang Fu as an intermediary. Huang Fu then was supposed to have contacted Yüan Liang, chief secretary of the cabinet, who was to make the overtures to Feng through Hsüeh Tu-pi. Feng was to be paid $20,000,000, of which $5,000,000 was given in cash and the rest on "delivery of the goods," and this money was advanced from the South Manchurian Railway. (U.S., Department of State 893.00/5949.) Although it is impossible to determine all the factors involved in the planning and execution of the coup, the above account seems most unlikely. In the first place, there would have been no need for Huang Fu to approach the problem in such a devious manner, because he was extremly close to Feng and could have gone to him directly. Furthermore, even if he had not approached Feng directly, it is doubtful that he would have contacted Hsüeh Tu-pi through Yüan Liang, because Huang was on intimate terms with Hsüeh, and the two might have approached Feng together. Yüan Liang was not at any time within the inner circle of either of these men or of Feng, and he certainly would hardly have been included in such a transaction. However, the suspicion of Japanese intrigue continued to exist, and it was heightened by the *Japanese Times* (Tokyo) and the *Manchurian Daily News* (Dairen), both of which carried detailed accounts of the coup in their issues of the day following the events in Peking. The fact that they were able to report information not generally available to the rest of the Peking correspondents was interpreted to mean that they must have been forewarned. (*North China Herald*, Nov. 7, 1924, p. 217.)

28. The strongest statement to this effect was issued by the Kiangsu Provincial Assembly, which was under the control of Ch'i Hsüeh-yüan. (Sun Yao-pien, *Chung-hua min-kuo shih-liao* [Historical Data on the Chinese Republic], 3 vols., [Shanghai, 1930], vol. III, p. 101.) Other statements consisted of carefully guarded comments to the effect that Feng's actions were indeed treacherous, but justified because Ts'ao had established a corrupt regime. (*Tung-fang Tsa-chih* 21, no. 20, [Oct. 25, 1924], pp. 2–3.)

29. Before the Tientsin Conference of November 10–15 was convened, Chang Tso-lin ordered Chang Tsung-ch'ang to proceed with a campaign to the south to expand the area of Fengtien control, while Feng devoted his attention to the organization of the Kuominchün with the purpose of creating the impression that the coup had augmented his power. (*Tung-fang Tsa-chih* 21, no. 22 [Nov. 25, 1924], p. 3.)

30. Quincy Wright, *A Study of War* (Chicago: University of Chicago Press, 1924), vol. II, ch. 22; Sidney B. Fay, "Balance of Power," *Encyclopaedia of the Social Sciences* (New York, 1932); Hans J. Morgenthau, *Politics Among Nations* (New York: Knopf, 1944), ch. IX; Karl Polanyi, *The Great Transformation* (New York: Farrar, Rinehart, 1944), pp. 259–66; Edward V. Gulick, *Balance of Power* (Philadelphia: Pacifist Research Bureau, 1943), pp. 1–29.

31. Lin Ch'i-hung, *Political Parties in China* (Peking: Henri Vetch, 1930), p. 170. Actually, the main forces of the Fengtien Army were moving down the Peking-Hankow Railway under the command of Li Ching-lin, Kao Chao-hsi, and Chang Tsung-ch'ang. However, the initial clash on the Chin-Pu front was sufficient to rally the hesitant leaders to the support of Wu, and this demonstration of support for the Chihli cause forced Chang Tso-lin to withdraw his forces to the Great Wall. The defeat of Chang Ching-wei was not surprising, because he had shown signs of defection before the campaign and had even gone so far as to state that Chang Tso-lin was seeking to weaken him and his Sixteenth Division by ordering him to take over the entire Chin-Pu front. (U.S., Department of State 893.000/4761.)

32. See Chapter 7 of this volume.

33. *The Chinese Army as a Military Force* (Tientsin, 1926), p. 54.

34. U.S., Department of State 893.00/7499.

35. U.S., Department of State 893.00/5160.

36. For a graphic account of how Chinese doctors and medical students attempted

to serve as volunteers with the Chihli forces in the 1924 campaign and how they received little cooperation from the army, see Wen Han, "Tsung Chun Jih-chi" ("From the Diary of a Soldier"), *Ch'ing-pao Fu-hsin*, Peking, Oct. 10, 11, and 12, 1924.

37. Although there is little concrete evidence, it was reported that Wu actually had in mind the possibility that Sun might serve as a balance to Ch'i in case the Kiangsu commander became too powerful in the war with Chekiang. (U.S., Department of State 893.00/5816.) Wu ordered 22,500 men from Honan and Hupei, in addition to Sun Ch'uan-fang's troops, to assist Ch'i and to share in the spoils. (U.S., Department of State 893.00/5832.)

38. *North China Herald*, Sept. 6, 1924, p. 411. Lu Yung-hsiang had suspected that Sun Ch'uan-fang might have designs on moving into southern Chekiang in the event of a conflict, but his campaign plans called for the deployment of only his less reliable First and Second Chekiang divisions against Sun and the use of his Shantung troops against Ch'i. (*Kiang-che Chan-shih* [*History of the Kiangsu-Chekiang War*], vol. II, [Shanghai, 1926,] pp. 1–2.)

39. *Ibid.*, vol. III, p. 23.

40. *North China Herald*, Sept. 20, 1924, p. 452. The Chekiang commander was confronted with much the same problems as Ch'i Hsüeh-yüan. When it was necessary for him to apply greater pressure to resist the Kiangsu armies, he found it more difficult to maintain the allegiance of his less reliable troops who were opposing Sun Chuan-fang. (*Kiang-che Chan-chih, op. cit.*, vol. III, p. 27.) In fact, on September 18, the Second Division of Chekiang troops under Hsia Ting-ho issued a declaration that the Hangchow area would no longer directly support Lu. (*North China Herald*, Sept. 20, 1924, p. 452.)

41. Li Chien-nung, *op. cit.*, p. 585.

42. Because Sun had not had to call upon his forces for serious fighting, he was able to break down his two divisions into six mixed brigades. (Kiang-che Chan-shih, *op. cit.*, vol I, pp. 78–79.) This facilitated his occupation of strategic points, because each of his units could operate independently.

43. *Peking and Tientsin Times*, March 6, 1926.

44. *North China Herald*, March 2, 1926, p. 152.

45. T'ao Chü-yin, *Wu P'ei-fu chiang-chun chuan* (*Biography of General Wu P'ei-fu*) (Shanghai, 1941), p. 153.

46. U.S., Department of State 893.00/7388 (April 7, 1926).

47. The fact that the conference was to be held at T'angshan (to the north of Tientsin and within the Fengtien area of jurisdiction) was the first indication that Chang intended to use the meeting to strengthen his own power. The specific proposals that he made confirmed this suspicion because they included the appointment of Chang Tsung-ch'ang as inspector-general of Chihli and Shantung, under whom Chin Yün-ao (a Wu supporter) would serve as *tuchün* of Shantung. Sun Ch'uan-fang would be given the title of *tuchün* of Kiangsu and Chekiang, while Wu P'ei-fu was to be recognized as the commander in chief of the Yangtze regions. (U.S., Department of State 893.00/7388 and 893.00/7392).

48. U.S., Department of State 893.00/7392.

49. In particular, Wu turned to negotiations with Yen Hsi-shan during the last week in May. This move was especially significant because, at the time, Yen and the Kuominchün were engaged in an armed conflict in northern Shansi, but there were reports that this struggle was about to end with an agreement satisfactory to both sides. (*Peking and Tientsin Times*, May 15, 1926.) It appears that Wu was seeking to prevent such an agreement because it would have resulted in strengthening the position of the Kuominchün vis-à-vis Fengtien and add to the bargaining power of Sun Ch'uan-fang. Wu went so far as to make a personal trip to Shihchiachuang to confer with Yen, but he was unsuccessful in preventing Yen from reaching an agreement with the Kuominchün. (*North China Herald*, June 5, 1926, p. 431.)

50. *Peking and Tientsin Times*, June 3, 1926.

51. *North China Herald*, June 5, 1926, p. 429.

52. *Tung-fang Tsa-chih* 23, no. 10 (June 20, 1926), p. 6.

53. In this maneuver, Wu had to overcome the objections of some of his subordinates. His principal argument was that the weakening of the Kuominchün was the easiest way to undermine the power of Sun Ch'uan-fang short of a direct conflict in the Yangtze Valley. Wu also pointed out that, even if the Fengtien forces decided to move into Sun's territories, after the defeat of the Kuominchün, they would not be able to consolidate their position before they would have to meet the Kuomintang. It is significant that the argument that convinced the doubtful elements was that, even if Wu did succeed in defeating the Kuomintang, it would be meaningless since it would not increase his "prestige," because the Nationalists were still "nonentities" who had not proved themselves in previous conflicts among the *tuchüns*. (T'ao Chü-yin, *op. cit.*, pp. 148–49.)

54. During this inspection tour, which lasted until July 15, Sun sought to enter into negotiations with General Pai Shu-chen, a Fengtien subordinate of Chang Tsung-ch'ang, who commanded the Tsingtao area. Sun had hoped to persuade Pai to alter his allegiance. (U.S., Department of State 893.00/7913.)

55. *Peking and Tientsin Times*, July 13, 1926.

56. These negotiations, which were completed on July 28, were conducted through the mediation of ex-Premier Chin Yün-p'eng, ex-minister of communications Wu Yu-lin, and ex-minister of finance P'an Fu. The final agreement contained the following points: (1) The Shantung Mixed Brigade would be removed from the southern borders of their home province; (2) Sun Ch'uan-fang would reduce the number of Kiangsu garrison troops stationed along the Shantung border; and (3) Sun would return the portion of the railroad revenues collected within his area of jurisdiction that had previously been reserved for the support of the Shantung section of the Chin-Pu Railroad. (U.S., Department of State 893.00/7913.)

57. Department of State 893.00/7931.

58. In these negotiations of July 27 to 30, Wu agreed to permit Sun to send his troops into northern Kiangsu as far west as Hunan, but Wu specified that he would not tolerate Sun's sending any assistance to the Hankow area. (U.S., Department of State 893.00/7926.) During the negotiations, Sun requested that Wu desist from supporting the Fengtien operations against the Kuominchün so that the two of them could fully cooperate against the South. Wu replied with a curt telegram: "You want me to retire from politics. I want you to retire first." (T'ao Chu-yin, *op. cit.*, p. 168.) The tension between the two was at such a point that each was demanding of the other as a gesture of sincerity that he remove from power certain of his subordinates. In particular, Sun sought the dismissal of Ch'i Hsüeh-yüan, while Wu insisted that Sun give greater power to commanders who had formally served under Wu. (*Ibid.*, pp. 169–70.)

59. The American official who was informed of these agreements by an official in Sun Ch'uan-fang's headquarters remarked that it was amazing how carefully each of the commanders was measuring the sacrifice each would have to make in defending against the common foes and that only by arriving at equal sacrifices had any agreement been possible. (U.S., Department of State 893.00/7543.) Another American official discussed with one of Sun Ch'uan-fang's advisers the efforts that each of the *tuchüns* was making to maintain his power. The adviser also said that, should any of the leaders demonstrate weakness in his relations with the others, he would be inviting the enemy to attack at the weakest point in the Yangtze defenses and hesitate to threaten the strongest leader.

60. *Norh China Herald*, Aug. 28, 1926, p. 387.

61. *North China Herald*, Sept. 6, 1926, p. 423.

62. U.S., Department of State 893.00/7584. Although these troops were of secondary quality, Sun was clearly in a position to insist that Wu reduce his "reserve force" in return for any concrete assistance in the defense of southern Hupei, even though this area was of importance to both leaders. The fact that there was as yet no threat to Wuhu from the Nationalists indicates that Sun still thought in terms of balancing Wu's power in the Yangtze area.

63. *North China Herald*, Sept. 4, 1925, p. 434.

64. It was not until March 19, 1927, that Feng himself formally announced his association with the Kuomintang. (U.S., Department of State 893.00/9041.)

65. Sun Yao-pien, *op. cit.*, vol. III, p. 195.
66. U.S., Department of State 893.00/7932.
67. U.S., Department of State 893.00/7939. It is interesting that Wu always at-
    tached great importance to the independent control of finances and one of his
    last political acts concerned this subject. In 1939, when the Japanese were at-
    tempting to establish in North China a puppet government that would have pres-
    tige in the eyes of the Chinese, they offered its leadership to Wu P'ei-fu. Wu
    refused to leave his retirement except on the conditions that he be given com-
    plete control of the finances of the government and that he have full freedom to
    command all the troops in North China. (Owen M. Green, *The Story of China's
    Revolution* [London, 1945], p. 68.) The Japanese refused to consider such terms,
    and in 1941 Wu died. Although there seems to be no actual evidence, it was
    rumored that he died under peculiar circumstances. In 1947, he was given a
    second funeral, in which he was eulogized as a victim of "Japanese imperialism."
68. Wu responded on September 30 with a circular telegram proposing that the old
    Peiyang Army be restored and that all groups declare their allegiance to Ts'ao
    K'un. (*North China Herald*, Oct. 2, 1926, p. 8.) Although the proposals were
    preposterous if taken literally, the underlying implication was clear to all because
    Chang Tso-lin had never been a member of the Peiyang Army. Also, the sugges-
    tion of a return of Ts'ao K'un was recognized as a gesture for greater coopera-
    tion with Sun Ch'uan-fang, and possibly even Feng Yü-hsiang, because all of
    them had at one time been supporters of Ts'ao K'un's.
69. The preliminary agreements were definitely favorable to Fengtien and included
    the following points: (1) Sun Ch'uan-fang was to renounce all claims to the sec-
    tions of Anhwei and Kiangsu that lay north of the Yangtze; (2) Sun promised
    to contribute to the support of the Fengtien armies out of the Shanghai revenues
    he controlled; and (3) Sun could call upon four divisions of Fengtien troops to
    assist in the defense of his territories, and these troops would operate under his
    direct command. (U.S., Department of State 893.00/7996.)
70. *Ibid.*
71. Wu stated that by joining the Ankuochün he would have sacrificed his inde-
    pendence. However, he also suspected that Sun Ch'uan-fang and Chang Tsung-
    ch'ang would find it impossible to cooperate, in which case both would seek his
    support. By refusing to join the Ankuochün at this time, he hoped to increase his
    bargaining power. (T'ao Chü-yin, *op. cit.*, p. 173.)
72. U.S., Department of State 893.00/8335.
73. U.S., Department of State 893.00/8343.
74. *Peking and Tientsin Times*, Jan. 5, 1927.
75. *North China Herald*, Feb. 21, 1927, p. 117.

CHAPTER 7

1. *North China Herald*, Nov. 1, 1924, p. 211.
2. *North China Herald*, Feb. 12, 1927, p. 222.
3. Chapter 9 of this volume.
4. An example of this occurred on January 5, 1925, when Sun Ch'uan-fang issued a
   circular telegram in which he pledged to uphold the peace of the Yangtze area
   and ensure a stable currency. (Sun Yao-pien, *Chung-hua Min-kuo Shih-liao* [His-
   torical Data on the Chinese Republic] [Shanghai, 1930], vol. II, pp. 67–68.)
   However, Sun was at the time initiating his policy of seeking an alliance with
   Feng Yü-hsiang to oppose the Fengtien expansion into Central China and was
   preparing for campaigns that would seriously affect the credit and security of the
   Yangtze area. (Li Chien-nung, *Tsui-chin San-shih-nien Chung-kuo Cheng-chih
   Shih* [*Political History of China in the Last Thirty Years*] [Shanghai, 1930], pp.
   586–87.)
5. Thus, when, in 1922, Wu P'ei-fu announced that he was determined to "unify
   the country" by force, he found that even the previously loyal members of the
   Chihli alliance hesitated to support him, because he had made himself the clear
   target of most of the other military leaders in North China. (Cheng T'ing-sheng,

"Erh-shih Nien Lai Wo-kuo Cheng-chu Kan-kuan" ["A Consideration of Political Conditions in China in the Last Twenty Years"] *Tung fang Tsa-chih*, 21, no. 3 [Feb. 10, 1924], pp. 40–41.)

6. In many respects, this limitation on the free choice of propaganda themes is similar to the limitations that the race issue in the American South places upon Southern politicians, as has been pointed out by V. O. Key. (*Southern Politics*, New York: Knopf, 1949, p. 131ff.) Just as the Southern politician who sought to campaign on any "dangerous" issue would find himself confronted with a coalition of the other politicians, so did the *tuchün* who sought to become too bold in his statements find all others groups united against him.

7. *Peking and Tientsin Times*, Aug. 30, 1923. Such a statement coming from Li had particular weight because it was well known that he had been made the first Vice President of the Republic principally because he was acceptable to the Kuomintang and Sun Yat-sen.

8. T'ang Leang Li, *Suppressing Communist Banditry in China* (Shanghai: China United Press, 1934), pp. 2, 23.

9. When a representative of the American Legation questioned one of Feng's political lieutenants on this shift, the agent replied that there "was great speculation as to the relationships existing between various factions . . . and if he [Feng] were to make strong public statements it might create confusion in the public mind." Feng's agent "merely smiled when Mr. Peck hazarded the supposition that Marshal Feng was merely waiting to base his actions on events." (U.S., Department of State 893.00/6061.)

10. U.S., Department of State 893.00/6079 (Feb. 2, 1926).

11. U.S., Department of State 893.00/7025 (Dec. 14, 1925).

12. *North China Daily Mail*, Tientsin, Sept. 18, 1923, p. 1.

13. It is remarkable how often Westerners accepted such ideas. One of the features of the consular reports that often appeared was the statement of the American official to the effect that the *tuchün* in his area was a superior individual but that his assistants threatened to negate any good works the leader might attempt to institute. (U.S., Department of State 893.00/7253.)

14. *Weekly Review of the Far East*, Jan. 6, 1923, p. 225.

15. *Peking and Tientsin Times*, Oct. 11, 1923. It is noteworthy that Ts'ao K'un, while depreciating himself as a military man, emphasized, on the one hand, the newly developed concept of the importance to a republic of a basic constitution, while, on the other hand, he still defended the Confucian premise that good laws are not sufficient and that it is essential to rely upon talented and upright men in governing. Thus he showed that, although he was only a "humble" military man, he was aware of, and willing to pay deference to, the basic concepts of both the old and the new political theories.

16. U.S., Department of State 893.00/5796 (Aug. 19, 1924).

17. Sun Yao-pien, *op. cit.*, vol. III, p. 208.

18. *Millard's Review* 22, no. 11 (May 15, 1920), p. 536.

19. It is noteworthy that Lu's campaigns were not without effect in so far as some elements of the intelligentsia appeared to believe that Lu was sincere and that there was real hope that the *tuchüns* might recognize the folly of their ways and return to submission to the civil authorities. (*Tung-fang Tsa-chih* 17, no. 14 [July 25, 1920], p. 4.)

20. Sun Yao-pien, *op. cit.*, vol. II, pp. 37–38.

21. Only rarely did they become so bold as to propose that there might be a new role for the military in the society. Even though it was nothing more than an indirect hint, Sun Ch'uan-fang made such a proposal after his victory over Lu Yung-hsiang at Shanghai in October, 1924: "What we have got to do now is . . . to get rid of the old type military men; they know nothing. They have no modern ideas. We have to organize a new army with a new type of military man." (*North China Daily News*, Oct. 20, 1924.) It would appear that foreigners were more prepared to be optimistic over the possibility of a superior class of military leaders rising to power. An editorial in *The Weekly Review of the Far East* (17, no. 10 [Aug. 6, 1921], p. 283) was quick to point out that Feng Yü-hsiang

and Wu P'ei-fu represented substantial improvements over Tuan Ch'i-jui and Hsü Shu-cheng.

22. When, in 1924, Feng Yü-hsiang occupied the Forbidden City and declared null and void the Treaty of Abdication, he was able to justify his action with a claim that he was saving the country from a plot to destroy the Republic. Feng's action placed the other *tuchüns* in a difficult position because, if they condemned his move as a violation of a law of the land, they left themselves open to charges that they were at heart supporters of the monarchy and not stanch Republicans. In 1929, there was published what purports to be evidence of a plot to restore the monarchy. (*Chia-tzu Ch'ing-shih Mi-mou Fu-p'i Wen-cheng* [*Documentary Evidence of the Manchu Restoration Plot of 1924*] [Peking, 1929].) However, it is impossible to find any other evidence to confirm this charge of a plot to restore the Manchus, and the work appears to have been dedicated to the purpose of justifying Feng's action.

23. U.S., Department of State 893.00/3853.

24. U.S., Department of State 893.00/3862.

25. For examples of the arguments that the intelligentsia employed to explain the difficulties of the transition from the Imperial to a Republican system of rule, see Han Shih-yüan, "Tu-chüeh Chung-kuo Luan Yüan Chih San-ta" ("Three Main Ways of Suspending the Causes of China's Internal Disorders"), *Tung-fang Tsa-chih* 20, no. 16 (Aug. 25, 1925), pp. 17–36; Lo Ren-yen, *China's Revolution from the Inside* (New York: Abingdon Press, 1930).

26. *Peking and Tientsin Times*, Oct. 11, 1923.

27. *Ibid.*

28. Ts'ao paid further respect to Confucian concepts when he stated that "the nurturing of talents depends upon education." But he showed that this did not necessarily mean traditional education, when he followed with the statement that "the most urgent attention should therefore be paid to the maintenance and development of higher educational institutions." Because these institutions were predominantly based on the Western pattern of education, he was, in effect, supporting both the old and the new.

29. *North China Herald*, Jan. 3, 1925, p. 8.

30. From the time that the Ch'ing government first felt the need to adopt certain forms of Western technology, the issue arose as to the extent to which it would be possible to incorporate Western learning into Chinese society without destroying the traditional values. The great case for preserving the Confucian system of values while incorporating Western technology was made by Chang Chih-tung. (*China's Only Hope* [London: Oliphant, Anderson, and Ferrier, 1900].) He argued that China should use Japan as a mentor in the techniques of adopting Western science while refusing Western values. (*Ibid.*, pp. 90–93.) However, the issue of whether it was possible to divorce Western technology from the framework of values which accompanied it in the West continued to be a disturbing one for Chinese intellectuals, regardless of how they personally stood in respect to those values.

31. For a discussion of the problem of the foreign-trained students, see Chapter 9 of this volume.

32. Examples of such statements are to be found in Sun Yao-pien, *op. cit.*, vol. II, book 3, p. 37; vol. III, pp. 147–49.

33. For discussions of the appeal of the idea of a federal system of government for China, see Li Chien-nung, *op. cit.*, pp. 461–76; Ch'en Ju-hsüan, *Lien-pang Cheng-chih (Federal Governments)* (Shanghai, 1925), chs. I and II; Wang Hsüan in "Mei-kuo Ch'eng-shih Tzu-chih Te San-ta Ching-ch'a" ("Three Main Experiences in American Municipal Government"), *Tung-fang Tsa-chih* 19, no. 16 (March 25, 1922), points out that many of the intellectuals failed to realize that, although the concept of local autonomy may be admirable in terms of democratic principles, actually, if such a development should occur, it would mean the weakening of the political influence of the intellectuals as a group. The article argues that the power of the intellectuals was strongest on the national level and that they would have little influence in the local politics of any specific area.

34. The only *tuchün* who approached any such radical break was Chang Tso-lin, who, in 1922, showed signs of breaking completely the formal ties with the Peking government and attempting to establish an independent regime in Manchuria. On May 19, 1922, the Fengtien Provincial Assembly went so far as to pass a resolution stating that the province should "adopt a self-government system like that in vogue in various southern provinces." (U.S., Department of State 893.00/4441, May 20, 1922.) Chang at the time was endeavoring to obtain greater control over the surpluses of the Postal, Customs, and Salt Services and stated that he would refuse to make further remittances to Peking. (U.S., Department of State 893.00/4444 and 893.00/4446, May 20, 1922.) However, the combined pressures of the Peking government, the diplomatic corps, and Wu P'ei-fu's threats of invading Fengtien were sufficient to make Chang reconsider his actions. (U.S., Department of State 893.00/4456, May 24, 1922.)
35. Li Chien-nung, *op. cit.*, pp. 467–68.
36. At the time of the Feng coup in 1923, most of the leaders of the Chihli faction spoke of local autonomy until they were certain of the outcome of Feng's actions. However, once the situation was clarified the slogan lost its popularity. (*Tung-fang Tsa-chih* 20, no. 13 [July 10, 1923], p. 2.)
37. The failure of the initial attempt at a northern expedition in 1924–25 indicates that the success of the Kuomintang depended on its ability to support its propaganda with military power.

CHAPTER 8

1. To a limited extent, qualification must be made for the Ch'ing period. Owing to the vested interest of the Manchus in guaranteeing that policy decisions were not made that would lead to a weakening of their rule, the Chinese members of the bureaucracy were initially employed primarily as technicians. See Franz Michael, *The Origin of Manchu Rule in China: Frontier and Bureaucracy as Interacting Forces in the Chinese Empire* (Baltimore: Johns Hopkins Press, 1942), p. 103ff.
2. Li Chien-nung, *Tsui-chin San-shih-nien Chung-kuo Cheng-chih Shih* (*Political History of China in the Last Thirty Years*) (Shanghai, 1930), pp. 615–16.
3. U.S., Department of State 893.00/7535.
4. *North China Herald*, June 26, pp. 569–70.
5. U.S., Department of State 893.00/7113.
6. There appears to be no single source listing all the individuals who held cabinet offices during this period. Not only are the official records incomplete, but, since the Nationalist victory in 1927, no efforts have been made to clarify the record of the preceding decade. It was therefore a major task to determine precisely who these men were, and it was necessary to search systematically through the following sources: Chinese periodicals that recorded such appointments, Western-language newspapers, and the U.S. Department of State files. It was necessary to determine the precise dates of each man's appointment to office and of his retirement and to establish the succession and continuity of each ministry. In this search the author was unable in four instances to learn the precise date on which one official retired and the next recorded man assumed office. However, in each of these cases, the time interval was less than a month, and it might be assumed that no other individuals were appointed to office during this time.
7. The biographical background on the ministers was obtained from the following sources: *Chung-hua Min-kuo Ming-jen Chuan* (*Biographies of Famous Men of the Chinese Republic*) (Peking, 1932); *Chung-kuo Tang-tai Ming-jen Chuan* (*Biographies of Famous Contemporary Chinese*) (Shanghai, 1938); *Min-kuo Ming-jen T'u-chien* (*Biographical Directory of the Chinese Republic*) (Shanghai, 1928 edition); *Who's Who in China*, ed., published, *China Weekly Review* (Shanghai, 1925, 1931 eds.); the biographical section of *The China Year Book* (Tientsin, from the year 1919 to 1928 inclusive). The most complete source was the *Hsien-tai Chih-na Ming-chien* (*Biographical Dictionary of Famous Present-*

Day Chinese), compiled, published, the Japanese Ministry of Foreign Affairs (To-kyo, 1928). This work seems to be highly reliable and gives details of the careers of the men listed, as well as including information on their political associations and personality characteristics.

8. Many of the members of these revolutionary groups had identified themselves with the Canton government. However, the fact that each of the two govern-ments continued to vie with the other in professing that it alone represented the revolution still makes it striking that so few members of the revolutionary move-ments were in the Peking government.

9. The traditional disdain and distrust of the literati for the merchant class were based on several factors, among which were the low social status given to experts in market manipulation by an agrarian-Confucian society; the fear that the merchants' attitude that everything has a price might threaten the integrity of the bureaucracy because offices and posts might be made salable; the desire of the bureaucrats to maintain a monopoly, direct or indirect, over several fields of trade and commerce; the antagonism of an elite based on the control of land and land rents paid in kind against an elite that operated in a money market; and the scorn of the gentleman-scholar for the materialistic merchant.

10. Although it is difficult to obtain data giving a satisfactory indication as to how well these men had assimilated their Western training, the following facts are indicative: Of the men who received education in the United States, three ob-tained the degree of doctor of philosophy (Yale, Columbia, and Illinois), one received the master of arts degree (Cornell), and, of the three who received only undergraduate training, two were members of Phi Beta Kappa (Yale and Vir-ginia). The other student also graduated from Yale. Of those who were trained in Great Britain, two were admitted to the Inner Temple Bar and two completed sea tours with the British fleet after being graduated from Greenwich Naval Col-lege. One of the German-educated men received the degree of LL.B.

11. The data for the compilation of Table 8.1 were based on the listing of all for-eign-trained men in the following sources: *Who's Who in China*, (Shanghai: *China Weekly Review*, 1928 through 1931 eds.); and the Biographical Sections of the *China Year Book* (Tientsin, for the years 1919 and 1928 inclusive). These sources were employed because, being written in the English language, they include a high incidence of returned students. Often the sole justification for including particular individuals was the fact that they had received training abroad and thus were more likely to be known or have associations with those who had command of English. It should be noted that this does give the sample a definite bias. However, on the other hand, it might be expected that such sources would give a larger sample of the total universe of returned students. A comparison of the relative listings of returned students in these sources and the Chinese-language *Who's Who* might be of interest, but, for such a study to be of value, efforts should be made to determine the separate criteria of the two types of sources in selecting men for listing, and such a study would be beyond the scope of this work.

12. For discussions of the activities of the Chinese students studying in Japan, see F. G. Wang, *The Japanese Influence on Educational Reform in China, 1895–1911* (Peiping, 1933); Kiang Wen-han, *The Chinese Student Movement* (New York: King's Crown Press, 1948); and Frederick MacCormick, "Japan, America, and the Chinese Revolution," in *Japan and Japanese-American Relations*, ed., George H. Blakeslee (New York: G. E. Stechert, 1912), p. 340ff.

13. The sources in compiling this table were the same as for Table 8.1. However, it should be noted that the figures in the two tables differ because several men occupied posts in more than one ministry and were listed under all the offices that they held.

14. No explicit statement was found that would indicate why the *tuchüns* hesitated in appointing members of their own profession to this very important office. As will be seen, this position was one of the more desirable ones for the *tuchüns* to control, but also it was one that carried with it heavy responsibilities. The finance minister was usually burdened with problems of unstable revenues and the siz-

able debts of the Peking government. It would appear that the *tuchüns* recognized the need for specialists to cope with the fiscal problems and that they preferred to appoint civilians to administer the office. Perhaps they believed that in this way they could benefit from the revenues controlled by the ministry without assuming the responsibilities for the debts of the government. Also, possibly, the *tuchüns* hesitated to trust a fellow member of the military profession to control such an important post, because it might give him the opportunity to obtain greater independent power.

15. The average age of the ministers appears to be young even in terms of what might be expected in societies that do not place such emphasis on the values of maturity as Chinese culture has been characterized as doing. Nevertheless, it is necessary to keep in mind the relatively low life expectancy of citizens of China and the comparatively young population of the country. Although detailed statistics are not available, it has been calculated on the basis of relatively large samples that the life expectancy of a male at birth was only 34.85 years, and those who reached twenty years of age could have an expectancy of 40.74 years. (Ta Chen, "Population in Modern China," *American Journal of Sociology* III, no. 1 [July, 1946], part 2, p. 36.)

16. These figures were arrived at by taking what were regarded as the thirty-one different major organizations of the cabinet and considering them as separate "governments." The occupants of each of the posts in these ministries were then listed according to their relative ages, with the youngest minister given the rank of "1," the next youngest that of "2," and so on, until the oldest was given the rank of "10." After this was done for all of the "governments," the average age ranks of the ten positions were computed.

17. The exceptionally high age rank of the ministers of navy is explainable in terms of the relative unimportance of this position for the politics of the *tuchüns* and the fact that it was dominated by the senior admirals of the Chinese Navy. For the most part, four admirals, Li Ting-hsin, Sa Chen-ping, Tu Hsi-kuei, and Lin Chien-chang, shared in controlling the ministry. Li, Sa, and Lin had all served in the Fukien navy, which had been organized under British guidance before 1895, while Tu, though a native of Fukien, served in the Northern Fleet based at Weihaiwei during the same period. Only Tu Hsi-kuei, through his close personal association with Wu P'ei-fu, was recognized as having engaged in political activities extending beyond the field of naval affairs. The Ministry of Navy could contribute little of importance to the *tuchüns*, and it was even insignificant for purposes of patronage because it had only five hundred employees. (*North China Standard*, Jan. 13, 1926.) In fact, the Navy had been recognized as a semi-autonomous organization after an agreement reached between Tuan Ch'i-jui and Li Ting-hsin in 1917, by which it was to be excluded from the political arena of the *tuchüns*.

18. Students of constitutional law have made the point that, under the Chinese Constitution of 1913, it was in fact impossible to achieve effective cabinet rule. This was the case because, under the Constitution, the Prime Minister was designated to serve as director of the executive organs of the government, but he could not hold the separate ministers responsible, because the Senate had full power to approve and dismiss ministers. It was therefore impossible to insist upon joint cabinet responsibility. For a discussion of the inability of Chinese cabinets to serve either as governing organs or as bodies of advisers to the executive because of constitutional difficulties, see J. J. Heeren, "Cabinet Government in China a Failure—Why?," *The Weekly Review of the Far East* XXIII, no. 7 (Jan. 13, 1923). However, in the Constitution of October, 1923, this stipulation was changed and the Prime Minister was recognized as having full responsibility for the appointment and the functioning of all members of the cabinet. Actually, none of the cabinets had such a relatively calm career that they found the legal ramifications of the Constitution particularly disturbing.

19. Chin Yün-p'eng, the Prime Minister, had been a member of the Peiyang Army, a student of Tuan Ch'i-jui's, and a favorite of Yüan Shih-k'ai's. However, in early 1920, Chin recognized the weakening of the Anfu power, and, although

he remained loyal to Tuan personally, he sought to disassociate himself from the Anfu Club and to re-establish relations with the Chihli leaders. (*Millard's Review* XI, no. 13 [Feb. 28, 1920].)

20. Tung K'ung at this time was little more than a personal friend of Wu P'ei-fu's. However, Tung did become one of Wu's trusted followers, and, during his term in office, he was successful in exploiting his position to embarrass all of his fellow cabinet ministers by instituting a major investigation of the ministries and reporting irregularities and unscrupulous actions, particularly on the part of Minister of Finance Chang Hu. Although the Chihli faction controlled only the Ministry of Justice, it was successful in discrediting Chang's domination of the government and in making this ministry politically significant.

21. U.S., Department of State 893.002/58 (May 10, 1921).

22. *The Weekly Review of the Far East* XIX, no. 6 (Jan. 7, 1922), p. 230.

23. *Ibid.*, XX, no. 2 (June 10, 1922), p. 42.

24. U.S., Department of State 893.00/523.

25. Two such men, Wu T'ing-fang and T'ang Shao-i, refused to accept their appointments and never held office. The designation of these men, who represented the Canton regime, indicates another feature of the use to which cabinet appointments could be put as long as the posts did not guarantee the holders real power. This was the possibility that offices with only ceremonial value could be offered to dissident leaders without fear of compromising the power of the dominant *tuchüns*. For example, Wu P'ei-fu, after defeating the Fengtien forces, sought on June 11, 1922, to establish a government that, on the surface, would be acceptable to the South as a demonstration of his sincere desire to reunite China. He designated Wu T'ing-fang for the Premiership, but, although Wu hesitated and appeared tempted, he finally declined. Again, in November, 1924, after the Tientsin Conference had placed Tuan Ch'i-jui in the office of provisional chief executive, an effort was made to gain the support of the South, and T'ang Shao-i was appointed Prime Minister. T'ang waited to observe the outcome of Sun Yat-sen's trip to Peking, and, then, with the death of Sun and the decline of Feng Yü-hsiang's influence, he refused the offer. However, by these gestures, the *tuchüns* were able to claim that they were sincerely interested in reuniting the country and that they were willing to make concessions to the South, even to the point of offering them the highest posts in the Peking government.

26. Chang Shao-tseng was one of the early graduates of the Paotingfu Military Academy and was selected as a member of the first group of Chinese to be sent to study military science in Japan in 1901. Although his point of view was that of the traditional literati, Chang had joined in the revolutionary movement and was one of the "Three Heroes of North China." (The other two "heroes" were Wu Lu-chen and Lan Tien-wei, who were both executed by order of Yüan Shih-k'ai after he had secured control of the Revolutionary movement in North China.) Chang was well respected by the military leaders as a senior member of the Peiyang Army, but he had not commanded large numbers of troops since Yüan had removed him from posts of command to serve in the administrative office of the inspector general of the Chinese Armies. (*Hsien-tai Chih-na Ming-chien, op. cit.*, and *Who's Who in China, op. cit.*, 1925 edition.) Chin Yün-p'eng was a graduate of the Peiyang Academy and had served under Tuan Ch'i-jui before the revolution. After that event, he was a supporter of Yüan Shih-k'ai, and, because of his administrative responsibilities at the capital, he was never again in a position to command effective forces.

27. Although these ministries were far from solvent and the responsibilities for the nearly bankrupt government were numerous and heavy, the *tuchüns* had an unflagging confidence that more money could be squeezed from the government coffers or, by some miracle, the government would achieve an economic surplus while they controlled the critical ministries. It is impossible to obtain any accurate estimate of the sums the *tuchüns* exacted from the government. An American employee of the Engineering Office of the Grand Canal reported that the *tuchüns* obtained relatively large sums from government resources, including the Customs Service, but that accountants recorded these "transactions" in such a

manner that even the closet auditing would not disclose irregularities. (U.S., Department of State 893.00/4022.)

28. The selection of men prominent in business and financial circles was not solely based on considerations of the skills they possessed. It was also assumed that their personal associations with other leaders in these fields would lead not only to greater confidence in the financial position of the government but also to more positive assistance in obtaining markets for government bonds and sources for loans. Frequently this resulted in a *tuchün's* applying pressure on the ministers to obtain financial assistance from their business associates and acquaintances. For example, on April 24, 1921, Chang Tso-lin demanded that his minister of communications, Yeh Kung-cho, demonstrate his "loyalty to the cabinet" by securing a loan of $5,000,000 (Mex.) from his banking associates. (U.S., Department of State 893.00/3904, April 25, 1921.)

29. It is significant that, when the *tuchüns* chose to attack the official position assumed by the government on a particular issue in the area of foreign relations, they directed their criticism at the Prime Minister rather than the foreign minister. For instance, at the time of the Washington Conference and the negotiations with Japan on the Shantung Settlement, the Chihli leaders criticized Prime Minister Liang Shih-i as being pro-Japanese and did not mention Minister of Foreign Affairs W. W. Yen in their statements. (*China Review* II, no. 1 [Jan. 1, 1922], p. 3; U.S., Department of State 893.002.70.)

CHAPTER 9

1. *The Tiger* I, no. 10, quoted by Hu Shih, "Chinese Renaissance," *China Year Book, 1924–25* (Tientsin, 1926), p. 643.
2. For a discussion of the risks that students assumed in joining demonstrations, see Rodney Gilbert, "The Role of Students in Chinese Politics," *North China Herald* (June 6, 1925), p. 158; Lo Ren-yen, *China's Revolution from the Inside* (New York: Abingdon Press, 1930), pp. 64–78.
3. Some Chinese intellectuals did propose that the only hope for China was for the students to enter into the armies. See Yang Tuan-liu, "Chung-kuo Kai-tsao te Fang-fa" ("Methods of Reconstructing China"), *Tung-fang Tsa-chih* 18, no. 14 (July 25, 1921). Yang indicates that this suggestion is "impracticable" because the students would "lose their idealism" if they were in the armies and removed from intellectual activities.
4. "A Challenge to Western Learning," *News Bulletin*, Institute of Pacific Relations, Dec., 1927.
5. Many of these recordings are highly impressionistic because the data were quite limited. However, it was assumed, for instance, in such a case as that of the holder of a doctor's degree in agriculture from Cornell University who was serving as a private language tutor, that he was not applying his training. Most of the doubtful cases were listed under "Partially Applied" and included such examples as "holder of master of arts degree in business from the University of Illinois . . . serving as principal of a girls' school." It should be added that a great number of the students did not list their current occupations, and it might be assumed that an even larger proportion of these had not been successful in applying their Western training.
6. An excellent study of this attitude is to be found in Hu Shih, "Tu-wei Hsiensheng Yü Chung-kuo" ("Mr. Dewey and China"), *Tung-fang Tsa-chih* 18, no. 13 (Jan. 10, 1921). Hu Shih comments, "We can say that, from the time of the meeting of Chinese and Western cultures, there has never been a foreign scholar who has had as great an influence on Chinese intellectual life as Mr. Dewey" (p. 121). However, he adds that Dewey's "anti-intellectualism in an intellectual spirit" had made it possible for many Chinese to claim to be "practical thinkers," when in fact they were acting in the very manner that Dewey criticized.
7. The Chinese intellectuals' concern with, and division over, ideological issues led to the establishment of innumerable movements and sects. Almost any work pro-

duced during the period reflects this feature of Chinese intellectual life, but it is possibly best demonstrated in Sun Chih-tseng, *Hsin Chu-i Tz'u-tien* (*A Dictionary of New Ideologies*) (Shanghai, 1936). This work lists and describes an incredible number of sects and ideologies. Almost all of them are identified as Western in origin, and most of them carry English titles, but it is impossible to find mention of many of them in Western sources.

8. It is striking that, although Chinese political-science literature after 1926 did include a discussion of the Kuomintang party organization, there was almost no treatment of the role of parties in a democratic society. Another indication of this attitude is that, in the Commercial Press's prodigious effort to translate Western works into Chinese, such classical works as Robert Michels, *Political Parties*, tr., Eden and Cedar Paul (New York: Dover, 1959); M. Ostrogorski, *Demorcacy and the Party System in the United States* (New York: Macmillan, 1910); and others are conspicuous by their absence, whereas many of the works dealing with idealized systems of government were included. (*Catalogue of Foreign Works Translated into Chinese*, ed., published, Commercial Press [Shanghai, 1928].)

9. *Peking and Tientsin Times,* April 19, 1923.

10. For studies of the attitudes and roles of the traditional merchant as well as the modern merchant class, see Shih Kuo-leng and Marion J. Levy, *The Rise of the Modern Chinese Business Class* (New York: Institute of Pacific Relations, 1949); Richard Wilhelm, *Chinese Economic Psychology*, tr., Bruno Lasker (New York: Institute of Pacific Relations, 1947).

11. For statistics on the exchange, see *Shanghai Huo-chia Chi-k'an* (*Report on Shanghai Market Prices*), Tsai-cheng Pu (Ministry of Finance) (Shanghai, June, 1926), p. 17.

12. For discussions of the problems of the Chinese dollar, see Charles W. Brown, "Silver Saps Chinese Economic Vitality," *China Review* IV, no. 4 (April, 1923), p. 165ff.; C. F. Remer, "Price Maintenance and the Silver Market," *Millard's Review* XIV, no. 5 (Oct. 2, 1920), pp. 218–25; Chang Su-min, *Pai-yin Wen-te Yü Chung-kuo Pi-chih* (*The Silver Question and Chinese Currency*) (Shanghai, 1934), esp. pp. 102–63.

13. This separation of political decision-making and the exchange market exposed the *tuchüns* to sharp criticism from Chinese economists who argued that China was attempting the impossible by being the only country that operated on an unqualified silver standard, and that it was necessary for China to adopt some form of managed currency. However, at this point, the economists were frustrated because, being sane men, they realized the nation's currency was too precious a thing to be left to the manipulations of the *tuchüns*. (Ch'en Ch'i-hsiu, "Chung-kuo Kai-tsao Ho T'a-ti Ching'chi te Pei-ching" ["Chinese Reconstruction and Its Basic Economic Foundations"], *She-hui K'e-hsüeh Li-k'e* [*Social Science Quarterly*] I, no. 2 [Winter, 1923], pp. 273–85.) However, most of the members of the new commercial elite had far greater confidence in an impersonal market than in the notion of planning, as indicated by their reactions to the U.S. Treasury's policies of controlled buying and selling of silver. In 1920, this feeling that the United States was interfering with "normal" market conditions reached such a point that Thomas Lamont felt it advisable to give a public address to the Chinese business community defending American policies. (*Millard's Review* XII, no. 7 [April 17, 1920], p. 318.)

14. For an analysis of the inability of the Shanghai market to absorb imports during the Kiangsu-Chekiang war of 1924, see U.S., Department of State 893.00/6354 (Oct. 3, 1924).

15. *North China Herald*, April 4, 1925, p. 7.

16. The following figures give the value in Chinese dollars of Chinese imports and exports during the period under study:

1920	$1,342,870,818
1921	1,379,301,482
1922	1,560,833,778
1923	1,659,910,649
1924	1,726,782,369
1925	1,831,778,103
1926	2,029,367,460
1927	1,973,749,018

These statistics are based on the Maritime Customs Reports and have been adjusted in terms of the value of the 1919 Chinese dollar. ("China in Statistics," *The Chinese Social and Political Science Review* XIV, no. 4 [Oct., 1930], p. 461.)

17. See Eduard Kann, *The Currencies of China* (Shanghai: Kelly and Walsh, 1926), especially pp. 6–15.
18. Srinivas R. Wagel, *Finance in China* (Shanghai: North China Daily News and Herald, 1914), pp. 231–34.
19. *North China Herald*, June 26, 1926, p. 570.
20. Charles W. Mason, "From Skin Money to Bank Notes," *China Review* IV, no. 1 (Jan. 23, 1923), p. 34.
21. Eduard Kann, *op. cit.*, p. 516.
22. U.S., Department of State 893.00/5652, Sept. 26, 1924.
23. U.S., Department of State 893.00/3764, Jan. 15, 1921.
24. U.S., Department of State 893.00/3766, Jan. 18, 1921.

BIBLIOGRAPHY

Western Books

ABEND, HALLETT, *Tortured China*, New York, 1930.
BAKER, JOHN EARL, *Explaining China*, London, 1927.
BALES, WILLIAM L., *Tso Tsung-t'ang: Soldier and Statesman of Old China*, Shanghai, 1937.
BORG, DOROTHY, *American Policy and the Chinese Revolution, 1925–28*, New York, 1947.
CHAPMAN, H. O., *The Chinese Revolution 1926–1927*, London, 1928.
CH'EN, JEROME, *Yüan Shih-k'ai 1859–1916*, London, 1961.
CHI CH'AO-TING, *Key Economic Areas in Chinese History as Revealed in the Development of Public Works for Water Control*, New York, 1936.
CH'IEN, TUAN-SHENG, *The Government and Politics of China*, Cambridge, Mass., 1950.
CLARK, GROVER, *The Great Wall Crumbles*, New York, 1935.
CLUBB, EDMUND, *20th Century China*, New York, 1964.
GILBERT, RODNEY, *What's Wrong with China*, London, 1926.
GILLIN, DONALD G., *Warlord: Yen Hsi-shan in Shansi Province*, Princeton, N.J., 1967.
GREEN, OWEN M., *The Story of China's Revolution*, London, 1945.
HAIL, WILLIAM J., *Tseng Kuo-fan and the Taiping Rebellion*, New Haven, Conn., 1927.
HIGH, STANLEY, *China's Place in the Sun*, New York, 1922.
HOBART, ALICE TISDALE, *Within the Walls of Nanking*, London, 1928.
HOLCOMBE, ARTHUR N., *The Chinese Revolution: A Phase in the Regeneration of a World Power*, Cambridge, Mass., 1930.
HORNBECK, STANLEY K., *Contemporary Politics in the Far East*, New York, 1916.
HOUN, FRANKLIN W., *Central Government of China 1912–1928*, Madison, Wis., 1957.
HUMMEL, ARTHUR W., ed., *Eminent Chinese of the Ch'ing Period*, 2 vols., Washington, D.C., 1943.
IMPEY, LAWRENCE, *The Chinese Army as a Military Force*, Tientsin, 1926.
KING, LOUIS M., *China in Turmoil, Studies in Personality*, London, 1927.
KOTENEV, ANATOL M., *The Chinese Soldier*, Shanghai, 1937.
————, *New Lamps for Old*, Shanghai, 1937.
LANG, OLGA, *Chinese Society and Family*, New Haven, Conn., 1946.
LEVY, MARION J., *The Family Revolution in Modern China*, Cambridge, Mass., 1946.
LINEBARGER, PAUL M. A., *Government in Republican China*, New York, 1938.
LIU CH'I-HUNG, *Political Parties in China*, Peking, 1930.
MacNAIR, HARLEY FARNSWORTH, *China in Revolution: An Analysis of Politics and Militarism Under the Republic*, Chicago, 1931.
————, *China's New Nationalism and Other Essays*, Shanghai, 1925.

MICHAEL, FRANZ, *The Origins of Manchu Rule in China: Frontier and Bureaucracy as Interacting Forces in the Chinese Empire*, Baltimore, 1942.

MILLARD, THOMAS F., *China: Where It Is Today—and Why!*, New York, 1928.

MONROE, PAUL, *China: A Nation in Evolution*, New York, 1928.

PAO, CHAO-HSIEH, *The Government of China 1644–1911*, Baltimore, 1925.

PEFFER, NATHANIEL, *China: The Collapse of a Civilization*, New York, 1930.

POWELL, RALPH L., *The Rise of Chinese Military Power, 1899–1912*, Princeton, N.J., 1955.

REINSCH, PAUL S., *An American Diplomat in China*, Garden City, N.Y., 1922.

REMER, CHARLES F., *A Study of Chinese Boycotts*, Baltimore, 1933.

RUSSELL, BERTRAND, *The Problem of China*, New York, 1922.

SELLE, EARL S., *Donald of China*, New York, 1948.

SHERIDAN, JAMES E., *Chinese Warlord: The Career of Fen Yü-hsiang*, Stanford, Calif., 1966.

SHIH KUO-LENG and LEVY, MARION J., *The Rise of the Modern Chinese Business Class*, New York, 1949.

SOKOLSKY, GEORGE E., *The Tinder Box of Asia*, Garden City, N.Y., 1932.

TAMAGNA, FRANK M., *Banking and Finance in China*, New York, 1942.

T'ANG LEANG-LI, *The Inner History of the Chinese Revolution*, New York, 1930.

TAWNEY, R. H., *Land and Labor in China*, New York, 1932.

VAN DORN, HAROLD ARCHER, *Twenty Years of the Chinese Republic*, New York, 1932.

VERBRUGGE, RAPHAEL, *Yüan Che-k'ai, sa vie, son temps (Yüan Shih-k'ai, His Life, His Times)*, Paris, 1904.

VINACKE, HAROLD M., *A History of the Far East in Modern Times*, New York, 1950.

————, *Modern Constitutional Development in China*, New York, 1922.

WANG CHING-WEI, *China's Problems and Their Solution*, Shanghai, 1934.

WANG TSI C., *The Youth Movement in China*, New York, 1928.

WARD J. S. M., and STERLING, W. C., *The Hung Society or the Society of Heaven and Earth*, 2 vols., London, 1925.

WEALE, PUTNAM (B. L. SIMPSON), *The Fight for the Republic of China*, New York, 1917.

WEBER, MAX, "The Chinese Literati," *From Max Weber: Essays in Sociology*, tr., H. H. Gerth and C. W. Mills, New York, 1946.

WHEELER, W. REGINALD, *China and the World War*, New York, 1919.

WIEGER, P. LEON, *Chine Moderne (Modern China)*, Hien-hien, 1922.

WILHELM, RICHARD, *Chinese Economic Psychology*, tr., Bruno Lasker, New York, 1947.

WILLIAMS, E. T., *China Yesterday and Today*, New York, 1923.

WOODHEAD, H. G. W., *Occidental Interpretations of the Far Eastern Problem*, Chicago, 1926.

————, *The Truth About the Chinese Republic*, London, 1925.

WOU, ODORIC YING-KWANG, "Militarism in Modern China as Exemplified in the Career of Wu P'ei-fu," Ph.D. diss., Columbia University, 1970.

YANG, MARTIN C., *A Chinese Village*, New York, 1945.

ZI, ETIENNE, *Pratique des examens littéraires en Chine (The Literary Examination Practice in China)*, Shanghai, 1894.

CHINESE BOOKS

CHANG CHIA-SEN, *Chung-nei Chan-cheng Liu-chiang (Six Lectures on the Civil Wars)*, Shanghai, 1927.

CHANG CHUNG-FU, *Chung-hua Min-kuo wai-chiao hsih (History of the Foreign Affairs of the Chinese Republic)*, Peking, 1927.

CHANG SU-MIN, *Pai-yin wen-t'i yu Chung-kuo pi-chih (The Silver Question and Chinese Currency)*, Shanghai, 1934.

CHANG TSU-SHENG, *Jen-hsu cheng-pien chi (The Civil War of China in 1922)*, Shanghai, 1924.

CH'EN JU-HSÜAN, *Lien-pang cheng-chih* (*Federal Governments*), Shanghai, 1925.

CH'EN KUNG-FU, *Chung-kuo Tsui-chin San-shih-nien Shih* (*History of China in the Last Thirty Years*), Shanghai, 1928.

CHIA I-CHUN, *Chung-kuo min-kuo shih* (*History of the Chinese Republic*), Shanghai, 1930.

CHIANG T'ING-FU, *Chung-kuo Chin-tai Shih* (*History of Modern China*), Changsha, 1938.

CH'IEN TUAN-SHENG *et al.*, *Min-kuo cheng-chih shih* (*History of Government in Republican China*), 2 vols., Chungking, 1945–46.

CHU HSIN-FAN, *Chung-kuo ke-ming yu Chung-kuo she-hui chieh-chi* (*Chinese Revolution and Each Class in Chinese Society*), Shanghai, 1930.

CHU PIN-YUAN, and CHUANG TSE-YEN, *Chin shih-nien lai Chung-kuo ts'ai-cheng kai-k'uang* (*General Condition of Central Government Finance in the Last Ten Years*), Shanghai, 1926.

FEI PAO-YEN, *Shan-hou Hui-i Shih* (*History of the Reconstruction Conference* [1925]), Peking, 1927.

FENG YÜ-HSIANG, *Feng Yü-hsiang Jih-chi* (*The Diary of Feng Yü-hsiang*), 2 vols., Peking, 1930.

————, *Wo ti sheng-huo* (*My Life*), 3 vols., Chungking, 1949.

FU HUAN-KUANG, ed., *Chiang-su Ping-tsai Tiao-ch'a Chi-shih* (*Factual Record of a Survey of the War Devastation in Kiangsu*), Shanghai, 1924.

HSIEH PIN, *Min Kuo Cheng-tang Shih* (*History of Political Parties Under the Republic*), Shanghai, 1926.

HUA KANG, *Chung-kuo ta ke-ming shih* (*1922–27*), (*History of the Great Chinese Revolution* [1922–27]), Shanghai, 1928.

Hung Wen Library, ed., *Chiang-che Chan-shih* (*History of the Kiangsu-Chekiang War*), Shanghai, 1924.

————, ed., *Feng-chih Chan-shih* (*History of the Fengtien-Chihli War*), Shanghai, 1924.

KU CHUNG-HSIU, *Chung-hua Min-kuo K'ai-kuo Shih* (*History of the Founding of the Chinese Republic*), Shanghai, 1926.

LI CHIEN-NUNG, *Chung-kuo Chin-pai-nien Cheng-chih Shih* (*Chinese Political History of the Last Hundred Years*), Shanghai, 1947.

————, *Tsui-chin San-shih-nien Chung-kuo Cheng-chih Shih* (*Political History of China in the Last Thirty Years*), Shanghai, 1930.

LO ERH-KANG, *Hsiang-chün Hsin-chih* (*New Gazetteer of the Hunan Army*), Shanghai, 1938.

LU KUANG-YU, *Min-kuo Shih-yao* (*A Historical Summary of the Republic*), Shanghai, 1920.

MA TA-CHUNG, *Ta Chung-hua Min-kuo Shih* (*History of the Chinese Republic*), Shanghai, 1929.

PAI YING-HSING and CHIN YU-K'UN, *Kuo-min-chün Shih-kao* (*Draft History of the Kuominchün*), Peking, 1930.

Palace Museum, ed., *Chia-tzu Ch'ing-shih Mi-mou fu-p'i Wen-cheng* (*Documentary Evidence of the Manchu Restoration Plot of 1924*), Peking, 1929.

SHEN CHIEN, "Hsing-hai ke-ming ch'ien-hsi wo-kuo chih lu-chun chi-ch'i chun-fei, She-hui k'o-hsueh" ("The Chinese Army and Its Finances on the Eve of the 1911 Revolution"), *The Social Science Quarterly*, III, no. 2 (Jan., 1937).

SUN YAO-PIEN, *Chung-hua Min-kuo Shih-liao* (*Historical Data on the Chinese Republic*), 3 vols., Shanghai, 1930.

TAI CH'UAN-HSIEN, *Chung-kuo tu-li yun-tung ti chi-tien* (*The Foundations of the Chinese Independence Movement*), Shanghai, 1928.

T'AO CHÜ-YIN, *Wu P'ei-fu Chiang-chun Chuan* (*Biography of General Wu P'ei-fu*), Shanghai, 1941.

TS'AI TUNG-FANG, *Min-kuo T'ung-shu Yen-i* (*A Popularized Discussion of the Republic*), Shanghai, 1930.

WEN KUNG-CHIH, *Tsui-chin San-shih-nien Chung-kuo Chün-shih Shih* (*History of Chinese Military Affairs in the Last Thirty Years*), Shanghai, 1930, 2 vols.

Wu LIAO-TZU (*pseudonym*), *Hsien-tai Chih Chang Tso-lin* (*The Present-Day Chang Tso-lin*), Shanghai, 1924.
Wu T'ING-FANG, *Min-kuo T'u-chih Ch'u-i* (*Essays in the Practical Problems of Government Under the Republic*),
YANG YU-CHIUNG, *Chung-kuo Cheng-tang Shih* (*History of Chinese Political Parties*), Shanghai, 1936.

ARCHIVES

U.S., Department of State Files (China, Political), National Archives, Washington, D.C. Political reports of U.S. civil and military officials in China for the period 1920–28.

REFERENCE WORKS

Biographical Dictionary of Republican China, ed., Howard Boorman, 4 vols.; New York: Columbia University Press, 1967–70.
The China Year Book, 1919 through 1929 editions, ed., H. G. W. Woodhead, Tientsin.
Chung-hua Min-kuo Ming-jen Chuan (*Biographies of Famous Men of the Chinese Republic*), Peking, 1932.
Chung-kuo Tang-tai Ming-jen Chuan (*Biographies of Famous Contemporary Chinese*), Shanghai, 1938.
Hsien-tai Chih-na Ming-chien (*Biographical Dictionary of Famous Present-Day Chinese*), Tokyo, 1928.
Min-kuo Ming-jen T'u Chien (*Biographical Dictionary of the Chinese Republic*), Shanghai, 1928.
Who's Who in China, China Weekly Review, Shanghai, 1925 and 1931 editions.

NEWSPAPERS AND PERIODICALS

Central China Post, Hankow.
China Quarterly, Shanghai.
China Review, Shanghai.
China Weekly Review, Shanghai.
Chinese Social and Political Science Review, Shanghai.
Ching-pao Fu-k'an, Peking.
Kuo-wen Chou-pao, Shanghai.
Millard's Review of the Far East, Shanghai.
Nankai Social and Economic Quarterly, Tientsin.
New York Times, New York, N.Y.
North China Daily News, Shanghai.
North China Herald and Supreme Court and Consular Gazette, Shanghai.
North China Standard, Peking.

INDEX